Personnel Administration in the Courts

Also of Interest

Managing Local Government for Improved Performance: A Practical Approach, Brian W. Rapp and Frank M. Patitucci

Alternatives for Delivering Public Services: Toward Improved Performance, edited by E. S. Savas

The Foreign Service Personnel System: An Organizational Analysis, Patrick E. Linehan

A Westview Special Study

Personnel Administration in the Courts
Harry O. Lawson, H. R. Ackerman, Jr.,
and Donald E. Fuller

This is the first text that fully treats personnel management in a court environment. The authors cover in detail both the broad range of personnel management tools and the problems and processes unique to courts and judicial systems. Also providing a framework for understanding the objectives of court personnel systems, their approach covers the entire spectrum of theory and practice and will be useful to academicians as well as practitioners.

Harry O. Lawson is professor of judicial administration and director of the Master of Science in Judicial Administration Program at the University of Denver College of Law. He was state court administrator in the Colorado Judicial Department for ten years and has been consultant to the court systems in thirteen other states.
H. R. Ackerman, Jr., is personnel director for the Colorado Judicial System.
Donald E. Fuller is director of the Judicial Administration Program, School of Public Administration, University of Southern California.

Personnel Administration in the Courts

Harry O. Lawson,
H. R. Ackerman, Jr.,
and Donald E. Fuller

Westview Press / Boulder, Colorado

A Westview Special Study

All rights reserved. No part of this publication may be reproduced or transmitted in any form or by any means, electronic or mechanical, including photocopy, recording, or any information storage and retrieval system, without permission in writing from the publisher.

Copyright © 1979 by Westview Press, Inc.

Published in 1979 in the United States of America by
    Westview Press, Inc.
    5500 Central Avenue
    Boulder, Colorado 80301
    Frederick A. Praeger, Publisher

Library of Congress Catalog Card Number: 79-5133
ISBN: 0-89158-588-5

Composition for this book was provided by the author.
Printed and bound in the United States of America.

Contents

List of Figures xii
Preface xiii
Acknowledgments xvii

SECTION ONE - OVERVIEW

1 THE NEED FOR PERSONNEL MANAGEMENT IN
  THE COURTS. 1

  Introduction. 1
    Reasons for Growing Court Interest. . . 2
  What is Personnel Management? 3
    Scope of Personnel Management 3
    Accomplishing Goals and Objectives. . . 4
    Interrelationship with Other Manage-
      ment Functions: Some Examples 4
  Personnel Management in Courts:
    Whose Responsibility?. 5
    Executive Branch Involvement. 6
    A Separate Judicial Personnel System. . 7
    Court Personnel Administration
      Standards. 10
  Legal Requirements and Court Personnel. . 15
    Federal Requirements. 16
    State Constitutions and Statutes. . . . 17
    Court Rules 18
    Model Judicial Articles and
      Legislation. 19
    Summary 20
  The Court Environment 21
    Specific Areas of Concern for
      Personnel Management 23
    Elected Court Clerks. 25
    Other Examples of Court Personnel
      System Fragmentation 27
    Summary 28

2	COURT PERSONNEL SYSTEMS	33

    Background. 33
        Patronage 35
        Merit Systems 36
        Collective Bargaining 37
    Personnel System Models 38
        State System. 41
        Local System. 41
        Mixed System. 42
    Summary 43

SECTION TWO - TOOLS AND PROCESSES OF
PERSONNEL ADMINISTRATION IN THE COURTS

3	CLASSIFICATION: THE ESSENTIAL BUILDING BLOCK.	45

    Introduction. 45
        Classification and Other Terms
        Defined. 45
    Classification Plan Development 49
        Ranking System. 49
        Position Classification 49
        Point Rating System 52
    The Classification Process. 54
    Determining Classification Study Need . . 55
    Judicial Support Needed 55
    Making the Classification Study 56
        In-House or Consultants 56
        Questionnaire Preparation 59
        Charting the Results. 59
        Pre-Desk Audit Allocations. 59
        Desk Audit. 61
    Writing the Class Description 62
    Employee Review and Appeal. 63
    Plan Maintenance. 64
    Reclassification. 64
    Periodic Class Review 65

4	RECRUITING: A MEANS TO AN END.	69

    Matching Needs and Supply 69
        Labor Needs 69
        Labor Market Survey 70
    The Recruitment Process 70
        Extent. 70
        Minority Recruitment. 71
        Personal Contact. 72

       Intergovernmental Efforts 72
       Private Agencies. 73
       Word-of-Mouth 74
       Using the Media 74
       National Recruiting 75
   Job Announcements 76

5   EXAMINATIONS. 81

   Introduction. 81
       Testing in the Courts 82
       Definitions 82
   Critical Issues in Examinations 83
       Open or Promotional Exam. 84
       Affirmative Action Implications 84
   The Examination Process 85
       The Application 85
       Types of Tests. 87
       Eligibility Lists 89

6   COMPENSATION AND BENEFITS 93

   Developing the Compensation Plan. 93
       Entry Level Classes 94
       Pay Differential Among Classifica-
         tion Groups. 94
       Other Important Considerations. 95
   Compensation Plan Maintenance 96
       Comparability with Executive Branch . . 96
       Salary Surveys. 96
       General Increase. 97
       Cost of Living. 97
       In-Grade Hiring 98
       A Different Approach. 98
   Fringe Benefits 99
       Annual Leave. 100
       Sick Leave. 101
       Maternity Leave 101
       Injury Leave. 102
       Military Leave. 102
       Educational Leave 103
       Administrative Leave. 103
       Leave Without Pay 103
       Health Insurance. 104
       Retirement. 105
       Overtime and Compensatory Time. 106
       Holidays. 107

7   RETENTION AND PROMOTION 109

   The New Employee. 109

	Initial Orientation	110
	On-The-Job Training	110
	Probationary Period	110
	In-Service Training	112
	Performance Evaluation.	112
	Who Should Do the Rating?	113
	Uses of Performance Evaluation.	113
	Types of Performance Evaluation	114
	What Plan Should Courts Use?.	118
	Employee Evaluation and Compensation. . .	120
	Promotion and Career Ladders.	121
	Promotional Opportunities	122
8	EMPLOYEE TRAINING	125
	Purposes of Training.	125
	Types of Training Programs.	126
	Orientation Training.	126
	In-Service Training	129
	Management Training	130
	Communication Training.	131
	Functional Training	131
	Problem Solving	132
	Supervision Skills.	133
	Team Training	133
	External Training Programs.	134
	Decentralized Programs.	135
	Designing Training Programs	135
	Determining Needs	135
	Establishing the Program.	137
	Training Program Evaluation	138
9	DISCIPLINE AND EMPLOYEES' RIGHTS.	141
	Employee Discipline	141
	Corrective Actions.	141
	Disciplinary Actions.	142
	Causes for Corrective or Disciplinary Actions	143
	Grievances and Appeals.	145
	Grievances.	145
	Appeal Procedure	147
	Limitations on the Right of Appeal. . .	148
	Making the Process Work	149

SECTION THREE - SETTING THE FRAMEWORK

10	PERSONNEL RULES	151

	Introduction.	151
	State Systems	152
	Trial Courts.	152
	Personnel Rules Content	152
	Rule Format and Organization.	153
	Content	158
	Drafting Personnel Rules.	169
	Preparing the First Set of Rules. . . .	170
	Continued Rule Revision	172
11	ADMINISTERING THE COURT PERSONNEL SYSTEM	177
	Introduction.	177
	Statewide Systems	178
	Over-all Authority and Responsibility .	178
	Local Authority	179
	Personnel System Adoption	180
	Local Systems	181
	Authority and Responsibility.	181
	Responsibility of Trial Court Administrator.	181
	Staffing the Personnel Unit	182
	Staff Size.	182
	Personnel Staff Qualifications.	183
	Personnel Staff Compensation.	186
	Personnel Record Keeping and Information Systems.	187
	Basic Personnel Form Content.	187
	Fiscal Information Requirements	187
	Personnel Reports	188
	Determining Personnel Needs	190
	Factors Affecting Needs Assessment Methodology.	190
	Accounting for Court Employment Diversity.	193
	Deciding on and Applying Measures . . .	197
	Summary	201
	Budgeting for Personnel Needs: An Example	201
	Position Costs.	201
12	COLLECTIVE BARGAINING	207
	Introduction.	207
	Taft-Hartley Act.	207
	Public Employee Collective Bargaining	208
	Issues.	211

	Who is the Employer?.	211
	Management Rights	212
	Civil Service	213
Strikes		214
	Wayne County Strike	214
Collective Bargaining Experience		
and Developments		216
	Overview.	216
	Individual States	216
Summary		221

Appendixes

A.	Bibliography	227
B-1.	Court Clerk II Job Description . . .	229
B-2.	Judicial District Administrator I Job Description	231
C.	Instructions and Suggestions for Filling Out Position Classification Questionnaire	233
D.	Civil Action 76 M 910	239
E-1.	Colorado Judicial System Personnel Rules.	261
E-2.	Maine Court System Personnel Policy and Procedures Manual	315
E-3.	Circuit Court of Oregon, Multnomah County, Personnel Plan	345
F.	The Judicial Cost Model	389

Figures

2.1	Key Distinguishing Factors Between State Personnel System and Local Personnel System	34
2.2	Key Distinguishing Factors: State, Local, and Mixed Personnel Systems.	39
3.1	Occupational Index to Classes	48
3.2	Example of a Compensation Plan, Showing Grades and Steps	50
3.3	Formal Organizational Chart	60
4.1	Job Announcement.	78
7.1	Uses of Appraisals or Ratings in 316 Leading Industrial Corporations. . .	114
11.1	Average Minutes Per Filing.	200

xii

Preface

In the past few years, increasing attention has been given to personnel administration in the courts, and significant changes have taken place in a number of jurisdictions in the management of nonjudicial personnel. National standards of court organization and administration, adopted in the mid 1970's, stress the importance of competent supporting personnel in the courts, appointed, compensated, and retained under a merit system operated independently by the judicial branch.

State funding of the judicial system, a reality in several states, and under consideration in some others, makes it possible to establish a state-wide judicial branch personnel system. A number of locally funded trial courts, especially in the urban areas, have also developed and implemented personnel plans. Public employee collective bargaining has now expanded in some jurisdictions to include court personnel, spurring even greater interest by judges and court administrators in personnel management. In short, personnel management is now accepted as an important part of the court improvement package, when not so long ago it seemed of little concern to proponents of court reform or to students of judicial administration.

Despite the growing interest in court personnel administration, very little has been written about significant developments or to provide guidance to court managers on how to undertake the various tasks of personnel administration within a court setting. This book and the monograph which preceded it were written to meet these two needs. Past and present personnel administration in the courts is discussed, as are personnel problems peculiar to the court environment. Classification, recruitment, compensation, and other aspects of personnel administration are covered within the court setting, and information is provided for court administrators on how these tasks may be initiated and carried out.

Special attention is given to collective bargaining in this volume, because, in some fifteen states, court employees have entered into collective bargaining agreements, and there appears to be a significant trend in this direction. A chapter is devoted to these developments and the major issues involved, such as who is the employer, retention of management rights, and the right to strike.

Initially, the authors intended to address another subject more extensively than it is covered in this volume, because of the importance of equal employment opportunity in the courts. This was not done, because the National Center for State Courts shortly will publish a comprehensive report on this subject after an extensive study funded by the Law Enforcement Assistance Administration, U. S. Department of Justice.

The authors are greatly indebted to the Criminal Courts Technical Assistance Project, Institute for Advanced Studies in Justice, American University Washington College of Law , and to the Law Enforcement Assistance Administration, U. S. Department of Justice. First, they provided funds for the field studies, research, and some of the writing involved in this effort. Second, as indicated, in the acknowledgments, they permitted us to use the material which appeared in the monograph with the same title in April 1978. This material has been updated and expanded for this book.

We thank the many state and trial court administrators who filled out and returned our lengthy and complex questionnaires and then, took the time not only to respond to follow-up questions, but to supply us with copies of personnel rules, collective bargaining agreements, and other pertinent material. Without their help, this book could never have been completed. The same is true for those court administrators and their staff members who took time from their very busy schedules to provide assistance during field visits.

We express our gratitude to Marion Weaver Lawson, who laboriously read and edited this volume and who made many clarifications in the text. Barbara Allen, University of Denver College Law Library staff, did her best to straighten out three very different and irregular footnote styles, and we thank her for her help. We would also like to acknowledge the helpful research assistance of Kandace

Van Sickle, graduate student and candidate for the Master of Science degree in Judicial Administration at the University of Denver College of Law. This is probably the place to state that any sins of **omission** or commission as to substance, style, or grammar are the authors' alone.

Finally, several people were involved in typing the manuscript in its various stages of draft and redraft. We appreciate their help and extend our thanks to: Nelle C. Ackerman, Kimberly E. Beckman, and Margo Guillen.

Denver, Colorado   Harry O. Lawson
                                    H. R. Ackerman, Jr.

Los Angeles, California   Donald E. Fuller

Acknowledgments

We wish to thank the Adjudication Division, Law Enforcement Assistance Administration, U.S. Department of Justice and the Criminal Courts Technical Assistance Project, Institute for Advanced Studies in Justice, American University Washington College of Law for granting permission to reprint the material in the monograph <u>Personnel Administration in the Courts</u>, published by the Criminal Courts Technical Assistance Project at American University and funded by the Law Enforcement Assistance Administration. (See further comments in the Preface.)

We wish to thank the American Bar Association for granting permission to reprint excerpts from American Bar Association, Commission on Standards of Judicial Administration, <u>Standards Relating to Court Organization</u>.

SECTION 1.
OVERVIEW

1. The Need for Personnel Management in the Courts

INTRODUCTION

All fifty states and most large and medium size counties and municipalities, as well as some of the smaller ones, have some sort of civil service or personnel merit system, usually including established classification and compensation plans for executive branch employees. Although state and local courts and related agencies employ at least 148,000 people, excluding probation and other court related ancillary services,[1] they have lagged behind other public entities in personnel administration.

Even though this is so, significant changes have been made in some jurisdictions in the past decade in the management of nonjudicial personnel in the courts. Some of these changes have been statewide; others have been limited to individual trial courts or circuits or to related agencies, such as probation departments. In almost all instances of change, some sort of formal personnel system has been created to replace the haphazard, personalized, and patronage methods and procedures of personnel management. These formal systems are generally similar to those in state and local executive branch agencies. Some of these, including the United States civil service system, had their origin in the nineteenth century.

A limited amount of the material in this chapter will appear in different form in a chapter on court personnel and facilities by the same authors in a monograph prepared and edited by Dr. E. Michael Wong and funded by the Law Enforcement Assistance Administration.

The relatively recent discovery of personnel administration by courts and judicial systems is related to and part of the major concerns of judicial administration today. As such, it is not a transitory phenomenon. Other judicial systems, courts, and related agencies are moving and will move in the direction of more sophisticated and systematic personnel administration.

Reasons for Growing Court Interest

There are several reasons for this emphasis on personnel administration, not the least of which is that appropriation bodies--whether state or local--are insisting upon greater productivity and efficiency from public employees and the development of new management techniques and technological applications to meet increasing workloads. This is an extremely important consideration, since personnel accounts for 75 to 80 percent of the operating costs of a court or judicial system, including furniture and equipment, but excluding building, maintaining, and remodeling facilities.

The second reason is the trend toward state-funded judicial systems. This has been a relatively recent development. While there were a few judicial systems predominantly state funded,[2] analysis of data from FY 1969 to FY 1972 led one author to conclude: "If there is a movement toward state financing of courts, it is moving much more gradually than the press releases and speeches on court reform might convey."[3] Since that time, another six states have assumed state funding of their judicial systems.[4] Two states (Nebraska and Virginia) now fund the court of limited jurisdiction, as has Maryland since 1971. Kansas, having unified its trial courts, has begun state funding of all court and probation personnel. This will take four years, beginning January 1, 1979. Missouri, which also reorganized its court system, will begin state funding of most court personnel in July, 1981. New York is phasing in state funding, and at least three states (Nevada, North Dakota, and Oregon) have state funding under study. State-wide judicial employee merit systems usually go hand in hand with state funding and administrative integration and unification of the judicial system.

The third reason for the increasing emphasis on personnel administration in courts is the emergence of public employee collective bargaining. Unionization of and collective bargaining by public employees have been on the scene for a number of years, and many states have legislated in this area, although the legislation is by no means uniform from state to state in its application either to state or local employees. Judicial systems and individual trial courts have had limited experience in collective bargaining as compared with other sectors of public employment, but this situation is changing and will change markedly in the next few years. Without a rational personnel system and skilled personnel administrators and negotiators, the courts are at a distinct disadvantages in the bargaining arena.

Fourth, judicial systems and individual courts are not exempt from federal statutory requirements and regulations concerning equal employment opportunity and affirmative action. This is especially true for those courts and related agencies which receive federal funding. It is extremely difficult, if not impossible, for a judicial system or an individual court to comply with these requirements or even to determine whether it is in compliance without some sort of formalized personnel system and some degree of personnel management sophistication.

Last, but certainly not least, is that good management of the public's courts dictates that trained, qualified personnel be recruited to handle the courts' business and that they be retained, promoted, disciplined, or removed according to their abilities and job performance. This is necessary for the effective, efficient, and equitable management of the courts' most important resource--personnel--regardless of the concern of appropriation bodies. A personnel merit system, properly managed and maintained, provides the framework for good personnel administration both on the state and trial court level.

WHAT IS PERSONNEL MANAGEMENT?

Scope of Personnel Management

Personnel administration, whether in the public or private sector, probably touches on or is involved in a wider range of activities than any other management function. It is concerned with compensation, retention, promotion, and discipline of employees on an equitable basis related to job content and employee performance. In addition, it is concerned with employee orientation, morale, and motivation. It is directed toward providing an adequate number of qualified employees to meet the agency needs, allocated and supervised in such a way as to carry out required functions as effectively or efficiently as possible. In the broadest sense, any person who supervises others is involved in and part of personnel management.[5]

Accomplishing Goals and Objectives

The accomplishment of the goals of personnel management requires:
1) understanding and determining employee skills needed;
2) gaining knowledge of the labor market and its various components;
3) developing and implementing an effective recruitment program designed to attract the best-qualified employees available in the labor market and to reach all segments and groups within that market;
4) developing and implementing training programs, both for new employees and those already on the job, including the development of supervisory skills and adaptation of and to technological change;
5) understanding budgetary needs and constraints;
6) forecasting personnel needs;
7) determining and improving adequacy of work space and equipment;
8) developing and implementing sound career ladder and promotional policies and opportunities; and
9) developing and implementing adequate fringe benefit programs to attract, retain, and maintain the morale of qualified and motivated employees.

Interrelationship with Other Management Functions: Some Examples

These are not easy or uncomplicated tasks, and their successful achievement requires the integration of personnel management and the other management skills and functions needed for proper administration.

The relationship between personnel management and budget and fiscal administration is illustrated by the personnel functions described above. Personnel need forecasting is an integral part of the budgetary process. It is also an integral part of both short-range and long-range planning, especially where planning is concerned with: 1) technological innovation to augment or supplant personnel; and

2) facility needs, including size, location, new construction, or remodeling.

Good personnel forecasting involves both good estimating techniques for determining future work levels and the development of realistic employee workload measures. It also involves determining the impact on personnel needs from a change in procedures or the introduction of technological change, such as the use of computers.

Budgetary constraints have a direct impact on improvements in fringe benefits or revisions in the compensation plan. These limitations might be offset to some extent by improvement in employee efficiency and better development of personnel. Both of these can be affected by training programs and cost-effective technological change.

Decisions on whether and how soon vacant positions should be filled are affected by expenditure patterns and fiscal controls, as well as by personnel needs. This is yet another reason for good communication among the various management disciplines and for the development of a system of shared management decisions.

To be effective, personnel managers must have knowledge of the agency's major functions, activities, goals, and objectives and should be involved in planning (including determination of facility needs), budgeting, fiscal administration, management studies, and any other major management activity.

PERSONNEL MANAGEMENT IN COURTS: WHOSE RESPONSIBILITY?

The importance of personnel management in the efficient and effective operation of public agencies has long been accepted. As previousl discussed, judicial systems, individual courts, and related agencies are recognizing the need for personnel administration in the court environment. With this recognition has come judicial understanding that personnel management is part of the professional training and skills expected of court administrators and their staffs, whether at the state or local level.

Beside determining the kind of personnel system best suited to meet court needs, a major question is who is to be responsible for managing and operating the system. Previous comments imply that personnel administration should be a responsibility of the judicial branch, but this is not a foregone conclusion, especially the definition of what constitutes "responsibility" and how it relates to "authority." This is a matter of such significance that considerable discussion is warranted.

Executive Branch Involvement

The executive branch may consider court employees to be the same as other government workers, failing to differentiate among the three branches of government or, in some cases, to recognize that there is a meaningful distinction. This is especially true at the trial court level for those trial courts supported primarily by local funds. County and municipal governments tend to think of court employees as similar to those in the public works or health department and, that, consequently, their recruitment, conditions of employment, etc., should be governed by the same rules and regulations under the county or municipal governing body. This is the practice in a number of jurisdictions today, as will be discussed in the next chapter.

Very often legislation (both state and local) will authorize the placement of judicial branch employees under the executive branch personnel system, although legislative bodies protect their own independence in the selection and management of their own personnel.

Even if the executive branch recognizes the distinction and implication of separate branches of government, it may still offer--rather insistently in some cases--to provide personnel services for the courts. An example would be Maryland, where the state-funded consolidated court of limited jurisdiction is under the executive branch personnel system.

In at least two states, Alaska and Colorado, there have been law suits to establish the authority and responsibility of the judicial branch over its own personnel. In Alaska, the matter was settled through a memorandum of agreement between the Department of Administration and the State Court Administrator as to the responsibility and authority of each.[6] In Colorado, the Supreme Court ruled that judicial employees were not subject to inclusion in the executive branch personnel system.[7]

It took until July 1, 1977 for the Hawaii judicial system to gain legislative authority to operate its own personnel system.[8] Even though the judicial system has been state funded, since 1966 the Department of Personnel Services of the executive branch had been the central personnel recruiting and administering authority for all state employees.

A Separate Judicial Personnel System

At first sight, it may appear that it is a sensible arrangement for the executive branch to provide personnel services for the judiciary, thereby eliminating duplication of administrative staff and services by using an established and experienced agency. Nevertheless, there are several reasons why it is not only desirable but necessary for the judiciary to have the authority and responsibility for its own personnel system. These were expressed very well in a 1972 study setting forth recommendations for improving the Utah court system:

> The creation of a separate judicial personnel system is basic recognition of the separation of powers concept in our form of government. The judiciary should be treated in the same fashion as the executive and legislative branches in its ability to select and retain qualified personnel. The separation of powers concept in Utah State Government has not always been adhered to. For example, Section 1 of House Bill 22 passed by the 1972 Budget Session (amending Section 67-13-12 of the Utah Code) provides that by July 1, 1973, the State Director of Personnel, an executive employee, shall prepare and administer a position classification plan for all positions in the executive and judicial branch of state government. Interestingly, employees of the Legislature are exempt from the authority of the Personnel Director to devise and administer such a plan.
> The power to control the qualifications and salaries of employees is tantamount to the ability to control an organization. Especially if a personnel office in exercising its statutory prerogatives begins to make what amounts to "line" as opposed to "staff" decisions on who can be hired, when, and at what salary.
> There are many positions in the judiciary which are not comparable to those in the executive branch. There is, for example, nothing in the executive

branch directly comparable to a court administrator, court clerk or bailiff. Requiring that these judicial positions be comparable, in qualifications and/or pay, to positions in the executive branch complicates the ability of the court to secure the kind of people needed for jobs that are unique to the judiciary.

By merging judicial and executive personnel systems, legislative intent in appropriating funds to the courts may be frustrated. The interposition of executive branch employees with authority to make judgments on court personnel matters can be quite critical when it is realized that over 75 percent of all funds appropriated for courts are for salaries and wages. . . .

Continuing the practice of using the same personnel or "merit system" for judicial personnel as that developed for executive employees is contrary to the concept of the administrative independence of the judiciary. It inevitably results in the courts being treated as departments of the executive branch in administrative affairs. It is important that one branch of government not become excessively dependent on another for essential administrative support, of which personnel is a large part.

The protections presumably afforded court employees under a state merit system designed for executive employees may be illusory because ultimately the sanctions that can be brought to bear for any violations of merit rules apply only to employers subject to executive powers. Employee rights and protections are important and should be contained in express personnel rules and regulations. But these should be promulgated by the judiciary for its own employees. Reasonableness and general comparability in salaries can be maintained by legislative approval of the judicial compensation plan if this is considered appropriate. This would be similar to the current practices in Colorado and the Federal courts.

A separate judicial personnel system,

> if properly created and administered,
> will not jeopardize reasonably uniform
> salaries for the same type of work (sub-
> ject of course to reasonable latitude
> for employees that have no parallel in
> the executive branch), adherence to
> merit principles, and adequate protec-
> tion for employees of various courts
> where the employees of some courts are
> subject to executive cotrol while others
> are not.[9]

The rationale for placing control in the judiciary over personnel management and other administrative functions in the courts is a constantly recurring theme in the literature of judicial administration. It is perhaps best expressed in the <u>American Bar Association Standards Relating to Court Organization</u>.

> Standard 1.00 provides:
> [1.00] Aims of Court Organization.
> The organization of a court system
> should serve the courts' basic task
> of determining cases justly, promptly,
> and economically. To this end, the
> organizational structure should facili-
> tate the selection and assignment of com-
> petent judicial and auxiliary personnel,
> sound financial administration, efficient
> use of manpower, facilities and equipment,
> and continuous planning for the future.[10]

The commentary on this standard discusses the two basic objectives of a court system. In brief, the primary objective is to determine the matters committed to its jurisdiction fairly, promptly, and economically. The secondary objective is set forth here in detail because of its bearing on the subject under discussion:

> A secondary objective of the court
> system is to maintain itself as an inde-
> pendent and respected branch of govern-
> ment. This objective is ultimately ful-
> filled by achievement of the court sys-
> tem's primary goal. <u>The courts must,
> nevertheless, direct attention and effort
> to their own maintenance problems. These
> include administering their affairs effec-
> tively, establishing and improving skill</u>

and morale of their judicial and auxiliary personnel, developing the popular and legislative support required to secure adequate resources, and planning to meet future demands.11 (emphasis supplied)

Examination of court personnel rules and policy statements reflects this concern for independent management within the judiciary. The following taken from the foreword of the Hamilton County (Ohio) Court of Common Pleas Personnel Rules is but one example:

> The Hamilton County Court of Common Pleas existing as entity of the judicial structure seeks to maintain its constitutional independence of the executive and legislative branches concerning organization and personnel supervision.12

Court Personnel Administration Standards

Both the American Bar Association and the National Advisory Commission on Criminal Justice Standards and Goals have specifically addressed personnel administration in the courts in the promulgation of standards related to judicial administration. Both stress the need for a separate, independent personnel system for the judiciary based on merit.

The American Bar Association Standards Relating to Court Organization deal extensively with this subject in Standard 1.42:

> 1.42 Nonjudicial Personnel of Court System.
> (a) Governing regulations. Nonjudicial personnel of the court system, including those performing the functions stated in Section 1.41(b)(ii)(2), should be selected, supervised, retained and promoted by the court system, in accordance with regulations adopted pursuant to Section 1.32. [relating to administrative authority] The regulations should provide for:
> (i) A uniform system of position classification and levels of compensation.
> (ii) A system of open and competitive application, and examina-

tion, and appointment of new employees that reflects the special requirements of each type of position in regard to education, professional certification, experience, proficiency, and performance of confidential functions. Employment should be made without discrimination on the basis of race or ethnic identity, age, sex, or religious or political affiliation, and should be administered to encourage members of minority or disadvantaged groups to seek employment in the court system.

   (iii) Uniform procedures for making periodic evaluation of employee performance and decisions concerning retention and promotion.

   (iv) Requirements that discipline or discharge be based on good cause and be subject to appropriate review.

   (v) Compatibility, so far as possible, with the employment system in the executive department. Transfer of individuals from one system to the other, without impairment of compensation, seniority, or fringe benefits should be facilitated.

 (b) Auxiliary staff classifications. Regulations governing nonjudicial employees of the court system should reflect the difference in duties and responsibilities of various types of nonjudicial personnel including the following:

   (i) Administrative personnel. Administrative personnel, such as the executive director of the administrative office, court executives of subordinate court units, and their principal deputies, should perform duties requiring managerial skills and discretion. Administrative personnel should have qualifications that include general education, appropriate professional experience, and education and training in court management or public administration. The executive director should be appointed and hold office as provided in Section 1.41(a)(i). The court executive of a subordinate court unit should be appointed and hold office as provided in Section 1.41(b)(i). The principal deputies of the executive director should be appointed by him and hold office at his pleasure, and a corresponding arrangement should apply to the principal deputies of court executives of subordinate court units.

    (ii) Professional personnel. Professional personnel include persons such as examining physicians, psychological and social diagnosticians, appraisers, and accountants, whose duties require advanced education, specialized technical knowledge, and the exercise of critical judgment. They should be selected on the basis of their competence within their own profession and adaptability to the working environment of the court system. The procedure for evaluating potential appointees to professional positions should include participation by persons of recognized standing in the professional discipline involved.

    (iii) Confidential employees. Confidential employees include secretaries and law clerks, and other persons whose duties require them to work on a personal and confidential basis with individual judges, judicial officers, administrative officials, and professional personnel. Confidential employees should meet qualifications prescribed in regulations adopted pursuant to Section 1.32, but their appointment and tenure should be at the pleasure of the person for whom they work.

    (iv) Technical and clerical employees. All other employees should be appointed by the chief administrative official of the administrative office in which they are employed.[13]

In its commentary, the American Bar Association Commission on Standards of Judicial Administration stresses the importance of selecting and retaining nonjudicial court personnel on the basis of competence, with a rational and uniform system of job classification. The classification plan should be designed to "assure parity of treatment of employees who do essentially the same work, to "assure fair relationships regarding compensation and responsibilities between levels of employee positions and to facilitate promotion and transfer of personnel within the system."[14]

The Commission observes that court employment policies should appear to the public to be even-handed and efficient. The Commission also voices its concerns about the application of the traditional civil service system to judicial system employment:

> The regulations relating to personnel policy may go so far as to amount to a civil service system for the administrative staff of the courts. Subject to the considerations referred to in paragraph (b) of this section [Standard 1.42], particularly those pertaining to administrative and confidential personnel, a civil service system may well be satisfactory in many jurisdictions. Indeed, in some states civil service systems are so fully established that anything different would be incompatible with locally prevailing practice concerning government employment. At the same time, some aspects of civil service systems have proved extremely burdensome and sources of serious inefficiency. This is particularly true of rigid seniority arrangements and requirements that an employee may be discharged only for serious cause. In the absence of strong local traditions that impel adoption of such provisions, these aspects of formalized personnel systems should be avoided.
> Whatever the arrangements concerning employment, retention, and advancement of court auxiliary personnel, they should reflect the important differences in the duties and responsibilities of various types of court staff members. Staff officials who serve as the immediate representatives of judges in positions of administrative responsibility require the personal confidence of the judge whom they serve, and should be employed on that basis. Professional personnel, who are retained so that the court system can have the benefit of advice and assistance from a professional expert, should be retained in terms of their professional competence. . . .[15]

It should be noted that Standard 1.42 and the commentary related thereto not only question the application of full civil service protections to certain categories of court employees, but also provide that personal employees of judges, such as secretaries and law clerks, be treated differently from other personnel as to employment and retention. In addition, the election of court clerks and appointment of any court personnel by anyone outside of the court system should be abolished. These are three of the major issues confronting court personnel administration and are discussed more extensively in a subsequent section of this chapter and in other chapters of this book. Stated specifically, these issues are:

1) the extent of employment safeguards which should be afforded court personnel who serve in high level administrative and professional positions;

2) the extent to which personal employees of justices and judges should be treated differently; and

3) the elimination of elected court clerks and appointment by them of their staffs outside of the court system.

In contrast with the American Bar Association, the National Advisory Commission deals with personnel administration much more generally and summarily. Standard 9.1 provides in part:

> 2. Personnel Policies. The state court administrator should establish uniform policies and procedures governing recruitment, hiring, removal, compensation, and training of all nonjudicial employees of the courts.[16]

A portion of Standards 9.2 and 9.3 also cover personnel administration:

> [9.2]1. Personnel matters. The presiding judge should have control over recruitment, removal, compensation, and training of non-judicial employees of the court. He should prepare and submit to the court for approval rules and regulations governing personnel matters to insure that employees are recruited, selected, promoted, disciplined, removed, and retired appropriately.[17]

[9.3]4. Recruiting, hiring, training, evaluating, and monitoring personnel of the court or courts with which he [trial court administrator] is concerned;[18]

While there appears to be some conflict among the portions of the three standards quoted above, it is clear that the National Advisory Commission's position is that personnel administration belongs within the judicial system.

Summary

Roscoe Pound once wrote, "The judiciary is the only great agency of government which is habitually given no control over the clerical force. Even the pettiest agency has more control than the average state court."[19]

In the past decade this continuing problem has been recognized both by state judicial systems and individual trial courts. In more and more jurisdictions, the judicial branch is exercising the authority and responsibility for personnel management, usually through the adoption of personnel rules and the creation of a system of merit employment for nonjudicial personnel. This has been and is happening at the state level where state funding of the judicial system has made statewide administration possible. In other places, individual trial courts have established personnel systems for their employees.

This trend is expected to continue, although there may continue to be executive and legislative branch opposition in some jurisdictions. Two sets of national standards dealing with judicial administration include personnel management among those ingredients necessary to operate a modern court organization effectively. Personnel administration in courts tends to vary from that in executive branch agencies as adaptations are made of personnel management principles to meet the peculiar needs of the court environment.

LEGAL REQUIREMENTS AND COURT PERSONNEL

The legal framework has been touched upon briefly in a previous section in connection with determining who should have the authority and responsibility for personnel management in the courts. An expanded discussion is warranted, because one conclusion to be drawn from those comments is that the way a court personnel system is organized and administered--indeed whether there is any system at all--may be determined by a variety of constitutional provisions, statutory requirements, or court rules; by a combination of the three or any two; or by statute or rule only. The content and mix of these provisions, requirements, and rules differ from jurisdiction to jurisdiction, and, in some states, there are no formal requirements or guidelines at all within the judicial system.

Where there are no judicial system or court formal requirements or guidelines, court personnel are usually administered in one of two ways. First, court personnel may be hired, retained, promoted, or terminated under traditional, unwritten practices-- usually found in patronage systems. Second, an agency outside the judicial system may step in to fill the vacuum--an executive branch personnel system at the state level or a county or municipal personnel system at the local level, as previously discussed.

Federal Requirements

Court personnel administration is subject to very few federal statutory requirements or rules. A relatively recent U. S. Supreme Court decision determined that state and local employees are not subject to the provisions of the Fair Labor Standards Act.[20]

The Equal Employment Act of 1972 applies to court personnel along with all others. The Act states that state and local governments are subject to the provisions concerning discrimination in the employment process as outlined in the 1964 Civil Rights Act. The courts are ordered to correct discrimination practices, both current and historic, and may order back pay for two years preceding the filing of a charge.

Although judicial systems and individual courts have been sued under the provisions of this act by persons alleging discrimination in hiring or other personnel practices, the main impact on courts has come through federal grant requirements, especially those made by the Law Enforcement Assistance Administration. LEAA requires an Affirmative Action/ Equal Opportunity Employment Program, if there are more than fifty employees, or if the population to be served has more than 3 percent minority representation, or if the LEAA sub-grants total more than $25,000.

State Constitutions and Statutes

Very few state constitutions make reference to court personnel, as such. One exception is Colorado, which provides: "The supreme court shall appoint an administrator and such other personnel as it deems necessary to administer the system."[21] Several state constitutions provide for the appointment of an administrator, but do not refer to other personnel.[22] Article VI, Section 11 of the South Dakota constitution provides in part:

> Section 11. ADMINISTRATION
>
> The chief justice is the administrative head of the unified judicial system. The chief justice shall submit an annual consolidated budget for the entire unified judicial system, and the total cost of the system shall be paid by the state. The Legislature may provide by law for the reimbursement to the state of appropriate portions of such cost by governmental subdivisions. <u>The Supreme Court shall appoint such court personnel as it deems necessary to serve at its pleasure.</u> The chief justice shall appoint a presiding circuit judge for each judicial circuit to serve at the pleasure of the chief justice. Each presiding circuit judge shall have such administrative power as the Supreme Court designates by rule and may, unless it be otherwise provided by law, appoint judicial personnel to courts of limited jurisdiction to serve at his pleasure. <u>Each presiding circuit judge shall appoint clerks and other court personnel for the counties in his circuit who shall serve at his pleasure at a compensation fixed by law.</u> Duties of clerks shall be defined by Supreme Court rule.[23]
> (emphasis supplied)

In many states, the only constitutional reference to court personnel usually is to elected court clerks.

An example of specific state legislation is an act adopted by the Kansas legislature in 1977, which provided for the establishment of a judicial personnel system for the nonjudicial employees of the supreme court, the court of appeals, and the judicial administrator. This measure provided in part:

> The supreme court shall establish for
> the non-judicial personnel of the su-
> preme court and the court of appeals
> a formal pay plan, a personnel plan
> and an affirmative action plan for the
> hiring of minority persons. Such pay
> plan and personnel plan shall include,
> but not be limited to, job descriptions,
> qualifications of employees, salary
> ranges, vacation, sick and other au-
> thorized leave policies. A copy of such
> pay plan, personnel plan and affirmative
> action plan shall be submitted to the
> legislature on or before January 15,
> 1978.[24]

Court personnel systems are usually not covered as extensively by statute in most states as in the examples cited above. Statutes in a number of jurisdictions, however, may specify the employee appointment authority of various courts or judges and may set salaries by statute.

Public Employee Labor Relations. Of considerable importance are laws providing for and regulating public employee labor-management relations. At least twenty-eight states have adopted comprehensive legislation relating to labor relations of state, county, and municipal employees. Usually, judicial branch employees are not directly addressed. Only three of the twenty-eight states which adopted comprehensive legislation specifically exempt or make specific reference to court employees (Connecticut, Iowa, and Vermont).[25]

These statutes--and those which may be adopted--in the other states will be of greater significance to the judiciary as court employees in more jurisdictions organize and enter into collective bargaining agreements. Because of the lack of specific reference to court employees in most of these acts, the amount of litigation and court decisions interpreting applicability to court employees can be expected to increase. (Collective bargaining in the courts is discussed in more detail in Chapter 12.)

Court Rules

Statewide personnel rules have been adopted in

most jurisdictions where the court system has been state funded, as previously indicated. In Colorado, these rules were adopted by the supreme court pursuant to the court's general rule-making authority and specific statutory provisions. In South Dakota, it was done under the supreme court's general constitutional superintending authority. This pattern has been followed in most of these states.

In those states where local courts have established separate judicial system personnel plans, usually it has been accomplished by local court rules.

Model Judicial Articles and Legislation

Model judicial articles drafted before state funding and judicial system control of its personnel became part of the court reform package make no reference to court personnel. The new American Bar Association model judicial article, based on the American Bar Association Standards Relating to Court Organization (adopted in 1978) provides that the rules of administration promulgated by the supreme court of judicial council shall include: "Procedures for selection and retention on a merit basis of all non-judicial personnel employed in the judicial system. . ."

The model judicial article proposed by the Advisory Commission on Intergovernmental Relations provides for the appointment by the supreme court of the administrator and his assistants, but goes no further.[26]

The A.C.I.R. court reform package also includes legislation establishing a separate statewide, state-funded court personnel system. This proposed model legislation is based on a similar Colorado provision and specifies:

TITLE VIII

COURT PERSONNEL AND FINANCES

....Section 2. Court Personnel and Compensation. (a) After [insert appropriate date] the chief justice shall prescribe by rule a personnel classification plan for all courts in the judicial department. Such a plan shall include; (i) a basic compensation plan of pay ranges to which classes of positions shall be assigned and may be reassigned; (ii) qualifications for all non-judicial positions and classes of positions which shall include education, experience, special skills, and legal knowledge; (iii) an outline of duties to be performed in each position and class of positions; (iv) the number of fulltime and part-time positions, by position title and classification, in each court in the state; (v) the procedures for and regulations governing the appointment and removal of non-judicial personnel; (vi) the procedures for and regulations governing the promotion of non-judicial personnel; and (vii) the amount, terms, and conditions of sick leave and vacation time and fringe benefits for court personnel, including annual allowance and accumulation thereof, and hours of work and other conditions of employment.

(b) The chief justice, in promulgating rules as set forth in this section, shall take into account the compensation and classification plans, vacation and sick leave provisions, and other conditions of employment applicable to the employees of the executive and legislative department. The chief justice shall be aided by the administrative office of the courts in the implementation of this section.[27]

The subjects covered in the A.C.I.R. model legislation are essential in any comprehensive set of personnel rules and provide the framework for effective personnel legislation. These subjects are included in most of the statewide judicial system personnel rules adopted in the past few years and in a number of local jurisdictions as well.[28]

Summary

Only in a very few jurisdictions are there constitutional or statutory provisions that relate to or provide for court personnel, except in the most narrow way, e.g., a constitutional requirement for elected court clerks or a statute setting the salary of court reporters. The judicial branch in a number of statewide systems has exercised authority for personnel management under general administrative or rule-making power. This has also been true in a number of trial courts which are locally funded.

The most immediate concern is with state laws providing for collective bargaining by public employees. In most of these, specific reference is not made to court employees, either as to inclusion or exclusion. Court decisions and experience in those jurisdictions where court employees collectively bargain will make this cloudy picture clearer.

THE COURT ENVIRONMENT

There are a number of reasons why the court environment differs from that of most other public agencies. Some of these were cited by Edward B. McConnell in an address at the National Conference of Judiciary in Williamsburg, Virginia, in 1971:

> a. First, the key people in the courts are high level professionals--judges and lawyers--who are accustomed to working as individuals, and do not take kindly to regimentation. The judge in the balck robe does not wear under it a gray flannel suit--he is not an organization minded man!
> b. Second, in our governmental system we place a very high value on judicial independence, and to insure it we have surrounded judges with a variety of protections against outside influences, even administrative ones. Thus, in our state [New Jersey] for example, while the Chief Justice is constitutionally the administrative head of all the courts, he has no authority to appoint, promote, demote or remove any judge; in fact, the only people in the system he can hire and fire are his stenographer, his law secretary, and me! As an executive in business or government can appreciate, this severely limits the pressures that can be brought to bear to produce administratively desired results.
> c. Third, many of the "dramatis personae" required for a successful judicial performance--these include practicing attorneys, jurors, witnesses, and litigants are not even public employees; and others who are so employed are not within the

> judicial branch of government--this is particularly true on the criminal side.
>
> d. Fourth, the various participants in the litigation process do not all have the same goal in mind, but often are pursuing conflicting objectives.[29]

There are further reasons why administration of a court system (including personnel management) is complex and different from other types of administration.

First, the structure and organization of a court system are established by constitutional and statutory provisions. Reorganization cannot take place by executive fiat (of the judicial branch) even with the concurrence of those responsible for managing the system. Constitutional or statutory change is often a time-consuming and difficult process, involving many who are outside the system.

Second, the courts have no control over intake. With limited exceptions, courts have to accept cases filed with them.

Third, there is the matter of tradition. While court administration as a concept is relatively new and personnel management in the courts even newer, the courts and the laws they interpret have their roots in medieval England. Judges and lawyers are traditionalists and are slow to accept change and are usually not innovators. The doctrine of <u>stare decisis</u> is the cornerstone of the American <u>legal process</u> and provides stability in the determination of legal issues, but it is an impediment when applied to administration of the courts' business.

Fourth, judges are very much involved in all aspects of court administration, and this is as it should be, because the nature of the judicial process is such that administrative policy decisions often affect the image and independence of the judiciary and the ways in which cases proceed through the court (just to cite two interrelationship examples). The court personnel manager, whether or not the court administrator, must recognize these interrelationships and work within this context to be effective. He must also recognize that his authority is not independent and separate, but derives from the authority of the judge or judges to whom he is responsible. This situation requires a clarification of administrative responsibilities between the judges and the administrator and his staff, definition of the scope of the administrative staff functions, and an enumeration thereof--not always easy to accomplish, especially in a court or court system where the approach to administration has been fragmented and relatively unsophisticated.

Specific Areas of Concern for Personnel Management

There are certain aspects of the court environment that may raise problems for personnel management not found in other public agencies.

Method of Judicial Selection. In those states where judges are appointed, especially those with merit systems of selection, the imposition of a court personnel system for nonjudicial employees usually does not pose any unusual problems. These judges do not need the campaign support of their employees to gain office in the first instance or to be retained. This is not necessarily the case in those twenty-eight states where all or part of the judiciary is elected on a partisan or nonpartisan adversary ballot.

It is primarily in these states that many court employees are hired and still hold their jobs under some form of patronage. As Chief Justice Edward E. Pringle of Colorado has observed:

> The election of judges may also result in the hiring of patronage employees, again very understandable, but often employee qualifications and competence take a back seat to loyalty and the ability to help the judge get re-elected.[30]

This situation has been overcome in a number of jurisdictions, and personnel systems for employees based on merit have been established. This has happened both at the state and trial court levels. Usually, it has been accomplished by allowing judges to retain certain employees on a personal or patronage basis, such as the judge's secretary, law clerk, reporter, and bailiff, or some combination thereof. Even so, in some places, it has been possible to include these employees in the personnel plan insofar as salaries, qualifications, and fringe benefits are concerned.

Experience in these jurisdictions has shown that it is possible to establish a system of personnel management where judges are elected, but it may be more difficult to accomplish, and those working in this kind of court environment should recognize potential problems, especially in gaining initial judicial acceptance for establishing a personnel plan.

Personal or Confidential Employees. The question of what to do about personal or confidential employees of a justice or judge is not limited to jurisdictions where judges are elected. In all court environments, there are employees who work on a personal and confidential basis with judges. Each court system or individual court, therefore, has to deal with this aspect of personnel management.

Justices and judges in most jurisdictions feel strongly that they need to command the personal loyalty of secretaries and law clerks (and, in some places, reporters and bailiffs), because of their close and confidential involvement with the judge for whom they work in expediting his or her judicial business. Judges feel that they should select whom they want and that these persons should serve at their pleasure. Some feel strongly that they should be able to set salaries, determine working conditions, and fringe benefits. In fact, the new A.B.A. model judicial article expressly provides that confidential employees serve at the pleasure of the appointing authority, notwithstanding merit selection and retention of all nonjudicial personnel. One may well question the wisdom of placing this provision in a state constitution, but it certainly signifies judicial reverence for maintaining confidential employee status.

Very often, an administrator or consultant making a study preparatory to establishing a personnel system not only has to deal with this situation, but often finds that the salaries and benefits are out of line with those of other employees, including personal employees of other judges. These practices are not compatible with the basic tenents of a personal merit system involving equal treatment of employees, comparable pay for comparable duties, standard fringe benefits, and comparable employment standards for similar positions. In fact, employee morale may be affected, because of the feeling on the part of some that there are two classes of employees in the court.

Most court personnel systems handle this situation by effecting a compromise. As previously indicated, justices and judges are given the direct authority to hire and remove confidential or personal employees. These employees, however, must meet employment standards as specified in the job description for the position, and they are subject to the same classification and salary plan and fringe benefits applicable to other employees. They do not have the protection of the grievance procedure or disciplinary appeal proceedings available to most employees in the classified service, which means they have no tenure protection. South Dakota appears to be the only jurisdiction where all employees, including those usually considered personal or confidential, are included within the classified service.

Reporters are removed from confidential service in jurisdictions, such as California, where they are pooled rather than assigned to a specific judge. This approach is possible only in large multi-judge courts and is not applicable in rural areas where reporters accompany judges on circuit. At least one jurisdiction--Colorado--provides that confidential employees of a judge are subject to reassignment by the chief judge when not needed in their own court.

No matter how this problem is handled, it represents a situation seldom found in other kinds of public employment. Its solution requires a great deal of tact and give and take by all involved. It is seldom solved to the complete mutual satisfaction of all concerned: the judges, the employees involved, the personnel managers, and other employees of the court. Short of eliminating this category, it is difficult for the employees involved, regardless of group, to overcome the feeling of separateness, but it can be mitigated. A court personnel system that does not come to grips with this problem and resolve it in some way is not likely to endure.

Elected Court Clerks

In thirty-seven states, at least some of the trial court clerks are elected. In some, the only duties of the position are related to the courts. In others, the position is combined with other functions, such as recording deeds and maintaining the election rolls. Elected clerks usually appoint their deputies and may operate independently of the judges as separately elected constitutional officers. The situation is further complicated in some places, because the clerk's office is operated from the fees it collects, and staff size and salaries depend on the revenue received.

A few states, such as Alaska, Colorado, and Hawaii, never had elected court clerks, and a few others, such as Kansas and South Dakota, have been successful in changing from elected to appointed clerks as part of a court-reform constitutional package and implementing legislation. In most jurisdictions, the election of court clerks is deeply rooted in tradition, and efforts to change this practice has been successfully resisted, even when included in a court-reform proposal.

In large jurisdictions, such as Maricopa County Superior Court (Arizona) and the superior courts of the larger counties in California, employees of the clerk's office may be under the county (executive branch) personnel system, while the other court employees are under a separate system. Employee morale problems are minimized, if the salary structure and fringe benefits under both plans are similar.

North Carolina's handling of personnel management with respect to elected court clerks may be unique. In that state, the judicial system is state funded. The elected court clerks still select their own court employees, but these employees must meet the qualifications and be selected according to the procedures established in the judicial system personnel rules promulgated by the Administrative Director of the Courts.[31] Salaries and fringe benefits are also specified by rule.

The ways in which the employees of elected court clerks might be incorporated into a state-wide judicial personnel system were among the major considerations of a 1974 state-wide court personnel study conducted by an interim committee of the Florida legislature. A further compounding factor was the disparity of the salary and fringe benefit plans affecting clerk's office personnel in most of the counties.[32] The results of this study were not adopted because the legislative decision was made not to consider state-wide funding, at least at that time.

The same management problems usually exist regardless of the personnel system covering the employees of the clerk's office. These problems are not limited to personnel management, but cover all aspects of court support operations and the relationship and degree of coordination between the judges (and their administrator, if they have one) and the elected clerk and staff. These vary among jurisdictions, and a separate treatise would be necessary to explore this subject in the depth it deserves. It is sufficient for the purposes of this book to highlight this situation as another important aspect of the court environments in many jurisdictions which cannot be overlooked in efforts to rationalize personnel management, as well as other aspects of court administration.

Other Examples of Court Personnel System Fragmentation

The discussion thus far in this section shows the difficulties inherent in establishing rational personnel management in the courts, because of fragmentation in administrative responsibility for court personnel, with personal employees of judges and elected court clerks cited as examples. The list is by no means exhausted. In some jurisdictions, bailiffs are employees of the sheriff. In others, employees working side by side may be funded by different levels of government and subject to different rules and statutory requirements governing their employment.

Perhaps a prime example can be found in the State of Maryland, where the status of court personnel was explained as follows in a 1976 report:

> There are approximately 2,250 employees in Maryland courts or related agencies. Those in appellate courts (64), Administrative Office of the Courts (30), and the District Court (826) are state funded. In a sense, the employees in the elected clerks of circuit courts (733) are state funded, in that the state makes up any deficiencies in operating expenses, if fees fail to provide sufficient revenue. Circuit court employees and employees of the Supreme Bench of Baltimore, other than those in the clerks' offices, are funded at the county level, except for employees of the Supreme Bench of Baltimore; they are funded by Baltimore City.
>
> There are a variety of personnel systems in effect, not necessarily related to the source of funding. The district court is under the state executive branch personnel system. The two appellate courts and the Administrative Office of the Courts have an ad hoc system patterned after the state system. With two exceptions, employees of the elected court clerks serve at the pleasure of the clerk. Personnel in the clerk's office in Washington County and in the Criminal Court of Baltimore City (part of the Supreme Bench) are in the state executive branch merit system. The nonclerks' office employees in Baltimore City are under the municipal personnel

system. In the circuits, generally, employees serve at the pleasure of the judges, even though the county pay plan may be used.[33]

Summary

The court environment is much more complex than that usually found in state agencies. The nature of the process, the concept of judicial independence, the many and varied actions, tradition, and the necessary involvement of judges in administration all contribute to this complexity. All of these factors must be taken into account, if court administration is to be accepted and effective.

Personnel management in this setting must be adaptable to still other conditions, such as how judges are selected, differential treatment for personal employees of judges, elected court clerks and staffs (where they exist), and the general fragmentation of court personnel. The task is not insurmountable, as attested by the success achieved in a number of state systems and individual trial courts. This experience shows generally that the traditional civil service system probably will fail if applied without modification in a court setting. Modifications are necessary given the nature of the court environment, but vary from place to place depending on local conditions.

It is little wonder that it has taken longer for professional personnel management to be accepted in a court setting than in other public agencies. The need is just as great and may be even greater, the longer it is postponed.

NOTES

1. The last published total (1975) shows 131,988 FTE's (full-time employee equivalents) employed in state and local judicial activities, Source Book of Criminal Justice Statistics, 1976, (Washington, D.C.: U. S. Department of Justice, Law Enforcement Assistance Administration, National Criminal Justice Information and Statistics Service, 1978), Table 1.12, p. 64. The average annual increase in FTE's between 1971 and 1974 was 6,215, some of which may be attributed to better reporting. Even assuming a somewhat lesser growth rate, the total FTE's at the end of 1978 can be conservatively estimated at 148,000.

2. Alaska, Colorado, Connecticut, Delaware, Hawaii, New Mexico, North Carolina, Rhode Island, and Vermont.

3. Carl Baar, Separate but Subservient; Court Budgeting in the American States (Lexington, Mass.: Lexington Books, 1975), p. 121.

4. The six are Alabama, Kentucky, Maine, Massachusetts, South Dakota, and West Virginia.

5. There are many personnel text books and handbooks that explain the importance of the various facets of personnel management in great detail and trace the historical development of civil service and personnel merit systems and personnel administration. It is not necessary for the purposes of this book to reproduce this material. Rather, the major functions of personnel management, especially as they relate to courts, are stressed and summarized here, with emphasis on the interrelationship of personnel and other management disciplines. A bibliography of some standard works on personnel administration is included as Appendix A for those readers who wish to cover this background material in greater detail. The major functions of personnel management with identification of the issues and a discussion of "how to do it" in courts are set forth in Chapters 3 through 10.

6. Memorandum of Agreement, signed by Robert W. Ward, Commission of Administration and John W. McMillan, Administrative Director, Alaska Court System, July 7, 1967.

7. In Re Interogatory of the Governor, Concerning Article XIII, Section 13 of the Constitution of Colorado 162 Colo. 158 [425 p2d 31].

8. Act 159, Ninth Legislature, State of Hawaii, 1977.

9. Utah, Legislative Council, Unified Court Advisory Committee, Utah Courts Tomorrow; Report and Recommendations (Salt Lake City: Utah Legislative Council, 1972), pp. 43-44.

10. American Bar Association, Commission on Standards of Judicial Administration, Standards Relating to Court Organization (Chicago: American Bar Association, 1974), p. 1.

11. Ibid.

12. Hamilton County, Ohio, Court of Common Pleas, General Division, Personnel Manual for the General Division of the Hamilton Court of Common Pleas (Cincinnati: Hamilton Court of Common Pleas, 1975), p.1.

13. American Bar Association, Commission on Standards of Judicial Administration, Standards

Relating to Court Organization, pp. 91-93.
    14. Ibid., p. 94.
    15. Ibid., pp. 95-96.
    16. National Advisory Commission on Criminal Justice Standards and Goals, Report on Courts (Washington, D.C.: U. S. Govt. Print. Off., 1973), p. 176.
    17. Ibid, p. 180.
    18. Ibid, p. 183.
    19. Roscoe Pound, "Principles and Outlines of a Modern Court Organization," Journal of the American Judicature Society, 23 (April, 1940) p. 229.
    20. National League of Cities v. Usery, 96 Sup. Ct. 2465, 49 L. Ed 2nd. 245.
    21. Colorado Constitution, Art. 6, Sec. 5(3).
    22. For example, Alaska, Arizona, Hawaii, Illinois, Missouri, and New Jersey, among others.
    23. South Dakota Constitution, Art. 6, Sec. 2.
    24. S.B. 460, Kansas Legislature, 1977 Session; also see Institute for Advanced Studies in Justice, Criminal Courts Technical Assistance Project, Development of a Comprehensive Personnel Plan for Non-Judicial Employees of the Kansas Appellate Courts (Washington, D.C.: The American University Law School, 1977).
    25. George C. Cole and John R. Wadsworth, Unionization of Court Employees: A National Survey (Paper presented to the Conference of State Court Administrators, Minneapolis, August 1, 1977), p. 9.
    26. Advisory Commission on Intergovernmental Relations, Court Reform (Washington, D.C.: Advisory Commission on Intergovernmental Relations, 1971), p. 5.
    27. Ibid., p. 20.
    28. Statewide system examples are: Alaska, Colorado, Maine, New Mexico, and South Dakota among others; at the trial court level, the circuit court of Multonomah County (Oregon), the Hamilton County Court of Common Pleas (Ohio), and the Superior Court of Alameda County (California) are just a few of many examples.
    29. Edward B. McConnell, "The Role of the State Administrator," Justice in the States; Addresses and Papers of the National Conference on the Judiciary, March 11-14, 1971 (Washington, D.C.: U. S. Department of Justice, Law Enforcement Assistance Administration, 1971), pp. 89-90.
    30. Edward E. Pringle, "The Role of the State Chief Justice," Justice in the States; Addresses and Papers of the National Conference on the Judiciary, March 11-14, 1971 (Washington, D.C.: U. S. Depart-

ment of Justice, Law Enforcement Assistance Administration, 1971), p. 82.

31. North Carolina, Administrative Office of the Courts, <u>Personnel Manual</u> (Raleigh, N.C.: Administrative Office of the Courts, 1966).

32. Institute for Advanced Studies in Justice, Criminal Courts Technical Assistance Project, <u>Report on Technical Assistance in Planning a State-wide Court Personnel Study for the State of Florida</u> (Washington, D.C.: The American University Law School, 1974).

33. Institute for Advanced Studies in Justice, Criminal Courts Technical Assistance Project, <u>A Request for a Proposal to Design and Develop a Personnel Merit System for Non-Judicial Court Employees in the State of Maryland</u> (Washington, D.C.: The American University Law School, 1976), p. 4.

2. Court Personnel Systems

BACKGROUND

Court personnel systems, as previously indicated, have tended to follow developments in the executive branch personnel systems, though usually some years later. For the most part, court personnel systems may be typified by three general models: patronage, merit, and collective bargaining. There have been mixes, of course, of all three in the same jurisdiction, as well as gradations which hardly fit in one category, let alone three. Though the general movement has been from patronage to merit and then to collective bargaining, there are many exceptions, and many judicial systems or courts remain stuck with some form of patronage or merit system. Collective bargaining has probably stimulated greater attention among court personnel in some jurisdictions than either patronage or merit.

Operationally, a distinction exists between a statewide court personnel system and that of a trial court. This is so for a number of reasons, which are addressed in other chapters. As background for the discussion of models, it is useful to list the distinguishing factors between these two systems, as shown in Figure 2.1.

The differences enumerated in Figure 2.1 make it obvious that any use of models to describe court personnel systems must recognize the state dimension, if one exists, as well as the local one. It is for that reason that patronage, merit, and collective bargaining may exist, on occasion, in the courts in the same state. It is possible to describe patronage as a system, regardless of the number of employees affected, in the same way that merit and collective bargaining are described as systems. It is important to see how each of these concepts operates as a

FIGURE 2.1

Key Distinguishing Factors Between State Personnel System and Local Personnel System (trial court, limited, and special jurisdiction courts)

Factor	State System	Local System
Scope	Typically affects all courts in unified system, usually with unitary budget (state funding), central headquarters staff	Typically affects one court at local level for which funding is provided primarily by a local governmental body
Employer	Typically, Chief Justice or State Court Administrator	Typically, Presiding Judge or Trial Court Administrator, though may include funding body
Funding	State legislature typically funds judges and nonjudicial personnel	Local government typically funds nonjudicial personnel and may provide salary supplement to judges
Technical Responsibility	State administrator's office typically develops, monitors, and controls classification and pay plan, as well as rules and fringe benefits for all courts in unified system including headquarters, but hiring is a local responsibility	Local court typically develops, monitors, and controls classification and pay plan, as well as rules and fringe benefits system for its court only, though many courts yield to the executive branch (city or county)

system and then place the various systems together into a macrosystem which comprises all the judicial entities in a state.

A state then, for modeling purposes, will be made up of various entities which might constitute a state system as delineated earlier in the comparison chart, or a series of local systems. Of course, even a state system can have local exceptions which lie outside the unified system, such as municipal courts of limited jurisdiction. These courts are not covered in the models unless they are noteworthy, e.g., Denver, Colorado, is both a city and county, and the county court has both state and municipal jurisdiction, has local funding and a local personnel system, and is not part of the unified system (two tier). This court is a noteworthy exception to Colorado's otherwise state system.

PATRONAGE

Patronage in the courts derived its strength from the political process. It survives primarily in states wherein judgeships are contested on a partisan basis. Its decline can be traced in large measure to the introduction of merit selection of judges. Other factors in the decline of patronage include the introduction of merit systems in the executive branch, the unification of state courts and unitary budgeting, the complexity of court operations, attention to affirmative action (though some argue that patronage is more likely to be responsive to affirmative action than merit systems), and burgeoning numbers of well qualified court applicants.

For that matter, even political parties have increased their levels of professionalization, making it likely that, where patronage exists, the level of competence of appointees exceeds that of past generations. For the most part, increased levels of professionalization, whether patronage or merit, may be equated to increased education. This development has affected minorities, who traditionally have been excluded because of color and now may be excluded because of education (i.e., lack thereof).

A major difference between patronage and merit lies in the recruitment and selection process. In patronage, the appointment is limited to those persons who have assisted the judge or the political party in the election of a judge or some other official. Announcement of a job opening is typically by word of mouth. The selection interview, typically by the judge, is not recorded, need not conform to

standards, and is typically pass/fail. Other major
differences involve promotion, tenure, and parity in
compensation and working conditions.

Confidential/Exempt Employees

Closely akin to the patronage appointment is that
of the confidential or exempt employee, who serves at
the pleasure of the judge. Perhaps at its worst it
constitutes nepotism (familial relative) and crony-
ism (a friend). In other respects, the appointment may be the same as patronage with respect
to the announcement of a vacancy and the job interview.

A confidential or exempt appointment may occur
in a merit system or in a collective bargaining system. It may be unclassified, meaning that the position has no permanent status, no rights of appeal,
and terms and conditions of employment are not standardized. A confidential or exempt position may be
within the classified system for compensation, hours
of work, and fringe benefits, but still be without
any right of appeal or permanent status.

MERIT SYSTEMS

Merit systems, where they exist, are generally
similar to those governing executive branch agencies. They usually provide for open recruitment,
appointment, and promotion according to ability;
adequate compensation, equal pay for equal work, and
protection against arbitrary dismissal. There are
technical considerations as well:

A merit system typically consists of classified
positions. A classified position is one in which
permanent status can be achieved after a suitable
probationary period.

A merit system typically employs standardized
selection devices whether oral interviews, written
tests, performance tests, or combinations thereof.[1]
Whether these devices have been fair, predictive,
and selective of the best candidates, they have been
administered on the premise that each candidate
faced the same test. It was assumed that this equal
treatment would at least be nondiscriminatory and,
at best, produce the most highly qualified candidates from which to make the appointments.

A merit system bases its personnel action on
formalized rules which guide events such as status
changes (a status change is one which affects pay in
some fashion such as promotion, demotion, transfer,

discipline, dismissal, or freezing a salary step, fringe benefits, grievance procedure, classification, and pay plan, layoffs, etc.). Such rules control personnel actions, forcing individual actions to conform to the structure created. Rules, it is argued, make it more likely that employees will be treated equally in personnel actions.

A merit system provides for an appeal procedure from personnel actions. These procedures in court personnel systems are focused more on grievances from disciplinary actions than from matters affecting classification and pay. (These matters have not necessarily been excluded, although they have, to some extent, been neglected.) Appeal procedures typically provide for a hearing before a normal appeals board.[2] These boards vary in composition from completely independent bodies to committees appointed from within the agency. The courts typically hear such appeals, when so provided, before a board or panel of judges (sometimes including nonjudicial personnel) from within the system. Appeals boards may be assisted in their deliberations by a hearing officer who makes findings of fact with respect to the issues and recommends a disposition of the dispute. Boards usually sustain the findings of hearing officers.

As hearings officers are usually paid by the agency, normally the defendant in such cases, it is not surprising that they are viewed as pro-agency. After exhausting these remedies, litigants may turn to the trial courts. This poses an interesting dilemma, as the plaintiff, if suing in the state trial court, and if a trial court employee, must once again face a judge of the employing court, a situation which may prompt filing in the federal court in hope of finding a more sympathetic tribunal. As an alternative, an outside judge may be assigned upon disqualification of the local judges.

COLLECTIVE BARGAINING

Collective bargaining is described in detail elsewhere in this book. For purposes of the present discussion, two distinctions should be made with reference to the courts between:

1) collective bargaining which covers a court function, such as probation, which is in the executive branch; and

2) collective bargaining between the court,

at least as a co-employer, and at least one court function, such as clerical employees.

Collective Bargaining When the Court Function is in the Executive Branch

The court, in this instance, not only stands outside the funding relationship, but yields the hiring and firing responsibilities to another agency. Accordingly, the court is not considered the employer in collective bargaining terms, nor does it have management rights.[3] For the most part, such employees gained quick collective bargaining rights when a public employees' relations act was adopted. These employees had been typically lodged in the executive branch prior to passage of the act.

In states where court functions, such as probation, remain in the court and where executive branch employees enjoy collective bargaining there may be pressure from among these court employees for transfer to the executive branch. This can occur, as well, in court merit systems which may lag in comparability with the executive branch system.

Collective Bargaining in the Court

In this instance the court stands as the administrative authority, though typically not the funding agency. There is speculation about who may become the employer in a unified, unitary budget system. Massachusetts has named the state's chief justice as the employer, though he may delegate this authority. Presumably, since local courts stand as co-employers with local funding bodies, the state legislature will become involved at such time as state-funded court systems engage in statewide collective bargaining.

PERSONNEL SYSTEM MODELS

Earlier discussion of models considered the state and local systems with respect to scope, employer, funding, and technical responsibility. The type of personnel system: patronage, merit, and collective bargaining should also be added as key distinguishing characteristics, and a separate category, mixed systems, should also be added to characterize those jurisdictions with a combination or mix of the features of state and local systems. These are shown in Figure 2.2.

Figure 2.2

Key Distinguishing Factors: State, Local, and Mixed Personnel Systems

Factor	State System	Local System	Mixed System
Scope	Typically affects all courts in unified system, usually with unitary budget (state-funded), central headquarters staff	Typically affects one court at local level for which funding is provided primarily by a local governmental body	May affect a whole level of trial courts or certain categories of employees statewide, but otherwise affects individual courts because of local funding
Employer	Typically, chief justice or state court administrator	Typically, presiding judge or trial court administrator, though may include funding body	Diffused, depending on source of funding and type of personnel system
Funding	State legislature typically funds judges and nonjudicial personnel	Local government typically develops, monitors, and controls classification and pay plan, as well as rules and fringe benefits system for its court only	A mix of state and local funding, state funding may cover one level of trial court or certain categories of employees, such as court administration, reporters, and judges' secretaries

Figure 2.2 (cont'd)

Factor	State System	Local System	Mixed System
Technical Responsibility	State administrator's office typically develops, monitors, and controls classification and pay plan, as well as rules and fringe benefits for all courts in unified system including headquarters, but hiring is a local responsibility	Local court typically develops, monitors, and controls classification and pay plan, as well as rules and fringe benefits system for its court only, though many courts yield to the local executive branch (city or county)	Typically fragmented between executive and judicial branches and between state and trial court levels
Type of Personnel System	Typically some sort of merit system under the judicial branch, but with some exempt positions—top professionals and judges' personal employees	A merit system under the court, or a merit system under the executive branch, a patronage system or a combination may exist; if a merit system, there will be some exempt positions; collective bargaining is most often found in local systems	Any or perhaps all of the systems described in this chapter may exist in different combinations; where one level of trial court is state funded, a merit system is likely; collective bargaining is the exception rather than the rule

Judicial personnel systems should be classified as to both state and local dimensions. The state dimension in Michigan, for example, would include the Supreme Court, court administrator's staff, one juvenile probation officer in each county, and the basic salary of the state trial judges. The local dimension would include the trial judges' salary supplement, all other nonjudicial personnel, equipment, and facilities. Michigan and California stand, to some extent, midway between the decentralized, autonomy of Texas and the unified, unitary budget of Colorado and South Dakota.

Three basic personnel models: state, local, and mixed can be identified from those states and local jurisdictions which either responded to personnel questionnaires from the authors or which were visited. Each state for which responses were received has been classified within one of these three models. The distinguishing characteristics of each model are shown below.

State System

This model is characterized generally by substantial state funding, appointed clerks, and technical responsibility attached to the administrative office of the courts (or state court administrator's office); substantial merit features with exempt positions typically judges' personal employees and top professionals; and a statewide affirmative action plan. States categorized as state personnel systems include Alabama, Alaska, Colorado, Connecticut, Delaware, Hawaii, Maine, Kentucky, New Mexico, New York, North Carolina, South Dakota, and West Virginia. In some of these states, some courts may be excluded from the state system, such as municipal courts (e.g., Colorado and New Mexico), or the county court, (Denver, Colorado) as previously mentioned. Of these states, only Hawaii and New York have collective bargaining involving court employees. In Hawaii, the executive branch handles the negotiations, but the administrative office of the courts performs the function in New York.

Local System

This model is characterized by local funding, elected clerks (usually), technical responsibility attached to the local court or local executive branch, substantial use of patronage, exempt employees, and very little use of affirmative action plans. One exception is the Circuit Court of Multnomah County (Portland, Oregon), which has developed and adopted a comprehensive merit plan. Court employees may need to meet executive branch standards, though selection and retention is a court matter, as in the Hamilton County Court of Common Pleas in Cincinnati, Ohio.

States characterized as local systems include Arizona, Arkansas, California, Illinois, Indiana, Iowa, Louisiana, Michigan, Minnesota, Missouri, Mississippi, North Dakota, Ohio, Oregon, Pennsylvania, Texas, Washington, and Wisconsin.

Of these states, the following have some collective bargaining agreements, basically negotiated by the executive branch: California (meet and confer), Iowa (bailiffs only), Michigan, Minnesota, Oregon, Washington, and Wisconsin. Michigan conducts negotiations in various ways with the court as employer, the court and county as co-employers, and the county as sole employer. Pennsylvania has essentially reserved bargaining for wages and conditions of employment to the county and management rights to the court.

Mixed System

This model mixes state and local funding in interesting ways. In certain states, the court of limited jurisdiction is state funded, while the court of general jurisdiction is locally funded. This situation is found in three states: Maryland, Nebraska, and Virginia. In Maryland, the court of limited jurisdiction is under the state executive branch personnel system. In Nebraska and Virginia, the court of limited jurisdiction is under a separate state judicial personnel system. In other jurisdictions, the state funds the trial court administrators and judges, but not other nonjudicial employees, although court reporters and judges' secretaries may also be state funded in some places. In this model, certain clerks are elected while others are not.

Technical responsibility for personnel matters is fragmented between the executive and judicial branches and between the central administrative office of the courts and the local trial court. Both merit and patronage systems may exist side by side. Where affirmative action exists it usually applies to state-funded employees. Of the states reporting, only one has collective bargaining, New Jersey, and bargaining is conducted in the same

variety of ways as in Michigan. States included in
this model are Florida, Georgia, Idaho, Maryland,
Nebraska, New Jersey, Utah, and Virginia.[4]

SUMMARY

    The development of court personnel systems
among the states is marked by diversity. Some
states have unified their personnel systems along
merit principles, typically using unitary budgeting
as a means for statewide standards. Collective bargaining has been limited in these states. For the
most part, these states have been those having lower
populations and, if highly urbanized, having small
geographical boundaries, such as Delaware,
Connecticut, and Hawaii.
    A second group of states has clung to local per-
sonnel administration which, for the most part, has
been characterized by substantial use of patronage
and exempt employees. These states typically fund
courts at the local level. Collective bargaining is
more prevalent in these states. These states do not
share any common population or geographical similarities although, for the most part, they are more
highly urbanized.
    A third group constitutes a mixture of state
and local funding, state and local technical personnel control, and merit and patronage features.
These states are primarily in the southern and western portions of the United States.

NOTES

    1. That is not to say that such instruments
have not been attacked legally as being discriminatory, unrelated, and invalid. Such attacks are discussed elsewhere in this book.
    2. It is customary that such a hearing is pro-
vided <u>after</u> the action, disciplinary or whatever,
has been taken. The California Supreme Court found
fault with this procedure referring substantially to
<u>Arnett v. Kennedy</u> (1974) 416 U.S. 134 [40 L.Ed. 2d
15, 19 S.Ct. 1633]. Said California, "...due process does mandate that the employee be accorded certain procedural rights <u>before</u> (emphasis added) the
discipline becomes effective. As a minimum, these
pre-removal safeguards must include notice of the
proposed action, the reasons therefor, a copy of the

charges and materials upon which the action is based, and the right to respond, either orally or in writing, to the authority initially imposing discipline." The court held certain provisions of the State Civil Service Act (Sec. 19574), governing the taking of punitive action against a permanent civil service employee to violate due process. See Skelly v. State Personnel Board, 15 Cal. 3d 194 [124 Cal. Rptr. 14, P.2d 774].
     3. See discussion of management rights on p. 136, et seq.
     4. Questionnaires were not received from some states. Where sufficient information was available, these states are categorized as shown in the text.

SECTION 2.
TOOLS AND PROCESSES OF PERSONNEL ADMINISTRATION IN THE COURTS

3. Classification: The Essential Building Block

INTRODUCTION

Classification is, in essential terms, the basis, the building block, the foundation of functional, modern personnel administration, and nowhere is it more important than in the court or judicial environment. Classification turns chaos into order and shapes the senseless into a formed, structural, rational approach to personnel management.

Other than providing the information and system necessary to classify and pay employees in a clear, logical, and evenhanded manner, classification and work that goes into it supply the information which is basic to examinations and recruitment, placement, performance evaluation systems, training programs, systems analysis, planning, and just about anything else having to do with people and personnel systems.

Classification and Other Terms Defined

Whan then is classification? To understand classification, one must first understand what a position is. A position is a group of duties and responsibilities which require the employment of one person (either full or part time). These duties and responsibilities must be assigned by competent authority to the position. The classification of a position becomes, then, the manner or format used to describe the duties and responsibilities of a position. To be redundant, because it is important, a classification is no more and no less than a description of the duties and responsibilities of a position set forth on paper.

With a large number of positions, it is not necessary to have an equally large number of classifications. In a system of any size, there will be groups of positions which are similar in the nature of their duties and responsibilities. These positions will be close enough in their activities to be placed under one description. This group of positions is called a class. Aside from similar duties, a class that has the same grade level (pay level) requires the same education and experience, and uses the same testing device for all of its member positions.

Class Series. A class series is a group of classes which has the same general area of concern or responsibility. For example, Court Clerks I, II, and III all work in the same general area requiring court clerical skills, but with varying amounts of responsibility. Court Clerk I may be an entry, or lower level classification, and may be assigned to areas such as filing, entry of various prepared documents into docket books, or to a general apprenticeship throughout a number of divisions within a court. Court Clerk II may be a classification used to connote the journeyman level of expertise in filing cases, issuing various documents, bonding, etc. Court Clerk III can be used for those positions which supervise a unit of other clerical employees within a court clerical setting and which are responsible to an administrative superior.

As can be seen from the above, the higher the classification, the more responsible are the duties which are assigned to the position. An interesting approach to assigning class numbers in a series is to reverse this process. Instead of having the higher numbers denote the greater responsibilities, the lower numbers may carry the greater share of the duties. Court Clerk I then becomes the supervisory class. This approach has the advantage of forestalling the urge to create more and more classifications with higher responsibilities and pay, but it will also make the classification system less flexible and may inhibit the creation of a new class in a series when one is needed.

A class title is the title, or name, given to a classification. This seems readily apparent and taken for granted on first observation, but it should not be confused with a working title. For example, a Court Clerk III (classification title) may have the responsibility for supervising the activities of the criminal division of a court of general jurisdiction. The working title may be something like "Criminal Division Supervisor," but would carry a classification title of Court Clerk III.

Classification Plan. The classification plan is a grouping of all the classes by class series and of all the class series within the organization to form one entire, complete structure. It may include everything from court clerks and court administrators to probation officers and psychologists. (See Figure 3.1 which indicates a portion of a classification plan.)

Job Descriptions and Class Descriptions. Some mention, for purposes of definition, must be made of two other terms which are similar and, consequently, somewhat confusing. These terms are job description and class description. For the purposes of this work, a job description is the sum and substance of the duties of a position as described and defined by the incumbent of the position and his supervisor. A class description is a written document which sets forth the duties, responsibilities, and the activities of a classification and includes the levels of education and experience necessary for success on the job. In short, the class description is the written description of all similar positions and is prepared by the personnel analyst.

Desk Audit. A desk audit is a tool used by the personnel analyst to gather additional data about a position. These data are in addition to information already received from the job description and are used to supplement that information. The desk audit is an oral interview with the position's incumbent and his supervisor. This tool is rarely used in 100 percent of the positions in a large organization and, when used, is primarily for clarification purposes only. For example, it makes more sense to make desk audits on a larger percentage of a diverse classification, such as court clerks, than it does to make them on a generally uniform classification, such as court reporter, as all court reporters are required to do much the same thing.

Grade. A grade is a pay or wage term which denotes a level of salary. Classifications or classes are assigned to a pay grade. The federal government uses some eighteen different pay grades for all of its classes. Employees of the state of Colorado currently have some eighty-two different grades. The New Mexico judiciary uses thirty-two pay grades, while both Maine and West Virginia have thirty-three. Hamilton County, Ohio (Cincinnati) has a thirty-grade pay plan. The number of grades is not important. What is important is that, within a system, all incumbents, or member positions of a

FIGURE 3.1

OCCUPATIONAL INDEX TO CLASSES
(An Example)

Class
Code   Class Title

1XXX   ADMINISTRATIVE

    11XX   General Administrative

        1101   Planning and Development Director

        1111   Administrative Assistant I
        1112   Administrative Assistant II
        1113   Administrative Assistant III

    12XX   Administrative, Court

        1201   Assistant Director Juvenile Court
                Services
        1202   Director Juvenile Court Services

        1211   Clerk of Supreme Court

        1221   Court Administrator I
        1222   Court Administrator II
        1223   Court Administrator III
        1224   Court Administrator IV
        1225   Court Administrator V

    13XX   Administrative, Jury

        1301   Jury Commissioner I
        1302   Jury Commissioner II

2XXX   PROFESSIONAL

    21XX   Budget and Fiscal

        2101   Budget and Fiscal Director

class are paid at the same grade level. For example, all Court Clerk IIs within a system would be paid at the same grade level. It is important to note that they may not receive the same pay, but that they are at the same grade or pay level. Each pay grade typically has a series of steps from, for example, one to ten, with each step being a certain amount above the one which precedes it. (See example of grade/step chart in Figure 3.2.)

Job Analysis. Job analysis is a method used by the personnel specialist to determine the range and extent of the duties and responsibilities of a job or position. All facets of these duties and of the position itself are determined. This is the key tool to be used, not only in constructing the classification plan, but also in developing the remainder of the personnel plan.

Classification Plan Development

Ranking System. There are three prevalent systems used in establishing a classification plan, all of which rely upon job analysis for their validity. The first method is the ranking system. This is an intra-comparative system which compares, after job analysis, the duties and responsibilities of each position within an organization with the other positions in the organization. All of the positions are then ranked in order of their duties and responsibilities from top to bottom. This ranking indicates to the personnel analyst the order of responsibilities, allows him to classify each position, and assign it to a proper grade level.

The advantage of this system in that it allows a clear, concise method of comparing one position with another and for weighing the relative merits of each position. It is also relatively simple to use. The disadvantage is that it can be rather unwieldy when applied to a large, geographically far-flung organization, such as a state judicial system. For example, it would be difficult to weigh the merits of a position in a large metropolitan area with a position in a rural judicial district. A Court Clerk III (class title) may be the head of a civil division in the metro court, but the clerk of the entire court in a rural area.

Position Classification. A second method of classification may be called position classification. Under this method, all jobs are analyzed to determine the level of duties and responsibilities. Like or similar positions are then grouped together to

FIGURE 3.2

EXAMPLE OF A COMPENSATION PLAN,
SHOWING GRADES AND STEPS

STEP	1	2	3	4	5	6	7
GRADE							
1	543	570	598	623	660	693	727
2	557	585	614	645	677	711	747
3	570	598	623	660	693	727	764
4	585	614	645	677	711	747	784
5	598	628	660	693	727	764	802
6	614	645	677	711	747	784	823
7	628	660	693	727	764	802	842
8	645	677	711	747	784	823	864
9	660	693	727	764	802	842	884
10	677	711	747	784	823	864	907
11	693	727	764	802	842	884	928
12	711	747	784	823	864	907	952
13	727	764	802	842	884	928	975
14	747	784	823	864	907	952	1000
15	764	802	842	884	928	975	1023
16	784	823	864	907	952	1000	1050
17	802	842	884	928	975	1023	1075
18	823	864	907	952	1000	1050	1103
19	842	884	928	975	1023	1075	1128
20	864	907	952	1000	1050	1103	1158
21	884	928	975	1023	1075	1128	1185
22	907	952	1000	1050	1103	1158	1216
23	928	975	1023	1075	1128	1185	1244
24	952	1000	1050	1103	1158	1216	1277
25	975	1023	1075	1128	1185	1244	1306
26	1000	1050	1103	1158	1216	1277	1341
27	1023	1075	1128	1185	1244	1306	1372
28	1050	1103	1158	1216	1277	1341	1408
29	1075	1123	1165	1244	1306	1372	1440
30	1103	1158	1216	1277	1341	1408	1478
31	1128	1185	1244	1306	1372	1440	1512
32	1158	1216	1277	1341	1403	1478	1552
33	1185	1244	1306	1372	1440	1512	1588
34	1216	1277	1341	1408	1478	1552	1630
35	1244	1306	1372	1440	1512	1588	1667
36	1277	1341	1408	1478	1552	1630	1712

FIGURE 3.2 (cont'd)

STEP	1	2	3	4	5	6	7
GRADE							
37	1306	1372	1440	1512	1588	1667	1750
38	1341	1408	1478	1552	1630	1712	1798
39	1372	1440	1512	1588	1667	1750	1837
40	1408	1478	1552	1630	1712	1798	1888
41	1440	1512	1588	1667	1750	1837	1929
42	1478	1552	1630	1712	1798	1883	1952
43	1512	1598	1667	1750	1837	1929	2025
44	1552	1630	1712	1798	1888	1932	2081
45	1583	1667	1750	1837	1929	2025	2126
46	1630	1712	1798	1888	1982	2031	2185
47	1667	1750	1837	1929	2025	2126	2232
48	1712	1798	1883	1982	2031	2185	2294
49	1750	1837	1929	2025	2126	2232	2344
50	1798	1888	1982	2081	2185	2294	2409
51	1837	1929	2025	2126	2232	2344	2461
52	1888	1962	2031	2185	2294	2409	2529
53	1929	2025	2125	2232	2344	2461	2584
54	1982	2081	2185	2294	2409	2529	2655
55	2025	2126	2232	2344	2461	2584	2713
56	2081	2185	2294	2469	2529	2655	2783
57	2126	2232	2344	2461	2584	2713	2849
58	2185	2294	2409	2529	2655	2783	2927
59	2232	2344	2461	2584	2713	2829	2991

form a sort of loose class. Class descriptions are then prepared or, if already prepared, are analyzed and modified. The grouping of job descriptions in a loose class are then compared with the various class descriptions until the one most suitable is identified. Then the job descriptions which are borderline are moved into the higher or lower classes in the class series, or into an entirely different class series, if this move is warranted.

The advantage of this system is that all job descriptions are compared to the same standards across an entire system, and this can be done regardless of the size of that system. The big disadvantage is that it may be somewhat subjective, as the individual position tends to lose individual identity with other positions of the same class, and the uniqueness of the position tends to be leveled, with certain salient features being forgotten or ignored.

Point Rating System. The third method is the point rating system. In this system, as in others, a thorough job analysis must be performed prior to any further action taking place. Each duty of the position is given an assigned point value. For example, filing documents may have an assigned value of two points, whereas supervising persons who file documents may have an assigned value of ten points. When all the duties and responsibilities of a position have been identified, weighed, and assigned a point value, the numbers are totaled, and the full value of the position is calculated. The values of all of the positions are then entered on a log in numerical order, so that they may be compared with each other, and so that proper wage and classification levels may be determined. The advantage of this approach is that it is relatively scientific and sophisticated, and much of the work may be done by a computer. The disadvantages are that it takes a person with training and experience in the area to apply it correctly.

The following is illustrative of a point rating system, and is a portion of one which is currently used in the Massachusetts court system. The system uses as criteria nine job evaluation factors, all of which are present to a greater or lesser degree in all of the occupations covered by the reports. A survey was conducted to determine the degree of importance of four main factors. Based on the average responses the following degree pattern was established.

            Skill   38%
            Responsibility   48%
            Effort
             (physical & mental)   9%
            Working conditions   5%
Appropriate point values were assigned to each main factor based on the percentages. The total points number 1,000; thus, for example, the skill factor is worth at best 380 points.

Each of the main factors was then divided into the nine sub-categories with point values as follows:

    SKILL:

            Preparation and Training   145
            Work Experience Required   145
            Analytical Ability   90
    RESPONSIBILITY: 185

            Independent Judgment and
              Consequence of Errors   185
            Contacts with Others   85
            Work of Others   140
            Responsibility for Welfare
              of Others   90
    EFFORT NEEDED: 90

    WORKING CONDITIONS: 50

    The points to the right of each factor represent the highest possible points available in that factor. It should be understood that it is almost impossible for a job to be valued at the highest 1,000 points.

    The next step is to take each factor and break it down further to establish degrees or levels of each job. This degree or level measures the requirements of any job being evaluated. A definition of each degree was written to aid the personnel administrator in obtaining the correct degrees for each position. These definitions also aid the employee in understanding why his or her job is given a certain point value.

    The third step is the comparing of each job against each factor and assigning a degree factor which best measures the requirements of that job. The points for the factors are added and the total provides a point score reflecting the entire job content.

WORK EXPERIENCE REQUIRED

The degree of this factor is determined by the minimum amount of work experience that an average individual with the necessary preparation and training must have with the court, or elsewhere, in order to meet the quality and quantity standards for the job. The experience may be acquired on the job evaluated or a related one. Under this factor, do not consider the preparation and training required to provide the individual with the knowledge necessary to qualify for the job.

DEGREE	DEFINITION	POINT VALUE
1.	No work experience required (entry level)	0
2.	One week	10
3.	One through four weeks of work experience is required	25
4.	One through three months experience is required	40
5.	Between three and six months of experience is required	55
6.	Six through twelve months experience is required	70
7.	Thirteen through eighteen months of experience is required	85
8.	Eighteen through twenty-four months of progressively more responsible experience is required	100
9.	Between two and three years of progressively more responsible experience is required	115
10.	Between three and five years of progressively more responsible experience is required	130
11.	More than five years of progressively more responsible experience is required	145[1]

THE CLASSIFICATION PROCESS

The size of the court personnel system is unimportant for the purpose of classification. Classification is relevant or applicable regardless of the size of the system to which it is applied, except that, as the size of the system grows, the more structured and formalized the classification system becomes, with the result that there is less flexibility than in a smaller system.

In a smaller personnel system (fewer than 500 employees) more flexible, less rigid class descriptions can be used, while still maintaining control over the system. The smaller system can get by with terms such as "desirable" when applied to education or experience, and duties can be described in a more indefinite manner. The main reason for this is that the communications from top to bottom, bottom to top, and laterally in smaller systems are more clear than they are in larger systems. These communications help explain to people what is expected of them and, consequently, make much easier the process of classification control.

Determining Classification Study Need

The use and application of the principles and tenets of classification will make any personnel system function more efficiently and equitably. The first step is a classification study. There are several factors which must be considered prior to undertaking the study. Initially, several questions should be asked: Are there written class descriptions which set forth accurately the duties and responsibilities of the various formalized class descriptions at all? Do responsibilities appear to be commensurate with salary? Has a classification study been performed within the past five to seven years? If the answer to one or more of these questions is no, a study is probably needed.

Judicial Support Needed

At the outset, it is important to gain the support of the bench. This is necessary, because it is surprising to find the amount of fear and apprehension that the mention of a classification study can generate. If the judges, especially those with administrative authority and responsibilities, support a modern personnel program, including a classification plan, problems are minimized. If the judges are lukewarm or negative, the study must be sold on its merits, with no embellishment or promises which would well prove to be the undoing of the system later on.

Judges who are adamantly opposed to the idea of a study fall into two categories: those who can be convinced of such a system's merits, and those who will never be convinced. It is presumed that an administrator or other person proposing a classification study as the first step in developing a formal personnel system knows his or her environment. He or she knows or should know what is likely to be acceptable and how to present it so that it is.

Once the need for the study has been determined, and there is adequate support from the bench, the scope of the study should be decided, as well as the method of conducting the study.

In a circuit or district court or a state-funded judicial system where the administration and operation of probation services are also a judicial responsibility, there may be a need only to study court personnel or probation personnel rather than both. There may be some other reason, perhaps financial or political, why the decision may be made to study one and not the other. Such a decision must be made carefully, because either the studied or nonstudied group may feel it is being treated unfairly.

Another closely related problem is the inclusion or exclusion of personal or confidential employees of judges. These employees should be included, because the same classification scheme and salary schedule should apply to all employees, even if some are personally selected by judges as their confidential staff members. Different salary schedules cause morale problems, and, even if the same salary schedule applies, a large number of exemptions from the classification plan disrupts the uniformity, fairness, and effectiveness of the system.

Making the Classification Study

This explanation of the classification process is aimed at the trial court level, assuming trial courts of both general and limited jurisdiction with responsibility for juvenile probation services. The principles are the same regardless of the size of court and auxiliary services included. Indeed, they apply to a state system as well. It is assumed that the study has the support of the bench.

Proper preparation and planning at the start of the study will save much wasted time in the future and will do much to alleviate the fears and concerns of the employees.

In-House or Consultants. First, it must be determined who will make the study. Should the study be done in-house, or should a consultant be retained? Each has distinct advantages and disadvantages. An in-house study costs less. The system is also familiar to the persons doing the study or will become so. The main concerns are in-house capability and capacity, because most courts and related agencies lack expertise in the area of personnel. Also, in-house staff may be less objective than someone from outside. In addition, the reaction to the study findings may result in a climate which may be so "hot" that it is difficult for in-house staff to maintain both its credibility and that of the study. This is especially true in smaller jurisdictions.

The use of an outside consultant is a way to avoid this problem. The consultant brings with him a great deal of expertise and objectivity in the area of personnel classification and can generally be counted on for a good work product, as his reputation and future contracts depend on it.

Another important consideration in determining who is to do the study is whether the decision has already been made to establish a formal personnel system following the classification study or whether the study is being made to determine whether a formal personnel system is needed.

In the former instance, the decision may be made to spend the money on augmenting in-house staff rather than employing a consultant, so that in-house staff will have gained the experience requisite to administering the system after it is established.

In the latter instance, a consultant is preferable, because the court has not made a staff commitment before it decides to establish a system. A consultant may also be seen as more objective in this situation, because he does not have a vested interest in seeing the system established. A consultant may also be preferable in a small court or agency, where the court administrator would be able to maintain the system without additional staff help once it is established.

There are drawbacks to the use of a consultant. The costs are greater, and a consultant frequently has to be led by the hand through the court organization maze. In other words, if he has not had judicial personnel study experience, he has to learn a new and different environment. These negating factors are usually outweighed by the consultant's ability to take the heat for the disappointments inherent in the classification process; he can train existing personnel to maintain the classification plan, and he can give management the option of implementing the plan either wholly or in part.

In selecting a consultant to do a classification study, it is important to know his background, or, at least, the background of the firm he represents. It is also helpful if the consulting firm has had experience working in the judicial systems.

Requests for proposals (RFP's) which detail the study to be undertaken should be sent to all organizations and individuals deemed eligible after investigation. The RFP must include all information pertinent to the study. This information must include, but is not limited to, the site of the study; the number of positions to be classified; the number and types of units to be considered; the general scope of the study; the on-site resources available to the consultant; who has the power to approve or reject the classification report; and the deadline for submitting the RFP.[2]

    a) Technical and Management Approach. Emphasis will be placed on depth of understanding and the soundness of the offeror's study approach and work implementation plan.

A clear statement of the project plan and use of resources should be provided to assure compliance with the requirements within the time limits and budget framework of the project. This statement should include study approach relationships and sequence of the tasks and methods for managing the study.

    b) Performance Credibility Based on Experience and Resources. Emphasis will be placed on specific experience in the court personnel field afforded by the offerer's staff to be employed on the study. This experience should be demonstrated by successful completion of projects of comparable work scope. Assigned key personnel must possess demonstrated familiarity with the structure, functional relationships and operational problems of a court system, with emphasis on personal administration.

    c) Price.[3]

Once the consultant is selected and under contract, the contractor should make sure that all lines of communication are open. Failure to do so can undermine the study from the start. The consultant should be furnished with all material that has a direct or indirect bearing on the subject matter at hand, including, but not limited to, all pertinent statutes, rules, organization charts, work-flow charts, any previous studies, and procedural manuals. All of these documents will give the consultant a broader understanding of the system.

In addition, the court administration should offer any assistance to the consultant that he may need. For instance, it will help him a great deal, if the administrator explains the purpose of the study to all the employees, allaying their fears and suspicions, and distributes the classification questionnaires. The questionnaires (see example, see Appendix B) should be distributed approximately three to four weeks prior to the arrival of the consultant on site, with a mandatory return date at least one week before the arrival of the consultant.[4]

Questionnaire Preparation. Who should prepare the questionnaires? Although some personnel specialists propose that the analyst or the supervisor do the preparation, it is these authors' contention that the person who knows the most about the position (i.e., the incumbent, or if the position is vacant, the supervisor) complete it. There should be a review of the statements made by the incumbent by the supervisor. This supervisory review, if done objectively, can cut down on the impact of the incumbent's ego, or lack thereof.

Once all the questionnaires have been filled out and reviewed, the consultant can begin his work in earnest.

Charting the Results. The consultant's first job should be to categorize the questionnaires in the form of a supervisory hierarchy. On the bottom of each questionnaire (see Appendix B), there is a section concerning whom the incumbent supervises, and who, in turn, supervises the incumbent. This charting will indicate to the consultant (and to astute management) how employees perceive the manner in which the organization functions, as well as possible sources of conflict (e.g., Position A indicates that it supervises Positions B, C, D and E, while Positions B, D, and E indicate they are supervised by Position C. (See example in Figure 3.3.)

The chart should also contain the position numbers of the employees, so that they can be cross-referenced to the questionnaire.

Pre-Desk Audit Allocations. After the charts

FIGURE 3.3

FORMAL ORGANIZATIONAL CHART

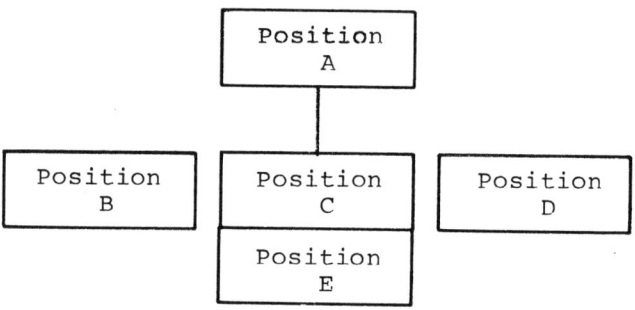

AS EMPLOYEES SEE IT

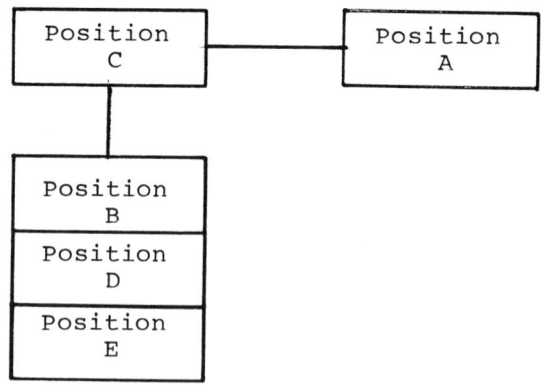

have been developed, pre-desk audit allocations may be made. To do this, the questionnaires are divided into groups which have similar responsibilities and duties. These groupings make it possible to identify the employee groups or classes, which will be used in position classification. In other words, all employees who have the responsibility for filing documents in various court records may be titled Court Clerk I; all employees who have the responsibility for supervising juvenile probationers may be titled Juvenile Probation Officer II, etc. This is done until all positions have been tentatively allocated to one group or another. These groupings are reviewed and reviewed again, shifting some up and some down, until the initial allocation process is deemed to be complete by the consultant.

Desk Audit. Desk audits are next performed to determine the validity of the questionnaire responses or job descriptions; to fill in or round out the information supplied in the questionnaires; to answer any questions which may have been raised by the questionnaires; and to convince employees that the person conducting the study is actually a human being, and not an office-bound technician who casts their fates to the winds, without even talking to them.

Desk audits, in a medium or small sized court, should be performed on all positions. This is especially true if the court has not had a classification system prior to the study. In larger systems, it may be difficult to do desk audits on all positions, even though it is desirable in a first-time study, but it can be done. It is interesting to note that Colorado performed what amounted to be a 100 percent desk audit on 1,206 positions during its initial study in 1968-69, and a 46 percent desk audit during the follow-up study in 1973.

A larger system which already has a plan should require only a 35 to 45 percent desk audit sampling, in subsequent studies. The reason is that there are many positions, such as court reporter or bailiff, each of whose job duties are similar enough to alleviate the need for more than a small general sample. Even so, it is important for all types of positions to have at least a small sample of the class audited, including, of course, one and two position classes.

During the course of the desk audits, it is important for the consultant or in-house analyst to put the position incumbent at ease and to allow the incumbent to expand upon his own duties and responsibilities, by asking open-ended questions. The consultant should guide the questions and the course of the conversation as much as possible to keep it centered on the subject at hand. The consultant must also watch out for the inevitable ego problems which crop up during the desk audit and make sure that the responsibilities are not inflated by larger egos, or deflated by smaller ones. All findings must be confirmed or discarded after discussions with the incumbent's supervisor.

Writing the Class Description

After the desk audits are completed, the class descriptions must be written. The information used in these descriptions is taken from the job description prepared by each incumbent and the subsequent desk audits performed on the positions.

The job descriptions are grouped, once again, by class, changing those descriptions about which additional information has been gathered through the desk audit, either up or down, depending on the nature of the duties and responsibilities. Remember--this is an important point--classification or reclassification does not mean that an employee can only be raised. It is a two-edged sword; the employee can be lowered too.

Salient and recurring features of the groups of job descriptions in the system are culled and noted. These recurring features are then set down in draft form and studied. In a group of questionnaires loosely entitled "Court Clerk," certain patterns will begin to emerge (see example in definition of "class series"). The common features in each of the classes in the class series are then used to write the final class description.

Each class description should have:

1) a Descriptive Title, or a title which states generally, but accurately, what the nature of the classification is;

2) a Definition of Work section which elaborates, in general terms, what the responsibilities of the position are;

3) an Examples of Work Performed section which defines more accurately what the classification is responsible for and what the nature of the work is;

4) a Skills, Knowledge, and Abilities section which sets forth the attributes necessary to perform the job effectively;

5) an Education and Experience section which defines the minimum preparation necessary to perform

the job effectively; and

    6) a <u>Necessary Special Requirements</u> section (if necessary) which states what, if any, special requirements are needed for a position (law degree, C.P.A. certificate, court reporting certificate, etc.). (For example of job description, see Appendix C.)

After the job descriptions are complete, the entire package, including the final allocations, are presented to the chief or presiding judge in conjunction with the court administrator. After, and only after, their review and approval, the allocations are announced to the employees, and a copy of each employee's class description is given to him/her for review.

<u>Employee Review and Appeal</u>

    This can be the most tense moment in the study. A wise move is to show the incumbent his or her salary at the same time the class description is reviewed. This will alleviate the suspense in that area. In addition, it would be wise for the consultant or the person making the study to hold an appeals session for those employees who feel they have been wronged by the classification study. This hearing, too, will relieve some of the pressure from a potentially difficult situation. The appeals session should include someone from the court sitting on the appeals board, as well as the consultant or his representative. This process will enable the consultant to receive information which is more in depth than that which was considered initially. Also, it can serve as a training session for the staff member selected to serve on the board.

    With the classification study essentially completed, the consultant moves on to a new job, leaving the administrator of the court to implement the plan.

    The court is not bound by the decision of the consultant. The court must decide for itself how much of the plan is to be put into effect. If the court feels that certain positions have been rated either too high or too low, it is free to change them. But, by and large, the recommendations of the consultant should be accepted as accurate and should be implemented with little or no modification.

    With the plan placed in operation in a smooth, efficient manner, management should make sure that it is maintained and not neglected.

Plan Maintenance

The classification study and the implementation of the plan are only half the battle in the classification process. True, it is a major step forward to have a classification plan in the court, as it leads to more progressive personnel administration, especially where none has existed before, but the proper maintenance of the system and the manner in which maintenance is carried out are the important factors in determining the viability of the classification plan.

To remain effective, the plan and the personnel charged with its administration must have the support of the chief or presiding judge and the entire bench, as well as nonjudicial administrative personnel. This support will allow those responsible for the plan's maintenance to monitor it and correct it as time passes, with little or no change of the plan's being set aside to allow a return to the old ways of personnel administration.

To maintain a plan in a trial court setting is somewhat more difficult than in a state-wide or more remote and centralized system. Trial court administration may have its view obfuscated by the various personnel interrelationships which exist within a court and may be incapacitated in rendering an objective decision. Any capable administrator should be able to recognize when this situation exists and should act accordingly by requesting help from the outside, if necessary. This help can come from the personnel analyst from the local city or county merit system, if one exists; from the state court administrator's office, if it has personnel who are capable; from the Intergovernmental Personnel Act staff members in the area, if they have the time and expertise; or from a consultant (as a last resort, as this can be fairly expensive).

These observations should not be interpreted to mean that the plan's maintenance should be shoved off on a third party. It only means that outside assistance may be needed for those positions where the administrator feels he is unable to render an objective decision. The remaining positions should be handled by in-house staff.

Reclassification

After the plan has been in operation for six months to a year, some dissatisfaction may set in with the incumbents of certain positions. These persons should be allowed to request reclassification of their positions. Reclassification requests stem typically from two areas. One is dissatisfaction with salary, which is not a concern of the classification process; and the second is a change in the duties assigned to a position, which is a concern of the classification process.

All positions for which classification is requested should have a position classification questionnaire completed and should have a desk audit performed. Care must be taken to determine the impact of decision regarding the reclassification request. Will changing the classification set off a wave of similar requests? Is the change warranted, based on new duties, or did the initial study overlook some of the more responsible features of the position? It should be noted, as in the initial study, personality, volume of work, efficiency of the incumbent, qualifications of the incumbent, diligence, length of service, recruiting problems, and financial need are not classification problems. The nature and difficulty of the work performed, the authority exercised by the position, the supervision exercised and received, and the qualification requirements of the work are classification problems or concerns.

The incumbent should have access to a classification appeals board, if he feels he has been wronged in the reclassification process, in the same manner as when the initial classification was determined. This board should be the "court of last resort," and its decision should be final.

Periodic Class Review

In addition to individual reclassification requests, it is wise to perform periodic checks on all of the class series within the organization. The only thing constant in personnel administration (as in so many other things) is change itself. Periodic class series checks give valuable information on the metamorphosis of a class series and allow the administration to restructure and act accordingly. These checks should be made every two to three years in smaller organizations and every three to four years in larger ones. Regardless of time limits used, a check should be made whenever it is felt that significant change has taken place.

Administration is also wise, if it reviews the nature of the duties of each position as it becomes vacant. Review of vacant positions allows for flexibility in position control both in classification and in meeting organizational needs. A vacant position which is classified properly may be moved to a different unit where the personnel needs are greater, be reclassified, and used more effectively without having an incumbent go through culture shock.

One final word on plan maintenance. In the larger systems, such as a state court system, the question of plan maintenance becomes one of centralization versus decentralization. Both approaches have their benefits, but centralized control of the classification process appears to be the better way to handle it. A centralized classification system relieves a lot of the pressure resulting from interpersonal relationships which exist at the local level. It may be better to blame classification problems on a remote state office than have intra-office hostility aimed at the trial court administrator, which could reduce his effectiveness. In addition, a state office can probably supply more expertise in the area of classification than can be expected to be found at the local level. After all, a trial court administrator has his hands full with the dockets, budgeting, accounting, and the public, without having the additional burden of the classification process. The local trial court administrator must be brought into the process by the personnel analyst, and he should be made aware of the potential consequences of the actions contemplated by the personnel analyst.

An example of personnel rules which govern the classification process, including the classification review board, are found in Appendix E.

NOTES

1. Excerpted from Office of the Chief Administrative Justice, <u>Request for Proposal for the Development of a Personnel System for the Trial Court Department of the Commonwealth of Massachusetts</u> (Boston: Commonwealth of Mass., 1978).

2. The Criminal Court Technical Assistance Project, Institute for Advanced Studies in Justice, American University Law School, has prepared RFP's for personnel studies in several jurisdictions through consultants funded by the Law Enforcement Assistance Administration. Copies may be obtained by contacting the Institute at 4900 Massachusetts Avenue, N.W., Washington, D.C. 20016.

3. Institute for Advanced Studies in Justice, Criminal Courts Technical Assistance Project, *A Request for a Proposal to Design and Develop a Personnel Merit System for Nonjudicial Court Employees in the State of Maryland* (Washington, D.C.: The American University Law School, 1976), p. 20.

4. While this discussion centers on the conduct of the classification study by a consultant, the same procedures and sequence of events would apply if the study were made in-house.

4. Recruiting: A Means to an End

MATCHING NEEDS AND SUPPLY

As explained in Chapter 3, the information gathered during the classification study is essential in the formulation of other positions of the personnel plan. One of the areas in which this information can be used most effectively is in the recruiting process.

Through the classification study, the minimum qualifications necessary for a person to perform effectively on the job are determined. These qualifications are established to be inclusive rather than exclusive. For example, a clerical position might be filled by a degree-holding individual, but it would not be desirable to make a college degree a minimum requirement for the position. The elimination of artificial barriers of this nature seeks to include people rather than exclude people from the system.

These minimum qualifications and the information concerning the duties and major responsibilities of the position are the items which are used to develop recruiting literature.

Labor Needs

The first step is to determine labor needs (once again the classification plan is extremely helpful) and to compare those needs with the type of labor market from which the court recruits. If the area is primarily blue-collar labor, there may be some problems recruiting persons for what are essentially white-collar jobs. This example, although extreme, indicates that recruiting may be somewhat more difficult in some localities and for some classes of positions.

Labor Market Survey

Courts usually employ persons in at least some of the following categories: clerical; secretarial; bookkeeping, administrative/supervisory (court administrators), professional (probation officers, psychologists, marriage counselors, etc.); and legal (law clerks, referees). There may be other categories, as well, if the court is responsible for juvenile detention or related services. Knowledge of the labor market will go a long way to insure that the applicants who come to the court not only are qualified, but may be the best available.

A labor market survey can accomplish several things for the administrator. It can provide information concerning the types of applicants an administrator can expect for open positions; it can indicate the unemployment rate and the types of persons unemployed in the recruiting area; and, based on the information gathered, can indicate what should be the size, type, and scope of the recruiting effort.

The most efficient manner in which a labor market survey can be conducted is to gather information from a variety of sources to give the administrator an over-all employment picture. The area of unemployment rate can be found by checking with the state department of labor or the federal government. Types of persons typically employed in the area can be checked with the local chamber of commerce or employers' groups and organizations. Types of persons graduated from high schools and colleges and their propensity to stay in the local recruiting area can be found by checking with the placement offices of these institutions or the state department of education.

Many other pieces of information can be discovered by consulting these and similar agencies. The information so gathered will give an accurate representation of the area's employment picture.

THE RECRUITMENT PROCESS

Extent

How extensive should the recruiting effort be? The local administrator is in a much better position to answer this question than someone from the outside. He or she should know after the completion of a labor market survey how widespread a recruiting campaign is required for any given position. He or she may find that the types of persons he or she seeks are not in the employing area and, therefore, efforts will have to be made outside the normal recruiting boundaries. He or she may discover that the types of persons sought are plentiful in the standard recruiting area, so that recruiting can be more selective, such as relying on those few agencies or other sources which can be expected to offer the most qualified talent.

What, then, are the appropriate target areas for recruiting efforts? Certainly, a court administrator would not seek qualified clerical workers from a factory assembly line or another traditional blue-collar field. He or she must determine where efforts logically should be directed. State and local agencies which deal with labor and employment matters are generally willing to aid almost any employer who requests advice. These agencies can also steer an employer to other agencies that can help in certain individualized areas, such as clerical, bookkeeping, professional, etc. An administrator should develop and keep updated a list of all agencies that perform recruiting and placement services in his or her employment field. This will enlarge and expand greatly the employment market he or she is trying to tap. Actions of this nature will enable the administrator to reach out to the most qualified persons available.

Minority Recruitment

A court administrator must be sure that he or she is reaching all sectors of the community in his or her recruiting efforts, because the courts are a public agency paid for by public funds. To facilitate the efforts, he or she should contact the heads of local, state, and federal civil rights agencies and enlist their aid in developing a list of organizations and groups which specialize in minority recruitment. This list should be incorporated in the full listing of agencies used for recruitment purposes.

The contact with and use of minority recruitment agencies will also help affirmative action efforts immensely. A good working relationship with these groups should furnish a steady stream of qualified minority applicants for available positions and will help in reaching the entire community. This is especially important when one realizes the importance of the courts in the evolution of this civil rights movement which has led to today's affirmative action plans and philosophies.

Personal Contact

Personal contact is necessary to insure that the recruiting/placement agencies are doing their best. Personal contact will relate a face to a name when subsequent telephone or written contacts are made and will tend to personalize the entire procedure. If an agency has not referred applicants for some period of time, the administrator should make personal contact with the agency head to determine if there is a problem, and, if there is, to move immediately to rectify the problem, so that the agency will once again furnish applicants to the organization.

The list of agencies which is developed may be anywhere from a handful to over 100 and depends on the size and scope of the judicial organization and the area covered. This list will become obsolete and useless unless it is kept up to date. Recruiting agencies come and go and depend largely on their success as a go-between for their applicants and employing agencies. In addition, many of the public agencies receive their funding from grant sources. When these dry up, the agency either goes out of existence or receives funding from a different source, changes its name, and continues to give service of the same or similar nature.

Intergovernmental Efforts

One example of a joint government effort in the recruiting area is the Intergovernment Job Placement Center in Denver, Colorado. This agency is supported by funds from the Intergovernmental Personnel Act and was set up to act as a centralized recruiting and information disbursement center for all governmental agencies in the Denver Area. The agency exhibits the job announcements of local, state, and federal systems and maintains a supply of each agency's application forms for distribution to interested applicants. If an agency of this type exists in a recruiting area, its use and support are strongly recommended. If one does not exist, intergovernmental cooperation between the courts and other employers is suggested to establish one.

Intergovernmental cooperation, an example of which was discussed above, is important in public personnel administration. The prudent court administrator must realize that his is a small agency when compared with the agencies of the executive branch of government; consequently, it is important to make sure that everything possible is being done to make the available positions attractive to applicants.

The esecutive branch, with its greater resources and number of available positions, is generally perceived by the public to be "the employer" in the public area. This misconception may hinder the recruiting efforts of the court. To combat this competition, it is important to inform the public of the availability of positions in the court area. This can be done through the agency approach, already mentioned, and through media announcements. The more the public knows about an employer, the better off the agency is in the recruiting arena.

One big advantage that the smaller judicial or court agency has is the speed with which it can move to fill positions. The executive branch bureaucracy frequently cannot, due to its ponderous nature, provide the fast personnel service that the smaller court agency can. For example, if both the executive branch and the courts are recruiting clerk-typists, and the courts can fill the position in two to three weeks from time of announcement, the recruiting advantage may very well lie with the courts.

One method of recruitment, that of using the job placement center or agency, has already been explored, but one type of agency has not been mentioned. The college placement agency frequently has a difficult time in placing graduates in governmental positions. The reason is that employers, such as court administrators, do not use these centers in their recruiting activities to the extent that they should. The college placement office is probably the best source of entry-level professional applicants there is. Administrators should use them, if at all possible.

Private Agencies

There are many private employment agencies which make their living by placing employees in jobs for a fee. These fees typically constitute a one-time charge of one month's salary for placing a person in a position. This fee may be paid by either the employing agency or the applicant. These agencies do a good job--their continued existence depends on it--but they should be used only if recruitment efforts through public and non-profit sources are not successful. Every citizen has an absolute right to information concerning jobs in the public area, and, consequently, should not have to pay for information which is a public right.

Word-of-Mouth

One of the most frequently used methods of recruiting is aptly called "word-of-mouth." This is a method which has been used historically by all agencies, both public and private. Its use may be either intentional or accidental. Word-of-mouth recruiting is exactly what its name implies; employees of the agency learn of a vacant position and tell their friends about it. These friends--at least, some of them--apply for the position and are accepted or rejected.

The advantage of this approach is that the friend of an employee is typically very much like the employee himself. Therefore, if an administrator has what he or she considers a good group of employees, word-of-mouth recruiting should perpetuate the quality of his or her work force.

There are disadvantages to this method of recruiting. One is that there is no agency acting as a screening agent to refer applicants with the minimum qualifications necessary to perform on the job. The other big disadvantage is that the "birds of a feather" approach alluded to above can have a backlash effect in the area of affirmative action recruting. If employees are predominantly Anglo, their friends will be, in all probability, predominantly Anglo. Therefore, an administrator will be tapping only one segment of the work force. Also, this type of recruiting has the effect of making employment by the courts appear to the public as a closed shop, depending on whom you know, and not on ability. Word-of-mouth recruiting, then, should not be relied upon as the sole recruiting method; rather, it should be used in conjunction with other methods.

Using the Media

Other sources of recruiting employees are the various media outlets available to employers. The big media outlet is, of course, newspaper want ads. Newspapers reach a large portion of the population at very little expense, but they may not reach everyone. Care must be taken here to assure that the newspapers selected to carry recruiting announcements are representative of the community.

The larger newspapers certainly should be chosen to publish job announcements, but consideration should be given to the smaller weekly journals which service minority or ethnic neighborhoods. Support of these smaller journals with the court administrator's recruiting literature provides another way to reach minority communities for applicants. In addition, by advertising in these publications, the court is helping to support a viable community force.

Trade journals or periodicals which may be available should not be overlooked by the court administrator. A local legal secretaries' association may have a regular periodical which can be used to advertise for the always needed secretarial/clerical employees.

Radio and television, while being considerably more expensive, have the capacity of reaching out to a large segment of the population and informing it of the job opportunities available in the courts. The court administrator's budget and needs are the key here. Will the expense incurred be justified by the increased exposure and a more plentiful supply of highly qualified applicants? This question must be answered before jumping into an expensive advertising market.

National Recruiting

At times, the court may be forced into stepping outside the normal recruiting area and procedure in order to fill certain positions. Jobs which are difficult to fill from the normal recruiting area include, but are not limited to, court administrator, probation supervisor or director, budget officer, personnel director, or any of the many other positions which require a specialized background.

A number of very good sources is available to the administrative officers of a court to effect a good nationwide recruitment effort. Among them are: The News and Views, publication of the American Society for Public Administration (moderate cost); the Criminal Justice News Letter (free); the Job Finder from the Western Governmental Research Association at the University of California, Berkeley (free); State Courts Reports from the National Center for State Courts; The Institute for Court Management; the Masters' Degree Programs at the University of Denver College of Law and the University of Southern California; The New York Times (relatively expensive); and The Wall Street Journal (very expensive and very effective). This list is not exhaustive, but gives examples which will give good results in any nationwide recruiting efforts.

One thing which must be guarded against in any nationwide recruiting effort is the practice of some agencies that prey on the public employer. An agency reads the announcement in one or more sources and runs the same advertisement in its own publication. The same agency then bills the court accordingly. This is all done without permission, and may cost the court, if its administrator is not careful, several hundred dollars. It is best to report an agency of this type to the local prosecutor, attorney general, and the attorney general of the state where the billing originated.

JOB ANNOUNCEMENTS

Regular announcements of vacant positions are a must, if the court expects to be a successful competitor in the recruiting market. These announcements can, of course, be regular only if there are vacancies on a weekly or monthly basis. Regular vacancies are symptomatic of larger agencies where there is more position turnover. A mechanism for a regular and orderly procedure must be set up for printing and distributing these announcements, if they are to be effective.

Job announcements should be distributed to all of the agencies with which the court has contact and should be posted in all court facilities, as well as offices such as the district attorney's, public defender's, and any other agency which interacts regularly with the court or court-related agency under the administrator's jurisdiction.

The job announcement, regardless of where it is sent, is a most important document, as it represents both the court administrator and the court. To be brief and accurate, the announcement must contain the following information:

1) <u>A descriptive job title</u>: This title may be either the <u>classification title</u> (See Chapter 3) or the working title, or both, and should be generally descriptive of the job to be performed.

2) <u>A brief summary of duties</u>: This may come from the "Definition of Work" section of the class description, or may be written especially to summarize the duties to be performed.

3) <u>Salary</u>: The salary range must be indicated unless the level of the wages is minimal for the

employing area, and may, consequently, repel rather than attract the prospective applicants. If the range is indicated, and there is a specific starting point above which an employee cannot be hired, this should also be indicated.

4) <u>Where application is to be filed</u>: Obviously, an applicant cannot file a resume or application unless the address of the employing agency or personnel office is mentioned in the job announcement.

5) <u>Closing date for application</u>: This is an absolute necessity, as no closing date mentioned serves no purpose other than to frustrate the applicant. If few or no applications are received, it is a simple matter to announce the position again and to intensify recruiting efforts.

6) <u>Type of examinations</u>: The type of examination to be given for the position should also be indicated in the announcement. Also, it is helpful to give the weighting value of each component of the examination. If the examination is to be 50 percent written and 50 percent oral, it should be so stated.

Figure 4.1 presents an example of a system's job announcement.

FIGURE 4.1

January 5, 1979

JOB ANNOUNCEMENT

1) COURT REPORTER III   GOLDEN   DISTRICT COURT
2) LEGAL STAFF
   ASSISTANT I   DENVER   DISTRICT COURT
3) DIVISION CLERK II   GOLDEN   DISTRICT COURT
4) COURT CLERK III
   (PROMOTIONAL ONLY)   GREELEY   COUNTY COURT
5) COURT CLERK II   COLORADO
   (.500 FTE)   SPRINGS   DISTRICT COURT
6) BAILIFF   DENVER   DISTRICT COURT

1) COURT REPORTER III $1,372-1,837
DUTIES: This is responsible stenographic work in recording and transcribing verbatim district court proceedings, hearings and conferences. Work involves responsibility for the verbatim recording and transcription of testimony at district court proceedings, hearings and conferences. Transcripts may be certified in judicial appeal proceedings in the courts, and the reporter is responsible for the absolute accuracy of the transcript. Employees of this job class perform under the general supervision of a district court judge and are evaluated on the basis of speed and accuracy of work.
DESIRABLE EDUCATION AND EXPERIENCE: Graduation from high school, including or supplemented by courses in typing and standard methods of taking dictation and experience as a shorthand reporter recording and transcribing verbatim proceedings of judicial or quasi judicial hearings, conferences and meetings.
NECESSARY SPECIAL REQUIREMENTS: Must have passed the Colorado CSR, or the Colorado Merit Exam.
APPLICATIONS TO: Dan Vredenburg, District Administrator, Hall of Justice, 1701 Arapahoe, Golden, Colorado 80401, by January 17, 1979. (#30004)

2) LEGAL STAFF ASSISTANT I $952-1,277
DUTIES: This is responsible legal and clerical work in serving as law clerk and bailiff. Work involves the performance of para-professional legal services

and assisting in courtroom procedures. Legal research which is performed requires the completion of at least two years of law school, and an employee of this class should currently be enrolled in his final year of law school. Work is supervised by a judge of a district or county court and is reviewed through conferences and written reports.

DESIRABLE EDUCATION AND EXPERIENCE: Graduation from an accredited four-year college or university and successful completion of two years at an accredited law school.

APPLICATIONS TO: Dean Nakayama, District Administrator, Denver District Court, City and County Building, Denver, Colorado 80202, by January 17, 1979. (#16143)

3) DIVISION CLERK II $907-1,216
DUTIES: This is varied secretarial and clerical work in support of a judge of a district court. Work involves performing secretarial duties and for relieving a judge of routine administrative duties. Work may also involve the performance of routine courtroom duties. Work is performed within established routine and is reviewed by the judge for adherence to established procedures and results obtained.

DESIRABLE EDUCATION AND EXPERIENCE: Graduation from high school, including coursework in office procedures and clerical routine; and considerable experience in court clerical or legal secretarial work.

APPLICATIONS TO: Dan Vredenburg, District Administrator, Hall of Justice, 1701 Arapahoe, Golden, Colorado 80401, by January 17, 1979. (#30011)

4) COURT CLERK III (PROMOTIONAL ONLY) $864-1,158
DUTIES: This is technical clerical and limited supervisory work in a court of the Colorado state court system. Work involves responsibility for performing a wide variety of technical operations, frequently requiring specialized clerical knowledges, and which may include supervisory responsibilities. Typical assignments include performing as the clerk of a small combined or district court or of a highly active county court. Other employees of this class typically are found in the largest district courts and are charged with unusually broad or technical responsibilities. Work is performed under the general supervision of a judge, court administrator, higher level clerk or other appropriate person and is reviewed through conferences, reports and on the basis of results obtained.

DESIRABLE EDUCATION AND EXPERIENCE: Graduation from high school, supplemented by completion of courses in business or legal training; and considerable experience in work involving familiarity with the procedures, policies, laws and operations of the court of assignment.
APPLICATIONS TO: Rosalie Adams, Greeley County Court, County Courthouse, P. O. Box 789, Greeley, Colorado 80631, by January 17, 1979. (#62409)

5) COURT CLERK II (.500 FTE) $373-500
DUTIES: This is technical clerical work in a court of the Colorado state court system. Work involves performing a variety of technical clerical functions which may require the application of independent judgment and the interpretation of routine policies and regulations on the basis of training and knowledge gained through experience on the job. Work is reviewed by a supervisor through observation of operations, and advice and assistance are available when unusual or difficult matters arise.
DESIRABLE EDUCATION AND EXPERIENCE: Graduation from high school, supplemented by completion of courses in business or legal training; and experience in work, including familiarity with procedures, policies, laws and operations of the court of assignment.
APPLICATIONS TO: Jack McLaughlin, District Administrator, Judicial Building, 20 East Vermijo, Colorado Springs, Colorado 80903, by January 17, 1979. (#21061)

6) BAILIFF $614-823
DUTIES: This is responsible work in maintaining order and providing general services in a courtroom. Work involves providing general services in the operation of a court. Work invludes maintaining order, calling witnesses, notifying interested parties, transferring prisoners, collecting case files for court cases and performing various services for a judge. Work is performed in accordance with established practices, procedures and instructions from a judge and is reviewed primarily through observation of performance and conferences.
DESIRABLE EDUCATION AND EXPERIENCE: Graduation from high school and some experience in routine clerical work or other public contact work.
APPLICATIONS TO: Dean Nakayama, District Administrator, Denver District Court, City and County Building, Denver, Colorado 80202, by January 19, 1979. (#16111)

5. Examinations

INTRODUCTION

With a few notable exceptions the courts have avoided formal testing of nonjudicial employees.[1] Courts have been slow to adopt testing practices which have been used by executive branch personnel agencies. That is not to say that testing is a panacea. Both private and public agencies have endured litigation attacking examinations. There is no indication that these attacks will cease. Few, however, suggest that tests be eliminated entirely.

It should be remembered that for all their frailties, tests in the civilian public sector came about to counter patronage methods. In the military, evidence somewhat to the contrary, examinations were used to assign GI's to appropriate duties. Though the military's examinations occasionally resulted in gross errors, the methods of testing fitted the need for processing large numbers of personnel. Following World War II, civilian jurisdictions, faced with large numbers of applicants, turned increasingly toward standardized tests. Such approaches were counter to patronage methods and only succeeded in jurisdictions having personnel boards or civil service commissions with some degree of authority.

As government, particularly local government, increased its personnel rolls, standardized tests became useful in screening large numbers of prospective public employees. Returning veterans expected consideration. They typically received special credit (veterans' preference points) after being admitted to civil service examinations. Where merit systems developed, then, standardized examinations found their place.

81

Testing in the Courts

The courts, except for Los Angeles and a few other large courts, did not for many years employ large numbers of employees. Often, the clerk was elected, as were the judges. These elected officials administered small, tightly knit staffs, using patronage as the primary selection device. Where probation officers were lodged in the executive branch, there was a higher probability of a testing program. As courts grew in size at the local level or became unified at the state level, and merit selection of judges was introduced, one began to notice some use of testing, primarily in the form of performance tests and unassembled examinations. Where testing is practiced in the courts, oral interviews predominate. Few standardized written tests are employed. Most oral interviews are unstructured. Virtually no examination used for court personnel has been validated in the courts.

Definitions

Examination. An examination embraces any device used in the selection of applicants for a job, or in cadre systems such as the military, law enforcement, and foreign service, for entry into the corps. Examinations for particular jobs of classes are more narrow than those designed for entry into a corps. The former tend toward examining for substantive knowledge, while the latter favor demonstration of skills and abilities. An examination may consist of various tests: written, oral, achievement, and performance, either administered individually or in combination.

Validity. An examination is said to have validity when it measures what it purports to measure. More simply put, a test is valid when it discriminates between those who can perform a task and those who cannot. If flying an airplane requires manual dexterity, then a valid test will accurately measure that skill without placing each applicant in an airborne aircraft. Validating an examination is merely an extension of the validity concept. The premise in a validated test[2] is that it will correctly screen out those not capable of performing a task and admit those capable of performing well.

The process of validating involves careful selection of existing employees generally rated as highly competent. The test to be validated is then administered to these employees. It is assumed that these employees will score well on the examination, particularly when compared with another group of employees generally rated as no higher than satisfactory. If both groups score equally well in the exam, it could not be considered a valid test. An I.Q. test, for example, would hardly predict successful performance as a court bailiff. Validation cannot really be complete until the performance of employees admitted through the testing procedure is monitored for some time thereafter. The results of that monitoring will indicate whether the examination process predicts successful job performance.

Reliability. An examination is said to have reliability when it consistently produces the same result. A group of persons taking a particular test should achieve essentially the same score if administered at different times. In like fashion, test takes should achieve similar scores, if the results are divided in half and a score computed for all even-numbered items and all odd-numbered items.

CRITICAL ISSUES IN EXAMINATIONS

Use of standardized tests can be costly. Such tests must typically be purchased, or in effect rented, particularly for proper interpretation in scoring. Certain tests may be available through executive branch agencies, lessening cost.
Whether such tests are valid for the courts must be carefully determined. Oral examinations, particularly unstructured exams,[3] are of questionable validity, though modest in cost.

In the courts, oral examinations seem most prevalent in selecting professional supervisory personnel. By far, the greatest need among the courts is to standardize oral examinations.

In today's labor market, particularly in metropolitan areas, an examination will attract large numbers of applicants. While the actual cost of administering the exam is a factor, the more critical factor is the cost of time in selecting a prospective group of eligible applicants. No administrator, least of all a judge, wishes to wait weeks or months before filling a vacant position. A merit system typically attempts to provide equal access to examinations for all persons possessing the minimum requirements. It can then be faced with the need to reduce 400 applicants to a manageable group from which to fill a limited number of positions. The method by which this is done will directly influence which types of candidates will be successful.

Open or Promotional Exam

The decision as to whether an examination will be open, that is, offered to the public, or promotional, so it is limited to employees of the court, turns on more than one factor. For the most part, entry positions such as junior clerk, probation trainee, and junior secretary will be examined for on an open basis. These positions are at the lowest salary levels for their series,[4] thus precluding interest among most existing employees. Secondly, it permits the court to seek new personnel who may be monitored and evaluated for positions of future responsibility. Training is virtually required for persons entering at this level.

The court may seek certain skills which are not prevalent in the organization, such as those required for court administrator, systems analyst, law clerk, court reporter, or budget officer. In these instances, the court may invite applicants from the public, even though these salary levels exceed entry levels. Promotional candidates may, of course, compete on an open basis. For the most part, promotions to higher levels in the series, in particular for supervisory positions, should be reserved for promotional candidates. It is sound personnel practice to promote qualified employees. The basic standard is that an examination should be held on a promotional basis whenever a sufficient number of qualified applicants exists from within the court.

Affirmative Action Implications

Courts will need to pay continuing action to affirmative action implications of the examination process. Bakke[5] notwithstanding, the courts have, over the years, held a number of examinations to be discriminatory. Griggs v. Duke Power,[6] certainly the most quoted case, held that an employment practice, such as a written intelligence test, that operates to exclude minorities and cannot be shown to be related to job performance is prohibited, notwithstanding the employer's lack of discriminatory intent. Put more simply, the court was saying that tests which are not validated for the job to be performed should not be used.

In 1965, the Equal Employment Opportunity Commission (EEOC) was created to enforce Title VII of the Civil Rights Act of 1964. EEOC is concerned with any employment and selection practices that may discriminate against minority groups and women. EEOC guidelines define test or selection standards in a broad sense and include any formal standardized measure or technique of appraising people that is used in employment decisions and covers decisions on eligibility for hire, transfer, promotion, and retention. The EEOC definition includes interview data, scored application forms, physical standards, and qualifying or disqualifying personal data.

THE EXAMINATION PROCESS

The Application

Following recruitment, described earlier, applicants must submit the job application. This, the first formal step taken by an applicant, sets the tone for the examination process. The court and the applicant begin to interact. This stage can run smoothly or seem not to run at all. An antiquated application form coupled with interminable delay may drive away desirable applicants. Filing deadlines not adhered to, confusion regarding out of state applicants, ambiguity concerning required documents to be included (e.g., transcript of grades), and uncertainty about the purpose of the application may jeopardize a successful examination. If, for example, the volume of applications is high, and the court decides to screen out applications without having communicated this intent in the examination announcement, the results will be uncertain. Applicants need to know whether they will have an opportunity to explain their applications at an oral interview or whether they will be judged solely on what is written.

Discriminatory questions continue to appear on job applications. Courts must recognize that certain information is not a valid determinant for job success. For the most part, questions relating to sex, marital status, ethnic background (e.g., requirement of a photograph), age, arrest records, and physical handicaps are discriminatory in nature. If these questions have any relevance, they should be so stated on the examination announcement: "Applicants for police officer must not have attained their 30th birthday." Inquiry into questionable items may be made after the candidate has been rated competitively with the other candidates. An arrest record, for example, should only be used to exclude a candidate entirely (because of the nature of the crime) rather than to reduce the candidate's score.

If applications are to be used for screening out candidates, a practice which should seldom be attempted,[7] it is essential that prior to submission, criteria for screening have been established. One cannot "take a look at what we get," and then screen. Such a procedure is inviting litigation. Each stage of the examination process requires specific criteria upon which decisions will be made.

The primary purpose of the application is to establish whether the applicant meets the minimum requirements. The examination announcement should state those requirements explicitly. If a bachelor's degree is not required, yet is desired, then the wording should state that a B.A. is desired. Similarly, the wording, "bachelor's degree in economics, business, psychology, or a related field" may be unworkable, unless a list of other acceptable degrees exists for inspection. For most jobs in the administrative and social fields, a bachelor's degree, regardless of major, will be acceptable. If a high volume of applications is expected, the applicants should be restricted to local residency.

The practice of raising the minimum requirements in an employer's market is counterproductive. Job analysis is a sound method for determining the requisite skills, knowledge, and abilities for a class. Requiring a master's degree when a bachelor's degree suffices will not produce the desired result. The employee will usually seek another position when such becomes available commensurate with his/her qualifications. The agency will experience turnover. Some courts will refuse to admit over-qualified applicants, particularly when more appropriate classes are available for application. This problem is known as "credentialism."

Some practitioners prefer to narrow the larger group of applicants by conducting a qualifying exam, most usually in written form. Candidates must achieve a passing score or be excluded from progressing to the next portion of the process, usually an oral exam. Though some written tests perform more admirably in this respect, they require high validity, if their primary goal is to screen out unacceptable candidates. Since written tests perform better in testing for intelligence or specific knowledge, they may not possess sufficient validity to screen for court jobs involving substantial public contact, such as probation officer.

Types of Tests

Written Tests. Written tests are primarily one of two types: short essay type and short answer. For all of the reasons stated previously, the essay exam, even short essay, presents major difficulties. Since answers are open-ended, scoring will tend to be subjective. Most typically, examiners are looking for a particular response. Their rating of unexpected answers will obviously influence the type of successful applicant. Secondly, writing ability is critical. If this skill is not highly important, the result may be disappointing. The essay test benefits from lower cost and ease of administering (careful validity and reliability checks are seldom made).

The short answer test permits standardized answers. Applicants must choose from a fixed number of responses. While more costly to administer, scoring is simplified. As mentioned earlier, the short answer test lends itself well to testing of intelligence or specific knowledge. Where validity of these tests can be established, they offer a benefit to the court. As has been mentioned, courts have seldom performed such validity analysis.

Achievement Tests. Achievement tests are specifically designed to measure a particular knowledge or skill that may be learned. Spelling for typists, bar examinations for lawyers, and CPA exams for accountants are examples.

A performance test is one which attempts to measure actual performance in an exam which simulates on the job situations. A court reporting test using actual equipment, a typing test with a typewriter, and a driver's road test are examples. Courts are most familiar with the typing test for clerical positions and, to some extent, a stenographic test for secretaries. Court reporters are often required to be certified before gaining a position with the court.

Oral Tests. The oral test, as previously indicated, is probably the most prevalent test used by courts. It suffers from all of the disadvantages of written tests plus more. It not only is seldom conducted as a structured oral,[8] it is seldom validated, nor tested for reliability. In addition, the opportunities for discriminatory evaluation abound. The unattractive, the handicapped, the female, the minority group member, and the uncommunicative applicant may all be at a disadvantage before an oral interview panel.

Selection of the panel will largely determine the outcome. Their biases are only balanced, not necessarily eliminated, by selecting three representative panel members. Courts frequently mix the membership of the panel to include both sexes, varying ethnic backgrounds, in-house membership, and public representatives.

An additional strain for the candidate is the tension of the actual interview situation. There is no excuse for a panel to cause tension in most court exams. It already exists. The results will be detrimental should panel members attempt to reproduce the actual job situation by simulating a hostile environment. Panel members are not professionally trained in such techniques. The reaction of the candidate may be neither valid nor reliable.

Despite the extraordinary difficulties in administering an oral exam, it has been used frequently in the courts. Many courts carefully select their panel members. It is substantially to their credit that oral exams have evolved without major litigation. To some extent, minorities have fared better in oral exams than in written tests. To the extent that panels appear to be asking valid questions, the candidates may assume that the test is at least fair. The appearance of validity is known as "face validity."

<u>Assessment Center</u>. A relatively new testing development is the assessment center.[9] For the most part, its use has found greatest favor at higher administrative levels. Most notably, it is used with great frequency in the selection of chiefs of police. The American Telephone and Telegraph Company has used the practice for many years. Perhaps the greatest limitation on its use among lower classifications is the cost of the process.

The assessment center is characterized by several critical features. Unlike most testing mechanisms, this method evaluates the candidates together rather than individually. Candidates in certain situations may find themselves in a group. In fact, they are competing with one another to demonstrate skill, usually, of an interpersonal or leadership nature. Naturally, for most applicants, this creates some degree of stress. They are aware that they must assert themselves for better or worse. Whether their subsequent behavior is valid or reliable may be open to question. Supporters of the practice believe it to be no less valuable than other methods.

The assessment center uses a number of evaluators typically called assessors. The ratio of assessors to applicants is very high. A ratio of one assessor to every two applicants is thought to be desirable. Assessors evaluate applicants when in groups or in certain phases of the testing. Naturally, the candidate group cannot reach a high number, as the number of assessors may be limited to five or six.

The assessment center measures the candidates along several dimensions. In order to mitigate the bias of any one test each candidate is rated (or scored) on a series of measures presumably different in form and in content. Candidates may be evaluated in group discussion situations,[10] in an in-basket exercise,[11] speech and writing exercises,[12] analysis problem,[13] and a paper and pencil test.[14]

The assessment center constitutes a major cost to the using agency. One or two days may be required by the assessors to rank the candidates. Naturally, outside assessors may project their own biases in evaluating the candidates. In-house assessors may lack the necessary training to perform the job adequately. Proponents of this method argue that the validity is at least as good as any other method. Courts, if they were to use this method, would do well to experiment with recognized, professional assessors. For many court examinations the cost would be prohibitive. Whether the costs ensure predictably more valuable results remains somewhat open to question.

Eligibility Lists[15]

Whatever method is used for ranking candidates, the court will need to produce a final list of those who are to be considered. The eligibility list will include those who have passed the examination and who might reasonably be considered for hiring over the life of the list. (Six months is usually the most viable time period.) If the court expects only one vacancy during the six months' period, there is little wisdom in placing 100 people on the list. Accordingly, the list should effect a balance between those who are acceptable to the court (i.e., would be hired if a vacancy exists) and those who might reasonably be reached on the list over a six months' period. The point at which all above pass and all below are eliminated is called the cut point or pass point.

The pass point is illustrated below:

CANDIDATES	RAW SCORE
A	99
B	97
C	96
D	93
E	89
F	88
G	88
H	86
I	83
J	79
K	77
L	73
....	....
M	68
N	67
O	66
P	65

    The pass point occurs above 68 and below 73. These raw scores happen to coincide with percentages, thereby, in this case, assuring that those who attained 70 percent were placed on the eligible list. The pass point may be moved upward or downward depending upon the desired size of the list. Care should be taken to find a natural break in the scores. In this case, performance tests may be similarly purchased or otherwise used. Executive branch agencies should be able to provide assistance to courts in test usage.

    Courts will continue to administer oral interviews. Though it is inherently open to misuse, steps can be taken to improve validity and reliability. The structured oral offers some advantages. Though time consuming, the oral exam provides the potential for equal access to the court's examining process. In avoiding the rather impersonal nature of a written exam, the oral exam brings the court in direct contact with the public. An opportunity is thus provided for the court to present the nature of its examining program on a personal basis.

NOTES

    1. Performance tests for clerical employees are somewhat more prevalant; where testing exists employees are frequently tied to procedures of the county or city executive branch. Testing does exist at the state level though almost always limited to the central administrative office for the courts.

    2. A technical discussion of test validation

may be found in Edwin E. Ghiselli, The Validity of Occupational Aptitude Tests (New York: Wiley, 1966).

3. A structural oral is a test in which the same questions are asked of each applicant. An unstructured oral permits the examiners to differentiate their questioning as the examination proceeds.

4. A series is simply a group of classes related vertically into which employees typically are promoted, such as Clerk I, Clerk II and Clerk III.

5. Bakke, 98 S.Ct. 2733 (1978), the leading reverse discrimination case.

6. 401 U.S. 424 (1971).

7. Despite the continuing practice of this method, there is a serious question whether quality of information provided by the applicant is comparable for purposes of selection.

8. See footnote 3 (above).

9. An illustrative handbook on the techniques used in the assessment center is that of George P. Tielsch and Paul M. Whisenand, The Assessment Center Approach in the Selection of Police Personnel, (Santa Cruz, California: Davis Publishing Co. Inc., 1977).

10. Assessors frequently observe groups in which a leader has not been assigned to note the emergence of a natural leader or leaders.

11. A simulation requiring the examinee to respond to notes, letters, memos, etc., and take appropriate action.

12. Typically, the candidate must respond orally and in writing to a hypothetical situation.

13. This might be a managerial or administrative problem requiring analysis typically analogous to that performed by an administrative analyst.

14. Most probably this would be an aptitude or personality test.

15. This section and the next are excerpted with permission from Courts and Personnel Systems, Institute for Court Management (Denver: Institute for Court Management, 1973).

6. Compensation and Benefits

DEVELOPING THE COMPENSATION PLAN

The information concerning duties and responsibilities of a position classification is extremely important in salary setting, especially that information which differentiates one classification from another, based on duties, responsibilities, and level of experience and education required.

These two integral sets of factors--education and experience, duties and responsibilities--play a large part in determining which classification receives more compensation than another and how much more it receives, expressed in an added percentage or grade differential. The fifty-nine grade salary chart shown in Figure 3.2 on Page 49 shows these grade differentials. In that chart, each grade is approximately 2 1/2 percent greater than the one which precedes it. Grade 46, Step 1 is $1,630 and $47 or 2-1/2 percent greater than the $1,583 which is indicated for Grade 45, Step 1. On the other hand, the horizontal axis of the chart has seven steps in each grade, with each step being 5 percent greater than the one which precedes it. Grade 46, Step 2 is $1,712 as opposed to Grade 46, Step 1 at $1,630, which is an $82 or 5 percent differential. This is shown in the following excerpt from Figure 3.2.

	Step 1	2	3	4	5	6	7
Grade 45 -	1583	1667	1750	1837	1929	2025	2126
Grade 46 -	1630	1712	1798	1888	1982	2031	2185

Entry Level Classes

An entry level class may have a larger differential between it and the next higher class than the differentials used between the other classes in a class series. This is for two sound reasons: one, the entry level, or training level, is of less use to the organization than the full-functioning higher level positions. Consequently, if it is of less use, then the pay grade assigned is lower; and, two, a larger differential will be an incentive to the incumbents of the lower classifications to move from the entry level to a higher level.

Other factors in setting the class differentials may include premiums for supervisory or lead work, exceptionally difficult or technical work assignments, or the possession of a necessary special license or certificate (i.e., more than the standard class differential within a class series could be applied to a classification requiring a court reporter's certification, or admission to practice as an attorney).

Pay Differential Among Classification Groups

The court should recognize that differing groups of classifications require differing amounts of pay and that each separate group requires a different pay structure. Clerical workers, for instance, are paid less than those workers carrying a professional level job classification, but how great should the difference be? Certainly there should be a large difference between the entry level clerical position and the entry level professional position, as there should also be a great variation between the high levels of clerical and professional classifications. In most state systems, the difference between entry level clerical and professional positions is 60 to 75 percent.

What differential should be applied between the top clerical classification and the entry level professional classification? As stated earlier, the entry level position does not require the skill, expertise, or training necessary to be of great worth to the court. On the other hand, the incumbent of the top level clerical position may have ten or more years in the court and frequently may know more about the day-to-day realities of working in a court environment than anyone else including the judges.

The setting of salaries or grade levels for these classifications may be difficult at best.

Parity can be achieved in this area by setting the grades of the top level clerical position and the entry level professional position at approximately the same level. This will allow the top level clerical employees an opportunity to switch from the clerical ranks to the professional ranks without having to overcome the hurdle of an artificial salary barrier and will allow for a more nominal increase, which may be 10 to 15 percent.

Other Important Considerations

Other internal considerations in setting salaries, beside classification, are: 1) employer's attitude and expectations, which may be raised by employee groups to which they belong; and 2) court or judicial system wage philosophy, such as setting artificially low wages on certain classifications to encourage turnover of incumbents.

There are also external forces which have an impact upon the pay level attached to a classification. One is collective bargaining agreements (discussed in Chapter 10). Another is legislation passed by federal, state, or local governments pertaining to or affecting salaries. An example is the Federal Fair Labor Standards Act, which was applied by the Congress to all levels of government in 1974. This act set the minimum wages to be paid to employees and, perhaps more important, set certain standards (time and a half) for work in excess of forty hours in any work week. The Supreme Court ruled in National League of Cities vs. Usery that the federal government has no power to regulate the wages and hours of state and local government employees.[1] Even though the law was reversed, state and local governments, including the judiciary, were forced to comply with the law and set their salaries accordingly for a period of approximately two years.

Another external force is compensation being paid by other employers who are competing for applicants in the marketplace. If the court's wages are too low, the court system will have a difficult time recruiting and retaining the best qualified applicants. If the salaries are too high, the taxpayers become upset; public pressure may well force salaries down to a more realistic level. This final consideration, that of other salaries paid in the court's recruiting area, is very important in establishing and maintaining a salary schedule.

COMPENSATION PLAN MAINTENANCE

Developing and adopting a compensation plan are only the first steps. The plan must be maintained; without updating, the plan will become useless in a short period of time. How should an administrator or personnel manager approach salary schedule maintenance? The most simple, most effective, and cheapest means available are to use a salary survey from another source and apply it directly to the compensation schedule used by the court.

Comparability with Executive Branch

When the classification study is made, the classes in the judicial system or court should be compared with the classes used by the executive branch for salary-setting purposes. Whoever does the study should weigh and compare the strength of each judicial class with the classes used in the executive personnel system. Obviously, not all classes can be related to those used in another system, as there are certain classes, such as bailiff, for which there is no comparison. These unique classes should be related internally to those judicial classes which are related to those in the executive branch.

Not every class within the judicial classification structure should be related to a class in the executive branch. Only the key classes of a class series need be related.[2] These key classes should be drawn from the entire spectrum of employment within a court. For instance, different classes (clerical, administrative, data processing) should be compared with their counterparts in the general labor force. In this manner, the administrator can determine that clerks are receiving comparable wages to other clerks, administrators are receiving approximately the same wages as other administrators, and so on through all of the various classes of employment.

Salary Surveys

If the judicial system or court has related its key classes to those in the executive branch, so that there are proper alignments, it becomes possible to apply the results of executive branch salary surveys to judicial branch classifications. It takes approximately one year to make and implement a thorough salary study for the average public personnel system, especially if certain senior level positions are surveyed regionally or nationally. The results of the study can be applied to any related system in a very short time, once the proper class alignments have been made. If in-house staff is not qualified to apply the survey results, a consultant can be retained at a nominal cost to analyze the salary data and to train staff in their application to court positions.

Most judicial systems and trial courts usually do not have the resources to conduct a separate salary survey, either by in-house staff or by hiring consultants. Funding bodies are likely to accept the application of executive branch salary surveys to court positions, especially if parity among the employees of the three branches is an established principle, and the alignment of key classes is supported by adequate documentation.

It might become necessary, under certain circumstances, for a judicial system or a trial court to conduct a separate salary survey, or at least a partial survey, even if the executive branch makes an annual study. The executive branch may have overlooked some key classes in the court or may not have made as comprehensive a survey as the judicial system or court considers necessary, e.g., court reporters may have been surveyed locally rather than nationally, when there is competition among states for qualified reporters. The judicial system or trial court may be concerned over the internal relationship of some classes in light of labor market developments. To assure valid results and their acceptance by the funding body, the person or persons conducting the survey should have personnel administration training and experience, with emphasis on wage and salary administration. Again it may be necessary to contract out to assure an adequate study is made.

General Increase

Another approach, used frequently by the United States Civil Service Commission, applies the same general increase to all classes of employment and, consequently, may short-change some employees, while overpaying others in comparison with the general labor market.

Cost of Living

Another method of maintaining the salary

schedules is by using cost of living (COL) increases. This method of salary setting is not prevalent in public agencies, but is used in the private sector. The COL method escalates salaries at the same rate as the cost of living index increases. This is done regardless of the type of work performed by an employee. Increments are applied to a certain base salary rather than to the total salary. For example, if an employee's base salary is $500 per month, and an increase of 1 percent is awarded, the employee receives $5. Succeeding 1 percent increases will be awarded to the employee at the rate of 1 percent on the base, or $5, not 1 percent of the total monthly salary. In other words, the increments are not compounded.

Another factor in the COL method of maintenance is that when the cost of living index drops, the employee's salary drops also. This can have a negative effect on morale. The biggest drawback to using COL to determine wages is that is is almost impossible to budget for unexpected increases. This may lead to a loss of credibility with the funding body when the use of COL places the court's budget in the red.

In-Grade Hiring

The salary schedule also has some built-in flexibility. If, during the middle of a fiscal year, or half-way through the wage survey cycle, it becomes apparent that certain executive classes have had dramatic wage increases, the entry level of the corresponding judicial classifications may be raised. This is done by setting an in-grade hiring rate for the class. That is, an employee, instead of being hired at Step 1, would be hired at Step 2 or 3 in the grade to compensate for the inequity between the judicial class and similar classes in other agencies. If an employee is brought in at a higher step in grade, the administrator should raise all persons in the class hired at a lower step to the in-grade step. This alleviates intra-system inequities, but may also lead to a serious budget problem, if the number of employees affected is large.

A Different Approach

The grade/step salary schedule is generally accepted in public employment, but all applications of this concept are not similar. Variations may relate to a number of different things, such as:

1) the number and time requirements for longevity steps; 2) the frequency of step increases; 3) the percent of increase between steps and grades; and 4) acceleration in step increases according to employee performance.

Perhaps, one of the most innovative and comprehensive variations is the new compensation plan adopted by the Maine judicial system.[3] This system has combined the usual salary plan objectives: 1) job value as related to other jobs in the system and in the labor market; 2) degree of learning on the job; 3) individual performance; and 4) value of extensive experience. It does this in a different way from other plans. Each grade has a target rate. This is the market level rate for satisfactory performance by a fully trained employee. The time necessary to achieve the target rate varies among job classes and pay grades.

Employees who have extensive experience and perform satisfactorily will be paid above market level--a different approach to the longevity concept. Employees whose performance is superior will be paid significantly above the target rate. For most employees, except those in professional classes in the highest grades, the maximum compensation is 25 percent above the target rate. Professionals in the highest grades have no maximum; their compensation depends on performance. Annual prevailing wage surveys will be applied to keep the grades adjusted to the labor market.

This plan is sound in its objectives, but it may be somewhat difficult to administer. Maine's experience should be watched closely, because of its innovative approach.

FRINGE BENEFITS

While wages are the most obvious benefit from working for any agency, whether public or private, the fringe benefits associated with an agency's positions must also be competitive with those offered by other employers. Fringe benefits differ from wages in that all permanent employees[4] receive the same amount, regardless of classification. This is true whether the employee is the highest administrative official or a clerk-typist.

Fringe benefits can be categorized in the following areas: annual, sick, and other types of leave; health and life insurance; holidays; retirement; and overtime and compensatory time.

Annual Leave

Annual leave is the leave which is accrued by an employee to be used for vacation purposes. An employee accrues annual leave at a set rate per month, year, or other designated time period. The employee uses this leave at times which are mutually convenient for the employee and his supervisor.

Annual Leave Accrual. Employees should be allowed to accrue and use leave at a rate which is competitive with other employers in the area. A suggested, but not mandatory, policy for leave accrual is to increase the rate of accrual for employees according to length of service. Following is an example of this type of system;

Years of Service	Accrual Rate
1 - 5	1 day/month
6 - 10	1 1/4 days/month
11 - 15	1 1/2 days/month
16 and up	1 3/4 days/month

An employee under this system can accrue from twelve to twenty-one days of leave per year.

An employee should also be allowed to carry over a certain amount of unused leave from one year to another, with a maximum amount of leave which he may accrue. This amount can vary according to the amount of time in service or the accrual rate of the employee. This is for two purposes: It forces the employee to use leave, as it is there for his use to keep him from getting too tired. It keeps the debit account of unused employee leave at a lower level, so that the organization will not be leave poor, because of excessive payoffs for unused leave.

Payment for Unused Leave. This latter reason is especially important, if the organization pays off unused annual leave when an employee terminates from the system. All annual leave accrued up to the limit allowed should be paid off in full when an employee terminates. The employee has earned the leave, and he should be compensated for the unused portion. The problem with annual leave payoff is that it is difficult to budget for (except for a rough estimate based on experience) and can, consequently, exceed budgetary estimates for personnel services. To help alleviate this problem, all but the most vital positions should be left open until the former employee's leave is paid off.

Sick Leave

Sick leave is leave which is accrued by an employee for use when he is ill or otherwise unable to perform his job. Sick leave may be accrued on an annual or monthly basis. Most public agencies allow accrual on a monthly basis at a rate of one to one and a quarter days per month.

Sick leave may be accrued at increasingly greater rates for length of time in service, or may be accrued at a standard rate for everyone. It is, however, a good idea to set a maximum for the number of sick leave days which can be accrued. The maximum allowed should be higher than the level set for annual leave days to allow an employee the time necessary to recover from a severe illness, such as a heart attack.

Payment for Unused Leave. Some jurisdictions pay off sick leave at retirement, some pay off upon any termination, and some do not pay off at all. Jurisdictions which do pay off sick leave sometimes pay off at a percentage of the total accrual.

The Colorado judicial system has found that by paying off 25 percent of total accrual at the time of termination (for any reason) the number of sick days used drops appreciably when compared with other public agencies' sick day absences. Employees of the Colorado judicial system use a yearly average of five days sick leave per person, whereas employees of other agencies in that state use approximately seven days yearly per person. The interesting fact is that the five days per year rate includes the number of sick leave days paid off to terminating employees. To keep the final payoff within reason, the Colorado judicial system has set a maximum accrual of one hundred eighty days with a maximum payoff of forty-five days.

Some public systems allow employees to convert a certain amount of unused sick leave to annual leave. This is done when an employee reaches the maximum amount of sick leave he can accrue. Time accrued over this amount can be converted on a one for one, one for two, or some other predetermined ratio. This is done to allow an employee to accrue extra annual leave to take a day or two at a time, e.g., to avoid having to cut short a two or three week vacation due to lack of leave.

Maternity Leave

Maternity leave is leave which is granted to a

pregnant employee whose continued employment constitutes a danger to the employee or to the unborn child. Maternity leave usually has a set period (from three to six months) and is made up of a combination of sick and annual leave and leave without pay.

Maternity leave allows a pregnant employee to leave the job, have the baby, and return to work without prejudicing the employee's position or salary. This is a benefit which most public agencies give to their employees. Typically, before taking maternity leave, the employee is requested to furnish a doctor's statement indicating the inadvisability of continued employment.

Injury Leave

Injury leave is leave which is given to an employee who is injured on the job or in the line of duty. This leave is used by an employee without prejudicing his sick leave account. Injury leave is usually a set amount of time, such as three or four months. When injury leave is exhausted, and the employee is still unable to return to his job, he can draw on his accrued sick and annual leaves.

Injury leave is usually granted by an employer only when the injury is determined compensable under the state's workmen's compensation laws. Because injury leave is given by an employer, he may require the employee to forfeit any workmen's compensation award received to the employing agency. As the courts are a low-risk employer, this leave is not used too frequently.

Military Leave

Military leave is leave which is granted to employees who are members of the National Guard or the active military reserve. Leave is generally for a two-week or fifteen-day period with pay and is granted annually to allow the employee to complete his military obligation. This leave is given without forcing the employee to use his annual leave.

Military leave without pay may be granted an employee who enlists in military service during a time of war or national emergency, allowing the employee the right to return to his position without prejudice after serving during that time.

Educational Leave

Educational leave is leave which may be granted to an employee who wishes to pursue his education in the specialty in which he is employed. This is a benefit to both the employee and the employing agency. The agency benefits from the employee's additional education, and the employee benefits both from the education and the chance to attain it in a short time.

Educational leave can be granted with or without pay. If the court can afford to give one employee educational leave with pay, it must afford the same opportunity to other employees similarly situated, or morale problems may result. The same is true for educational leave without pay. The administrator must be sure at all times that he is not granting so much educational leave that his court will be forced to operate with a short staff.

Administrative Leave

Administrative leave is leave with pay which may be granted to an employee at the discretion of the administrator or supervisor. This type of leave is granted to allow an employee to attend job-related clinics or seminars, although it may also be granted to an employee to attend to personal business (closing on a home, moving, etc.).

Jury leave or leave to be a witness in court generally falls under this category. Granting leave for these purposes is usually outside the discretion of the administrator. Any fees or payment to the employee for jury or witness service may be forfeited to the employer. Hawaii's collective bargaining agreement, on the other hand, allows employees to retain payments for juror service.

Leave Without Pay

Leave without pay may be granted to an employee for justifiable personal reasons in addition to those times where leave without pay is allowed in the foregoing sections on other types of leave. As a rule of thumb, leave without pay is given when other types of leave are exhausted or will be exhausted during the employee's absence. For example, if an employee has two weeks of annual leave accrued and desires to go on a package tour through Europe which lasts three weeks, then one week of leave without pay could be granted.

Health Insurance

It has become a practice for almost all employers to provide a health insurance package for their employees. This has been done to help curb the impact of rapidly rising medical costs. Health insurance is paid for in various ways. In some jurisdictions the employer pays the entire cost of the employees' health insurance; in others, the employer and employees split the cost of the insurance package at predetermined percentages or amounts. Some larger jurisdictions are using, or are exploring the use of, self-insurance for health purposes. As the amount contributed by the employer is nontaxable, this is a good benefit.

There are two types of insurance in frequent use today. One is the standard health insurance package offered by companies such as Blue Cross, Blue Shield, and commercial insurance companies, and the other is a relatively new concept known as health maintenance organizations (HMO's). Kaiser is an example of these.

Standard Coverage. Standard insurance works in much the same way as other insurances. Once the insured has incurred a loss, the bills are submitted to the insurance company which pays the portion(s) of the bill covered by the policy up to the extent covered by the policy. The remainder is paid by the insured. The costs of a group policy such as this depend on the extent of the coverage provided. "First dollar coverage," the insurance that pays almost everything, can be a very expensive package running well in excess of $150 a month. Insurance policies of this nature have a set amount that may be paid in each area of the medical bill. For example, the policy may cover the cost of a semi-private room up to $100 a day for 180 days in any policy year. Any costs above the maximum limit would be covered by the insured or the "major medical" provision (if there is such provision) of the policy.

Major Medical. Major medical covers otherwise uncovered costs after a certain deductible is reached. The costs in excess of the deductible are then paid on a percentage basis (typically 80 percent) by the insurance carrier. Major medical covers the insured for catastrophic loss.

Major medical, or percentage over deductible type of insurance, may also be used as primary insurance. This has the advantage of relatively low insurance premiums, while still providing coverage for the larger medical bills. For example, if the insured or a member of his family has a short stay in a hospital and the bill is $1,000, the insured would pay a $100 deductible plus 20 percent of the remainder, or $180, or a total of $280. The insurance company would pay $720. Under this type of policy, the insured generally pays only one deductible during the policy year. Consequently, any other costs during the policy year would be covered on an 80-20 percent basis, with no additional deductible. Furthermore, the major medical policies usually have a maximum limit for which the insured is liable at the 20 percent rate. Anything over this amount would be paid for entirely by the insurance company.

There are almost as many variations on this type of group policy as there are group policies. The administrator who has the responsibility of contracting for insurance coverage should be very careful to determine the best plan(s) for the employees.

Health Maintenance Organization. A type of health insurance plan that is becoming more and more popular is the HMO. HMO's provide medical services to the insured person at a low cost. The philosophy underlying the HMO concept is to keep the insured healthy to prevent major illness that may be very costly. This plan provides a clinic which is available to the insured for his medical needs. The per-visit costs for use of the clinic are very small when compared with the charge for a visit to a doctor's office.

The disadvantages of the HMO concept are that the insured usually has a choice of only those doctors associated with the plan and has the use of only one or two hospitals in the immediate area. In addition, only minimal coverage may be avaialble for insured persons who are hospitalized or who need medical attention outside of the immediate geographical area in which the plan functions.

Retirement

One of the most attractive features of working for a public agency has been the availability of good retirement plans. Most public employers provide retirement options for career service employees. These plans are funded by a combination of contributions from both the employer and employees and allow each employee to retire with a reasonable amount of income security.

Some public agencies establish a retirement plan through a combination of contributions to both social security and a local retirement fund, while others disregard social security entirely and place all funds in one retirement fund.

Vested Rights. Most plans provide features that are similar to the following. An employee, after contributing to the fund for five years has a vested interest in the retirement plan, which means that, with five years' service, the employee is guaranteed the right to a pension at the age of retirement. Usually when an employee has twenty years of service and has reached retirement age (between fifty-five and sixty-five years of age), he is eligible for approximately 50 percent of the average of his five years of highest salary earnings. For each year of service over twenty, the employee may be allowed to receive an additional percentage of his highest five year average salary up to a specified maximum. If an employee leaves the system at any time before five years, he may have his portion of contributions refunded, with or without interest. If an employee leaves the system after he has a vested interest, he may withdraw the amount he has contributed as mentioned above, or he may leave his share of the money in the fund and receive a pension when reaching retirement age.

Rule of Eighty. One new concept on retirement which is emerging is the "rule of eighty" (or seventy, seventy-five, etc.). This states that when an employee's age plus his years of service equals eighty (age fifty-five with twenty-five years of service, for example), he is eligible for retirement with 50 percent of his highest five year average salary. Additional years of service may be worth 2 percent per year up to a predetermined maximum.

The purpose of plans like the rule of eighty is to move employees out of the system, so that positions will be made available for the steadily increasing number of workers entering the employment market.

Overtime and Compensatory Time

Overtime is paid to an employee for work in excess of the standard number of work hours in a given time period. Overtime is generally awarded to an employee after he has worked more than forty hours in a work week. This is due to the impact of the Federal Fair Labor Standards Act, which was overturned in National League of Citys v. Usery. Overtime is generally paid at the rate of time and a half for each hour worked, although a union contract may modify the rate of overtime compensation.

Compensatory time, or "comp" time as it is frequently called, is also an award for time spent in work over the usual number of work hours. Instead of a monetary payment, the employee is granted time off for his extra hours of duty. Comp time may be granted at the straight time rate (one hour for each additional hour worked) or a time and a half rate (one and a half hours off for each additional hour worked). The danger inherent with comp time is that when employees must work extra hours to keep up with the work load in a court there is little opportunity for them to use that accrued time. As a result, employees frequently use the accrued comp time in lieu of annual leave allowance. This situation may lead to excessive annual leave accrual and the accompanying large payoff at termination.

Overtime should be granted only when prior approval of the court's administrative authority has been given.

Holidays

Public employment usually has more paid holidays than those found in the private sector, and this practice applies to courts as well. The most common holidays are New Year's Day, Lincoln's Birthday (some states), Washington's Birthday, Memorial Day, Independence Day, Labor Day, Columbus Day, Election Day, Armistice or Veteran's Day, Thanksgiving, and Christmas.

In addition, some jurisdictions celebrate the anniversary of statehood as a holiday, and religious holidays of various denominations are sometimes observed. There are also a few other holidays peculiar to one or two jurisdictions. Some examples are: Arbor Day (Nebraska and Utah); Jefferson Davis Day, Patriot's Day (Maine and Massachusetts); Confederate Memorial Day (Alabama and Mississippi).

As the courts are closed on official holidays, employees seldom work. If they do, for any reason, they may receive compensatory time or overtime pay.

NOTES

1. *National League of Cities v. Usery*, 96 Sup. Ct. 2465, 49 L. ed. 2nd 245.
2. Key classes are those classes which have

universally understood titles and which can be readily surveyed in most organizations. They can be defined easily from the type of work performed and the level of skill required to perform such work. Key classes are usually at the entry level of a class series whether the series is at the worker or supervisory level (Court Clerk I or Clerical Supervisor I) and have a fairly large numerical representation in the work force.

    3. See Appendix E, Rule 3 Compensation Plan, Maine Court System Personnel Policies and Procedures.

    4. The discussion of fringe benefits applies primarily to permanent workers. Temporary or contract workers may or may not receive them, as this depends on the management philosophy of the employing agency.

7. Retention and Promotion

THE NEW EMPLOYEE

It is unlikely that the new employees have had any court experience, especially those in lower level positions. Not all court positions differ substantially from those in other public agencies; some have essentially the same duties and levels of responsibility. Nevertheless, it is still necessary to provide training so the new employee can become as effective as possible in as short a time as possible.

Once the new employee has entered a training program and has proved his effectiveness on the job, efforts must be made to ensure that he stays within the system. Otherwise many hours and dollars will have been wasted in the training effort.[1]

One way an administrator can keep turnover at a low level is to show each new employee a route which he may follow to advance his career on the promotional ladder. This, then, is the thrust of this chapter: orienting new employees to retain and promote them within the system.

If a new employee is placed in his new role with no preparation and has no hope that he can pick up enough information to be successful on the job, the turnover rate will be abnormally high, and the administrator will spend most of his too-few hours in recruiting and examining prospective employees. A new employee should not be expected to take on a new work experience with little or no preparation. To do so will lead to a high frustration level for everyone concerned, especially the new employee.

Regardless of the size of the organization, it is very helpful to have an employee's handbook available for each employee to refer to when a question is raised. The cost of such a publication is minimal when compared with the benefits.

Initial Orientation

The first step for the administrator is to orient the new employee to his surroundings. This may be done either at formalized training sessions (in larger courts and jurisdictions) or at informal training sessions (in the smaller courts and jurisdictions where formal sessions are less cost efficient). At these training sessions, the administrator, or his designee, will explain the work environment and what is expected of that employee. A most rudimentary orientation system suggests that the employee be made aware of what his duties and responsibilities are and, in turn, what his rights and privileges are.

On-the-Job-Training

The simplest way for the new employee to learn is by doing the job under the guidance of a person who has considerable expertise about the job. This person may be the direct supervisor of the position, an employee who has just been promoted from the position, or possibly the court administrator.

Whoever is selected to perform the task of guiding the employee through the on-the-job training program should be aware that the new employee probably has no experience with the language and "buzz words" of the courts. The trainer needs to have the patience to answer all of the questions which will be asked and re-asked and should be selected with this attribute in mind. The care and patience with which the questions are answered will show in work performance and in the way in which the employee responds to the job.

Probationary Period

The employee should be told the length of the probationary period when he first begins work. A probationary period is that time during which the employee is expected to gain the ability to perform successfully on the job. It is also the period during which the supervisor and administrator evaluate the employee's performance and progress. The duration of the probationary period may be explicit (six months to a year) or may be general (the length of time required to complete a training program for the position). It is helpful if the training program coincides with the length of the probationary period.

During the probationary period, a constant check should be made on the employee by his supervisor. All too often an employee is not made aware of his weaknesses in the work environment and ends up being dismissed, when a few well-timed words would have corrected his deficiencies. Lack of communication between supervisor and employee is one of the most common causes for employee failure during the probationary period.

The orientation program should be carefully established to allow the employee to see what is expected of him and to allow the supervisor to chart the employee's progress. This does not mean that the program established for the new employee should be so rigid as to deny him access to other areas outside his principal purpose. To the contrary, the program should be set up in a way to allow all concerned the flexibility necessary to meet the changing environment of the job.

In addition to learning the job assigned, the new employee must be given the opportunity to learn about the rights, privileges, and benefits to which he is entitled. In larger organizations where there is a considerable amount of hiring, it is beneficial to have an orientation session for all new employees to explain the rights, privileges, etc., which go with each job. In smaller organizations, this may not be possible, as new employees may be hired at the rate of one per month, or even less frequently. In the smaller court organization, it is more feasible to have the supervisor sit down with the new employee and explain to him exactly what are the rights and benefits of the position.

When the employee has successfully completed his probationary period, it is necessary to continue to monitor his progress as he continues to learn his job. This may be very important in the employee's career, as well as in the over-all efficiency of the court's operation. The fact that the probationary period has been completed successfully does not mean that the employee has complete mastery of the position which he holds, nor that he has a complete understanding of the court environment. The supervisor should continue to review his progress with the understanding that rapid strides toward mastering the job are made during the early stages of employment and that expertise in completing assigned tasks is gained after the employee has been on the job for a longer period of time.

IN-SERVICE TRAINING

To that end, it is important that some sort of in-service training program be developed for those who have been employed for some time. The objective of in-service training is to enhance the employee's job skills and to improve his efficiency and competency.

It is more difficult to develop this type of training for lower level clerical positions (file clerks, etc.) than it is to develop a program for higher level clerical employees, clerical supervisors, and professional personnel involved in court operations. Because it is more difficult does not mean that some sort of job enrichment should not be attempted. Cross-training with employees at higher levels should allow the incumbents of lower level positions to gain the skills necessary to advance to better paying, more meaningful jobs.

Training programs for higher level clerks should concentrate on new techniques and systems for processing the work to be done and to prepare them for professional vacancies. A variety of programs may be designed and administered in-house to meet the needs of all these employees, and they may be used with outside training programs to achieve the desired results.

Training at all levels is essential to the goal of staff development. All too often training is viewed as an excessive luxury or governmental boondoggle by those who hold the purse strings. Excessive abuses of training may have led to these feelings. Every effort should be made to demonstrate to policy makers and appropriation bodies that proper training is imperative, if the court is to become efficient in its procedures and effective in its delivery of services to the public.

In addition to training employees, it is necessary for management to determine the relative value or merit of the abilities of the court employees. In other words, a performance evaluation system should be established and maintained for the benefit of both management and employees.

PERFORMANCE EVALUATION[2]

The American Bar Association's Commission on Standards of Judicial Administration recommends:

>Uniform procedures for making periodic evaluation of employee performance and decisions concerning retention and promotion.[3]

Performance criteria are the solid core upon which an effective performance evaluation program depends. In courts there are many jobs which cannot be easily measured, and there are many jobs in which the quality of performance is of greater importance than quantity. Accordingly, both quantity and quality of performance should compose the key elements in performance evaluation (also referred to as performance appraisal).

Performance-appraisal theory assumes that there are traits and characteristics which, when present in and applied by employees, result in productivity; these traits and characteristics can be perceived and isolated; they can be measured; and they should be rewarded.

Who Should Do the Rating?

One management concept that has withstood the test of time is that evaluations should be made at the lowest organizational level where there are sufficiane facts to make a valid determination. Thus, it follows that the evaluation of employee performance should be made by the employee's immediate supervisor, and the rating should be related to the characteristics, qualifications, traits, capacities, proficiencies, and abilities of the individual as demonstrated by him in relation to the job.

Uses of Performance Evaluation

In December, 1968, Fred E. Schuster, Associate Professor of Management, and Assistant Dean, College of Business and Public Administration, Florida Atlantic University, conducted a study of performance appraisal practices of 500 large corporations.[4] Out of 403 respondents to the survey, 316 used some type of performance evaluation plan. The uses made of employee appraisals by these 316 corporations are shown in Figure 7.1.

Data in that figure indicate that a substantial

Figure 7.1: Uses of Appraisals or Ratings
in 316 Leading Industrial Corporations

Uses of Appraisals	Responses No.	Percent
1. Merit increases or bonuses	238	75.3%
2. Counseling the ratee	278	88.0
3. Planning training or development for ratee	270	85.4
4. Considering the ratee for promotion	266	84.2
5. Considering retention or discharge	185	58.2
6. Motivating the ratee to achieve higher levels of performance	269	85.1
7. Improve company planning	178	56.3
8. Other	28	8.9

majority of organizations use performance evauations for multiple purposes, and it is recommended that courts do likewise.

Types of Performance Evaluation

The most widely used types of performance evaluations are:[5]

> performance checklists;
> graphic rating scales;
> narrative rating;
> forced distribution;
> forced choice;
> critical incident; and
> management by objectives.

Performance Checklist. The checklist consists of a series of scaled statements, phrases, or objectives characteristic of job performance to be checked by the supervisor. The rater checks items describing or which apply to a subordinate's performance. A performance rating is found by assigning a value, based on the job, to each item and averaging the scale values of all items.

The checklist is a person-oriented evaluation procedure and should contain factors that are objectively observable. Results from various tests indicate that the checklist reduces the errors of personal bias. Items to be checked can be closely related to or descriptive of actual job elements. The form also can aid in counseling and motivating an employee. Statements, phrases, and objectives to be checked should indicate typical performance or behavior observed of the employee. Descriptive statements are usually brief and may invite ambiguity, as the rater provides his own interpretation of the items checked. The form is relatively short and requires little time to complete. Best results are achieved when supervisors fully understand the system.

Graphic Rating Scale. The graphic rating scale contains a list of traits followed by a series of numerical or descriptive values to be used to designate the degree to which an employee possesses and displays a trait. The traits listed are explained by brief descriptions under each category. The rater is given a fairly broad score range within, which to determine the performance of the employee. An overall score is determined by adding up the scores given to specific factors. Often space is allotted for brief, written appraisals of a subordinate's work performance.

The graphic rating scale is the most widely used rating method due to its simplicity in design and facility of administration. The rating scale serves to differentiate employees on a series of given traits. It can be used in a small or large organization to rank or compare individuals in order of merit by giving an overall summary rating or score. The specific rating of a particular trait assists a supervisor in counseling an employee who needs development in certain areas of performance. The form may be used as an aid in designating employees who deserve pay increases, promotions, or employees who are in need of counseling or training.

The dysfunctional aspects of this type of rating concern:

1) using terms that are sufficiently vague and ambiguous as to make it difficult to distinguish between satisfactory and unsatisfactory performance; and

2) limiting the supervisor's rating to those traits and characteristics on the scale which may or may not be significant to the jobs being rated.

Narrative Form Rating. The narrative form of appraisal involves a written, subjective measure of job performance. The supervisor gears the rating to the particular job of the person being rated. Thus, the use of the same criteria by all supervisors is not required, and appraisal methods and factors are widely varied. But the narrative appraisal, due to its unstructured form, has an additional use in that it reveals a great deal about the values of the rater and his perception of what is and is not important to the jobs under his supervision.

The questionnaire type of narrative rating permits the rater to appraise the overall performance of the subordinate being evaluated. The form requires a subjective measure of evaluation and provides for an individual assessment. The rater is usually able to participate in the definition of the factors used in the evaluation. The form is most useful in small offices where the number of employees allows sufficient time to complete individual subjective appraisals. The completed form can serve as a counseling tool to motivate the employee for improved performance toward organizational goals. The questionnaire type of narrative rating does not require position description.

Forced Distribution. This system uses a ranking technique by which job performances are rated according to a "grading on the curve" to secure a technical, normal frequency distribution of individual performances. The rating results in ranking employees by class rather than assigning a set of values to an individual's performance. A five-point job performance scale is established ranking from top ten (outstanding) to low ten (unsatisfactory) thus creating a bell-shaped frequency distribution. Five areas of specific work habits are usually rated. There can be space given for a short narrative answer as to significantly good or bad performance at the end of the form.

This method eliminates the errors of leniency and central tendency and facilities intra-group comparisons. To secure normal distribution of scores, it must be explained to supervisors that a low score area does not necessarily indicate an ineffective employee. It should be used with caution in particular groups. Not all work groups reflect a normal distribution of individual performance. It cannot describe the absolute level of an employee's performance. This method has been most effective in small groups of under fifteen employees in a job class. It ranks order of merit, but not the area of difference in ability between ranks; it gives a graphic picture of a particular employee's performance in relation to fellow workers. An over-all rating of ability is made instead of a rating on a series of separate factors. This method of evaluation is relatively easy to administer.

Forced Choice. The forced choice system of rating uses a series of statements relevant to job proficiency or personal qualifications. The statements used fall into two categories: the most characteristic and the least characteristic of the person.

This system is thought by some to be the most advanced method to evaluate the job performance of individual workers. The method forces the rater to discriminate on the basis of concrete aspects of job behavior. The technique yields a numerical index by which persons in different occupations can be compared on factors found to be a significant part of job performance. The rater is unaware of the relative worth or value of the alternative statements, thus the subjective elements are minimized. The method is designed to produce a standardized, objective index of job performance. The underlying principle of this method holds that people are more apt to agree on description than evaluation, and the fact that the employee evaluated often agrees with the selected statements points out its usefulness for self-evaluation, counseling, and motivation. The job performance measured can be positively correlated with the review of other variables such as job satisfaction. The technique requires considerable time and expense to construct. The system is most useful in a large organization.

Critical-Incident. The critical incident technique of rating is a systematic and immediate recording of actual instances of significantly good or significantly poor performance. A list of credits and debits is maintained for each employee by the proper supervisor. A job description is used for each position rated as a tool for training supervisors to know what performance is expected of an employee. The emphasis should be on what is accomplished instead of how it is accomplished.

It has been found that the recorded incidents can be useful in predicting successful job performance. Using this technique, supervisors can anticipate job needs, improve job performance, improve results of work, increase the motivation of an employee, and establish a means of counseling. The facts gathered will provide the employee with an understanding of the requirements of the job at hand and help in developing potential for more responsible levels. It is a thorough procedure to insure that concrete events relevant to job performance are the basis of an evaluation.

This method requires that supervisors actually observe the work of employees and select important performance events for evaluation. The system gives added meaning to evaluation content, in that actual circumstances are recorded in specific terms; it evaluates results, not persons. It requires a great deal of the supervisor's time and effort to maintain a continuing performance record.

    <u>Management by Objectives</u>. This newer method of performance evaluation focuses on specific goals and results of performance rather than personal qualities and traits. It is an alternative to traditional forms of performance evaluation. This system is designed to evaluate results of job performance by four steps: 1) establishing organizational goals; 2) establishing unit objectives; 3) securing individual commitment; and 4) reviewing actual job performance.

    The system requires that each job be directed towards the objectives of the total organization. Evaluation of performance is measured by the contribution of each individual to the success of the whole.

    The design of the system and the philosophy of management by objectives involves the total organization and all its members in a common purpose. This method of evaluation holds an individual accountable for certain actions and their completion, thus setting a task guide to demonstrate how an individual's contribution fits into the over-all effort.

    The system offers an opportunity for the supervisor and subordinate to work together towards achievement of objectives. The evaluation form is designed to insure a means of accomplishing the individual work tasks necessary to goal fulfillment. It instills in the employee the idea that his abilities, skills, and knowledge will be as much a part of his or her work as the way it is done.

    The implementation of this method has positive effects in that employees are apt to grow as members of the organization, thus affecting their attitude and morale. The method is best facilitated when a clear explanation of the system is made. The initial effort of filling out the form must be sustained to insure positive participation and growth. This system does not have accompanying semantic problems. It is useful, as it does not require the supervisor to make ratings that he or she does not have the ability to make. Organizations can easily custom fit the form needed.

<u>What Plan Should Courts Use?</u>

    Until recently, most performance evaluation plans were based on the belief that the supervisor is in the best position to evaluate the behavior of subordinates. Thus, employee appraisals were primarily a trait rating by the supervisor, and, even though most plans required the supervisor to discuss the rating with the employee, the system was hierarchical, with little or no chance for input from the employee being rated. In the last twenty years, research, for example, by Rensis Likert, Peter Drucker, and Douglas McGregor indicates that the hierarchical trait rating approach tends to decrease motivation and inhibit individual development, while participatory and supportive management tends to increase motivation and foster personal growth and development.

It is understandable that courts, until recently, have not had professional administrators to devote the necessary time and attention toward developing employee appraisal plans. With the pressure of other administrative matters, the tendency is to copy those appraisal plans used by the executive branch of government. The danger in copying is that, in many instances, the problems associated with these plans have not been resolved. By blindly adopting these plans, the courts will inherit the unresolved problems.

There is no simple across-the-board answer as to which performance plan should be used by courts. There are some factors which should be considered by court administrators in deciding on a performance evaluation plan. These factors are:

<u>Nature of the Occupation</u>. Job content, skills, attitudes, and expectancies of individuals in various occupations; the organizational level of positions; and whether the occupation is professional, technical, or clerical should all be taken into consideration. Different position classes may require different employee evaluation methods, so as to account properly for the factors just enumerated.

<u>The Court's Management Climate</u>. The evaluation plan or plans should be viewed by all concerned as being in accord with the basic style of management prevalent in the court, e.g., management by objectives should not be used for employee evaluation unless it is a logical extension of other objectives of management philosophy.

<u>Difference Between Entry and Experienced Personnel</u>. If the person being evaluated is a beginning level employee, the appraisal might be limited to his grasp of the basic job requirements. If the person being evaluated is an experienced employee on that job, the appraisal might be more effective if it focuses on the extent to which his performance exceeds basic job requirements and expansion of the job to fit his own potential. Trainee or entry

level evaluations should be concerned with whether the employee has learned what he needs to know. The evaluation of jobs above the entry or trainee level should be concerned with how well the employee applies what he should apply to the work situation.

Employee Evaluation and Compensation

The steps involved in performance evaluation allow the incumbent employee to advance through the salary range at whatever rate is dictated by the salary grid in conjunction with the personnel rules.

Currently, there is a debate as to whether an employee's salary advancement (annual step increase) should be tied to his performance. The affirmative argument is that a salary increase at regularly recurring intervals over the first few years of employment is one of the better incentives for an employee to work at a greater capacity. The negative argument is that very few employees, regardless of their level of efficiency or inefficiency, are ever turned down for an annual salary step increase, so that it is better to give the increase automatically at designated intervals without regard to performance and to make an objective performance evaluation at other intervals. The theory behind this argument is that supervisors are reluctant to rate an individual as unsatisfactory when a salary increase is at stake.

No further argument is offered here to support either position, except to note that other factors, such as a reluctance by supervisors to confront an individual with any derogatory comments, may well be the overriding concern.

Varying Merit Increases. Another concept of performance evaluation the administrator may want to consider is the possibility of granting differing amounts of money for differing degrees of performance. In other words, a low level performer would receive little or nothing in the way of a merit increase, while a superior performer would receive more than the average amount. This system of wage increase distribution could be used compatibly with the forced distribution method of performance evaluation discussed in the preceding section. Before this is attempted, it is imperative than an evaluation system be devised which explores performance criteria objectively.

Even in the absence of such a system, some method should be developed to reward the consistently superior performer. One means is through promotion, which will be discussed later in the chapter; the other is through a mechanism known as a superior performance bonus or increase.

All too frequently employees who do average work and employees who do superior work receive the same compensation after the period of one year's service. To eliminate this disparity, it should be possible for the administrator to compensate the superior performer at a rate which is greater than usual. This amount may be given in one of two ways. The first is an increase of two steps rather than one on the salary scale; the other is to give the employee the equivalent of the second step in a lump sum. The former has its drawbacks, as the employee soon runs out of steps and becomes dissatisfied. The latter has much to recommend it in that the employee receives only one step increase and consequently does not reach the top of the range as quickly as he would with the other method.

With performance measures and performance evaluation related to salary increases, the incumbent who performs satisfactorily should be fairly secure in knowing approximately what his salary opportunities will be later in his career, even if he does not change classification or grade levels.

PROMOTION AND CAREER LADDERS

A career ladder expands the opportunities for advancement by an employee who comes into the system in an entry level classification (a classification which is designated to recruit applicants who have had no previous job experience in the field). The manner in which it works is that after sufficient time on the job to gain experience, after sufficient in-service training to polish skills, and with the approval and recommendation of the supervisor, if the budget permits, the employee is advanced from the first to the second level of his classification. This advancement continues until the employee reaches a certain predetermined point in the classification hierarchy, short of the supervisory levels, which may take as long as ten or twelve years to complete.

On the plus side of this system is improved employee morale, because the employee knows exactly what his opportunities for advancement are. The system also assures that only the most fit employees reach the top level and that those who reach it are highly trained and well thought of for their abilities.

There is a negative budget impact with a system of this nature. This can be compensated for by returning all positions which become vacant to the entry level classification. This will create a "vacancy saving" from the declassification of the position and will create extra funds to finance those persons who are on their way up the career ladder.

Promotional Opportunities

In the absence of a career ladder concept in the classification plan, an administrator can turn to a more traditional means of promoting the employees of his court. With normal turnover, employees leave upper level as well as lower level positions. These positions then become available to employees in the lower level classifications. This method of promoting employees through the system may take longer or shorter than the career ladder concept, as it depends entirely on the rate of turnover in the upper level classifications.

When a high level position becomes vacant, employees who are in the lower levels should have the opportunity to compete for the position through a promotional examination. To aid in the promotional examination process, it is helpful for the administrator or appointing authority to have at his disposal information from performance evaluations, a summary of the applicant's work skills, and any other information which may be pertinent to his ability to perform the job.

This system is self-regulating in that the higher the positions, the fewer there are. For example, a unit of employees may have four Court Clerks I, ten Court Court Clerks II, six Court Clerks III, two Clerical Supervisors I, and one Clerical Supervisor II, who has the responsibility for administering the work activities of all others below him. As may be seen from this pattern, a person can enter at the Court Clerk I level, progress rather easily to the Court Clerk II level, and, with a little more difficulty, to the Court Clerk III level. After that, promotion into the Clerical Supervisor levels would be highly selective and would depend upon turnover in those levels and the skill and expertise of the employee.

A similar system of promotion is used in New York City where a person enters the system as a Uniformed Court Officer, in the limited jurisdiction courts of that city. After some years of service at that level, the Uniformed Court Officer is eligible for promotion to a similar position with the Supreme Court of New York (general jurisdiction court). It is from the ranks of the Uniformed Court Officers of the Supreme Court of New York that persons are frequently selected to fill vacancies in the ranks of Court Clerks (these are administrative positions and should not be confused with the court clerks who have been discussed in this and other chapters). The system works quite well and has much to recommend it in that it is clear to each employee from the start what his promotional opportunities are and what he must do to rise within the system.

The problem with promotional systems, regardless of which kind is in use, is that they are internal systems as opposed to external systems and may lead to system stagnation or entropy. This problem may be dealt with by drawing persons from outside the system into some, but not all, of the higher level positions. This tends to inject new blood and fresh ideas into the system at higher levels, and helps combat the traditional "We've always done it that way" aspect of court administration. The selection of persons from outside the system must be made with caution, as too much use of outside personnel will create a morale problem with the existing employees. They will perceive outside recruitment as the denial of a promotional opportunity.

NOTES

1. A more complete discussion of employee training will be found in Chapter 8.
2. Much of the material on performance evaluation is taken with permission from Courts and Personnel Systems, Institute for Court Management, (Denver: Institute for Court Management, 1975), pp. 81-92.
3. American Bar Association, Commission on Standards of Judicial Administration, Standards Relating to Court Organization (Chicago: American Bar Association, 1974) p. 92.
4. See Fred E. Schuster, "History and Theory of Performance Appraisal," in Handbook of Wage and Salary Administration, ed. by Milton L. Rock (N.Y.: McGraw-Hill, 1972), p. 5:4.

5. See, in this connection, Rock, Ibid., chapters 22-27; and Joseph J. Famularo, ed., Handbook of Modern Personnel Administration (N.Y.: McGraw-Hill, 1972), chapters 40-45.

8. Employee Training

PURPOSES OF TRAINING

Courts and court systems, for the most part, have been slow to adopt training programs or procedures. While many of the larger court systems have adopted in-house training programs through grants supplied by the federal government (LEAA and Highway Safety, for example), other less formal or organized systems have depended on the same sources to establish funds to send judges and nonjudicial personnel to external training programs.

This is a sensible pattern of development. Larger systems with greater numbers of employees in diverse functions can generally justify the establishment of a training section or division to satisfy the needs of the organization. Smaller systems, on the other hand, might be misusing funds if they were to establish training departments. It is better in a smaller system with a more parochial staff to rely on sending the employees needing training to an external training center, or to retain the services of a consultant (if the number of employees to be trained justifies it) to conduct onsite training for court employees.

The purposes of training are many. An important purpose from the employer's view is to make more efficient use of existing personnel. This is a vital need in light of current and expected future fiscal conservatism of funding bodies. With increased workloads and fixed or diminished resources, it is imperative that training be aimed at increasing employee productivity.

Training is essential to organizational vitality, as it can prepare employees for advancement to higher level positions. Training is helpful in building organizational morale, because it demonstrates that the organization cares for its employees. Training programs also aid in the implementation of newly assigned duties and responsibilities. Finally, training programs hone or develop employee skills, so that a higher quality work product may be expected.

Training and training programs should not be confused with education in the formalized sense. Training differs from formal education in that training sessions are a more intense experience over a shorter time, typically, but not necessarily, involving one subject area. Also, most training does not carry with it credit or credit hours towards a degree. Rather, most training programs offer a certificate of completion, which may sometimes be required for an employee's promotion or continued employment.

Education, then, treats subject matter which is broader or more general in nature over a longer time, while training is more specific and direct and takes much less time.

TYPES OF TRAINING PROGRAMS

Orientation Training

Orientation training is designed to familiarize a new employee with the organization and job. Orientation training is used by most private employers and by many public employers. It gives the organization a chance to meet a new employee, and what is more important, it gives a new employee a chance to meet the organization. Because first impressions are lasting ones, the manner in which an orientation program is carried out is very important.

All court organizations, regardless of size, should establish an orientation program of some sort. As mentioned in Chapter 7, there is nothing more discouraging to a new employee than to be cast adrift in an organization without so much as a cursory overview of what is expected of him.

Orientation training should be designed to give a new employee some idea of how the court or judicial system is organized and how it functions, what the work rules are, what the organization offers in fringe benefits, and what is expected of court employees.

Orientation should occur as soon as possible after a new employee starts working in the court. Larger systems should hold orientation for employees on a regularly scheduled basis (once a month or once a quarter) while smaller systems or courts may choose to orient new employees individually, if the turnover rate is very low, shortly after they have commenced work. The time between the date of employment and commencement of orientation should be as short as possible, so that the possibility of the employee getting erroneous conceptions and ideas is at least minimized. A new employee needs guidelines at the beginning of his career, so that he will know what is expected of him.

The orientation program should be developed by the training director, if one is employed, or by some other responsible administrative staff member who has an interest in this aspect of training. The orientation program trainers should include representatives from the discipline or disciplines to be covered. Equally important is involvement in the design and conduct of the orientation program by key staff in the court or unit involved. The assistance of employees who know the job and its pitfalls is invaluable not only for orientation but for all training purposes.

The orientation training schedule shown below is designed for use with a group of new employees rather than the orientation of an individual or a few employees as might occur in smaller courts or jurisdictions.[1] While this session is designed for a larger group of employees, the size of the group is not necessarily related to the length of training sessions. Orientation sessions make take one day or several. It may be carried on for a fixed period each day for several days. Usually, when a small number of employees is involved, orientation tends to be more directly related to the job than to an understanding of how the judicial system functions.

<u>ORIENTATION FOR TRIAL COURT PERSONNEL</u>

<u>SCHEDULE</u>

8:30 a.m.	Registration	Director, Court Staff Development
9:00	History of Judicial System State Court Administration	State Court Administrator
	Trial Court Administration	President, Trial Court Administrators Association

9:00 a.m.	Roles of judge/clerk/ district administrator	Training Officer
9:45	Functions of Court Related Groups	
	Probation	Chief Probation Officer
	Public Defender	Deputy Public Defender
	District Attorney	Deputy District Attorney
10:15	BREAK	
10:30	Personnel Rules/ Fringe Benefits	Personnel Director
11:00	Legislative/Budget Process	Budget Officer
11:30	Using the Statutes	Staff Legal Officer
12 NOON	LUNCH	
1:00 p.m.	Dealing with the Public	President, League of Women Voters
2:00	General Overview of Courts	Trial Courts Coordinator
3:00	BREAK	
3:15	Case Flow Management	President, Trial Court Administrators Association
4:30	Evaluation of Program	Director, Court Staff Development
4:45	Credit Union Information, Employee Association or Union	Organization Representatives
5:00	ADJOURN [1]	

In a smaller court or unit, or, if the number of trainees is few, it is more economical to set up a schedule for the employees to visit different offices rather than to have office representatives contact the trainees in a group or work setting.

Each employee attending orientation training

should receive a prepared employee manual, which will give him or her something to refer to after orientation training has been completed. The manual should include an overview of the system and its purpose. It should also include pertinent personnel information, such as pay, hours, holidays, leave time, retirement, promotions, and health insurance, plus information on how to file a grievance and how to initiate other personnel actions. As court operations involve terminology generally unfamiliar to new employees, a glossary of commonly used legal terms should be included.

In-Service Training

On the Job. In-service training is offered to employees on the job to improve their skills and thier work habits.

One type of in-service training is commonly referred to as on the job training. This type of training has the advantage of providing employees the opportunity of learning while doing, and the cost is low, once the training schedule has been developed and implemented.

Most on the job training programs in courts require the time and attention of a supervisor to be effective. The supervisor can vary the pace at which the employee learns his job, or more about his job, to accommodate his ability. Also necessary for an effective on the job training program is a manual for employees' use and further instruction. This manual may include written assignments for the employee to complete and submit to the supervisor for grading and subsequent discussion.

An on the job training program may also include various components which increase in difficulty and perspective as the employee's skills are sharpened and his or her knowledge broadens. A program of this type is ideally suited for employees who are being trained for higher level positions having greater duties and responsibilities.

It can also be used in conjunction with a career ladder concept by which an employee enters the field at an entry-level classification and progresses through the training program, receiving higher classifications and pay levels until he reaches the full functioning juourneyman level. This approach provides the court with a group of well-trained journeyman employees in a short time at a relatively low cost.

Skills Development. Another type of in-service training is skills development. It is aimed at the journeyman employee who wants to increase his or her skills in a particular area, so that he or she will be eligible for promotion or be better able to handle a new or challenging duty. It can also be used to sharpen skills, such as typing or shorthand, that an employee already has. Time can be allotted from the workday to allow an employee to take advanced courses in the subject area, either in-house or through an external program.

One form of skills development which is beneficial to both the court and the employee is crosstraining. By definition, crosstraining means that two employees involved in different disciplines or duties are trained, or crosstrained, in each other's area, but crosstraining may be only one way. In other words, Employee A can learn the more advanced duties of Employee B and, therefore, be able to substitute for Employee A when he or she is either sick or on vacation. It will also allow Employee A to progress to the point where he or she can assume Employee B's position when that individual terminates employment.

Management Training

Management training has been developed in response to the needs of administrators and managers of both public and private systems. Training of this nature is designed to enable a manager to cope with the dynamics of an ever-changing environment and to improve skills as a supervisor. Typically, a management training program can involve one or all of the following areas: communication, functional training, problem solving, supervision or skills, decision-making, leadership styles, and team training. As a complete description and analysis of these types of training are beyond the scope of this book, the comments in this section will be confined to a general description of each, with some discussion of the value and use of each.

In general, management training programs are developed to make the organization more effective through uniform management principles uniformly delivered. Management training also enables lower level managers to train for higher level positions and provides for the training of new managers who have risen from the ranks, so that they are more likely to avoid the trap of the "Peter Principle." In addition, management training is the vehicle by which a court or court related agency can expose its managers and administrators to new management concepts which will improve the organization.

Communication Training

Important for all employees of an organization, and perhaps most important for the managers, is communication training.

Nothing is more disconcerting to an employer and employee than to discover that they are unable to understand each other, after working and communicating with each other over a period of weeks or months. Communication training has been developed to help people to understand others better and to send useful, clear messages.

Communication training, typically, is involved in how to speak clearly and to listen (as opposed to hear) attentively. It also teaches how to write effectively and how to read and retain what is written. Put in simpler terms, it trains employees and managers how to send and receive messages, both oral and written.

For the most part, courts will not have the in-house expertise available to carry out a self-contained program. At best, most courts or court organizations will have a training director or co-ordinator who has access to a communication skills trainer. This trainer can work with the court on a consulting basis in developing and carrying out an effective program. The consultant or person selected to develop the program should have an awareness of the court environment, so that pitfalls can be avoided.

Functional Training

Functional training is designed to heighten or increase the skills of managers or administrators in the fields or functions for which they are responsible. This type of training is aimed at keeping the professional administrator abreast of developments in his or her field. This training might be on new state or federal legislation and court cases which affect the field, or it may concern new and better ways of handling recurring work tasks or assignments, such as budgeting and personnel.

Obviously, not all functional training can or should be developed and administered in-house. Many programs are offered by different organizations nationwide which are designed to increase professional performance. While the costs of these programs are high, they do not approach the costs involved in developing and administering an in-house program. These external programs will be covered later in this chapter.

It is not too difficult to design and operate an in-house program to train professional administrators in the objective or definitive areas of their functions, such as those areas of legislation and case law which are important to the administrators' daily work. It is probably not cost efficient to design and administer a subjective training program on a one-time basis. Training in the subjective areas of a discipline may be better handled at an external facility. These include case load management and records management, which, while important, are more theoretical and not likely to be repeated with any degree of regularity.

Problem Solving

As most managers, especially those who are employed by a court system, have problems, training in problem solving is appropriate.

If the court or court organization is large enough to have a trainer of its staff, the problem-solving workshops can be presented in house.

Problem-solving training demonstrates how to analyse a problem and how to make decisions based on analysis. The methods used in this type of training are many and varied. One is the case method where an open-ended statement is made concerning a management problem. Then it is up to the individual or group to analyse and dissect the problem and come up with a viable solution.

Another problem-solving technique is a group session called brainstorming. The participants analyze the problem in a group setting, with participants responding to statements concerning the problem by other members of the group. The problem's solution is developed in the same manner after the problem's analysis is complete.

Another method or approach is through role playing the problem. This method requires the trainees to assume the roles of the individuals involved in the problem and then to interact with each other to effect a solution to the problem.

Another problem-solving method is to give each individual or group of individuals different pieces to a problem and then require them to come up with a solution by using teamwork and group interaction.

In short, there are almost as many approaches to problem solving as there are problems. Many of these approaches are packaged and may be purchased by any organization. If the court system has a training director, it can be left to this person to purchase those packages necessary to get the job done.

Supervision Training

Supervision training is intended to teach new supervisors or managers how best to do their jobs. It can also be employed to enhance the skills or alter the behavior of management personnel who have been performing their jobs in a routine manner for a considerable time.

Supervisor training should emphasize leadership and motivation of employees, so that an organization can realize its most efficient behavior and, at the same time, raise employee morale and keep it at a high level.

One of the most effective means of training managers in the art of supervision is through the use of role playing. These exercises can be performed either before a group of peers and evaluators, or they can be put on video tape for evaluation later in the training session. Video tape offers the advantage of action control, as the tape can be stopped to point out good or bad features of the trainee's approach to the role-playing problems.

The advantages of supervisor training are obvious, particularly when one considers the negative effect a new, untrained, insecure supervisor may have on the orderly work flow of an organization.

Team Training

Team training is especially important to courts or court organizations, especially when the relatively large number of jurisdictions and functions falling under the umbrella of the third branch of government is considered. The supervisors of different court units, or, as an alternative, all the employees of one court unit, are trained to act with a uniformity of purpose. The payoffs for the court organization can be great; for example, all unit supervisors share in and become aware of the problems their peers face in managing their respective units. It also gives top management (chief, presiding, or administrative judge) an effective team of professional supervisors and administrators who can deliver services to the public in an efficient manner. The training of one unit as a team makes that unit more cohesive and dedicated to performing its tasks well. It also gives the employees of the unit an appreciation of its over-all work objectives. This appreciation makes the unit supervisor's job much easier, and consequently, more effective.

To be comprehensive as well as effective, team training of the court's staff should be encouraged at both the unit level and the unit supervisor's level.

External Training Programs

External training programs are ideal for those courts or court organizations whose size is too small to justify the employment of a training director or coordinator. Unfortunately, the costs of most external training are rather high, and the subject matter available for use in the courts is relatively slight. Almost all of the training available is for court administrators who are midlevel managers, or higher. Little or nothing exists on an external basis (other than shorthand and typing classes) for the rank and file employee of the courts. This lack is probably because of little demand due to the high cost of training personnel in this manner and the fact that the results of this training would not justify the costs involved.

The Institute for Court Management, established in 1970, is the foremost example of an agency which offers external training to court administrators across the country. The courses include the whole range of administrative workshops, from one- or two-day seminars in a particular subject, to an extensive, long-term course leading to a certificate as a fellow of the institute. The costs involved in attending Institute of Court Management programs are competitive with similar offerings in other fields.

For several years, the National Institute for Corrections, under a federal grant, has been offering a number of training seminars in the field of corrections. The course matter offered deals with correctional administration only, and, to qualify for inclusion in these seminars, one must be in corrections or a closely related field. At least some of the courses offered are without cost to the enrollee.

Many colleges and universities offer external courses at moderate cost. Many of the offerings, e.g., collective bargaining in the public sector or affirmative action guidelines, are general enough to be of value to court administrative personnel.

There are other external programs available, such as the recently established continuing education program sponsored by Conference of State Court Administrators (COSCA) which is offered through the joint effort of the Institute for Court Management and the Master of Science in Judicial Administration program at the University of Denver College of Law, but, unlike this program, others may not be directly related to courts.

Decentralized Training Programs

Decentralized training programs are best used in areas where there is much geography to cover and where travel to and from a centralized training site becomes a problem.

Decentralized programs can be built or developed along a correspondence course guideline, with completed assignments being mailed to the training department for evaluation and grading. The correspondence course approach can be enhanced by the addition of video tape equipment at the remote court location. With video tape capability, programmed lectures can be duplicated and mailed to a number of court facilities at a reasonable cost.

Another approach to a decentralized training program is to send trainers out into the field rather than having trainees go to a centralized training facility. While this can be more expensive than the video tape approach, it can also be more effective due to the person-to-person contact involved. This approach can also be made more cost effective, if several employees in the same remote region can meet for the purpose of training at a location central to all of them.

While the decentralized approach to training may not have the immediate impact of a central training facility, it does have the advantage of relaying information of value to those who may not otherwise have the opportunity to receive it.

DESIGNING TRAINING PROGRAMS

Determining Needs

Nothing will undercut a training program in the courts more effectively than implementing a program that is ill conceived and unnecessary for the personnel involved. In short, training for the sake of training is wasteful and most likely will be resented by the attendants. Prior to instituting a training program of any type in a court or court system, those responsible for training must determine what the training needs of the employees are. The three most common methods of determining training needs are through questionnaires, brainstorming conference, and interviews with administrators and employees.

Questionnaire. The questionnaire is designed to be used by all levels of employees who are involved in the discipline that has been selected for training. For example, if a program is to be designed for probation officers, the sample used in the needs assessment questionnaire would be taken from entry level, journeymen, and supervisory probation officers.

The form would require the employee's name, classification, division or department, and where employed; a listing of the skill areas the employee is using on the job; a review of other positions the employee has held; the personal, career, and employment goals the employee has; and the training needs the employee sees as enabling him or her to reach those goals.

This information, when gathered from employees with a variety of backgrounds, both educational and experiential, gives those responsible for training a much better understanding of employee needs.

Brainstorming. Another method, that of brainstorming conference, elicits essentially the same information from a group of people smaller in number than those contacted in the questionnaire approach. This method requires that a group of the most knowledgeable employees in the area or discipline for which the training is being developed be gathered together in conference, so that they can express their more pressing training needs. The group should have between six and ten members from both metropolitan and rural areas and from differing jurisdictions within their disciplines, i.e., from both general and limited jurisdiction courts.

The data gathered at these brainstorming sessions are then analyzed and put to use much in the same manner as that information gathered by means of the questionnaire.

Interviews. Interviews by the training officer with different employees who have an interest in the training program and its subject matter are valuable to help sort out and sift through the large amount of information which has been gathered. In addition, these employees and their interest are important in supporting the training program and in gaining its acceptance amongst their peers, as well as in providing additional information about training needs.

Time and manpower permitting, it is a wise idea to use all three methods to develop training needs and to determine how and in what order these needs will be met.

If a recent classification study (see Chapter 3 of this volume) has been performed, there is almost certainly a vast supply of information available that can be put to use in establishing the training program.

Establishing the Program

Establishing the training program and having it accepted are much easier once an administrator understands training needs and can present them, when required, in an intelligent and practical manner.

This list of needs, presented to the judges of the court <u>en banc</u> will go a long way in establishing the support required for a training program to succeed. This support is necessary, if the employees are going to respect the training offered and, consequently, get something useful from it. In addition, if employees have had the opportunity to present their ideas, whether through needs analysis or in actual program development, they will more likely accept the training program.

Funding for training is becoming more and more difficult to obtain from appropriation bodies. In some jurisdictions, city councilmen, county commissioners, and state legislators seem to view training as a luxury. It is fortunate that money is available from grant-funding agencies, such as the Law Enforcement Assistance Administration and Highway Safety. These agencies, as well as others, have been willing to fund well conceived and constructed training programs in the courts. Not all of these funds are available on a 100 percent basis. Some of the programs require that the recipient of the funds supply a certain percentage of the total cost in either hard (cash) match or soft (in kind) match. Frequently, courts can obtain 10 percent of the total cost from local or state funding bodies to provide the cash match required to use federal funds for training purposes.

Training Program Evaluation

Because at least some funding bodies consider training a luxury, and because grants administrators have to account to their agencies for grants to courts and other public employers, it is necessary to evaluate the impact and effect of implemented training programs.

There are several ways in which the effect of a training program can be measured or evaluated.

If training is defined as a positive change in attitude, knowledge, and behavior beneficial to both the employer and the employee, then there should be a way to measure its impact. One method of evaluation is to measure the trainee's reaction to the program presented. Items which can be evaluated by the trainee are subject matter, its relevance, the manner in which it was presented, and the attitude of the instructor presenting it.

It is helpful for the trainer to have information from the trainee concerning his or her reaction to the training location or site and accommodations. While responses from trainees may seem somewhat superficial and subjective, they can provide the trainer with a fairly accurate evaluation and information about how the training program was received. If the content of the program is not valid and the delivery or presentation is poor, then it is likely that the trainee will get little or nothing from it. This reaction will show up in a negative manner in the trainee's evaluation instrument.

Another method of training evaluation is to measure the increased knowledge or skills of participating trainees. This measurement is much the same as any achievement test administered in an educational institution. A testing instrument of this nature is devised concurrent with the training program. The test should be set forth in the most objective manner available, i.e., true/false, multiple choice, or direct question, and it should be designed to avoid a rambling essay type of response. Essay responses are too subjective and cannot be readily used for comparative analysis against an established norm; also, they take much longer to grade. The test should cover only that information which has been made available to the trainees at the training session. An instrument of this nature is valuable in determining the training program's strengths and weaknesses. In no event should this instrument be used against an employee. It should be used to determine how much and what type of training the employee needs.

The testing instrument can be even more beneficial to the training director, if it is administered both before the training occurs and after the training has been administered. This approach allows the training director to qualify the results of the training program.

The third method of evaluating training effectiveness is to have the trainee's immediate supervisor evaluate the trainee's performance on the job when the employee returns from training. If the purpose of training was to improve the employee's knowledge in some job-related areas, such as case flow procedure, records management, or data processing applications, then the effect of training should be readily quantifiable. If the purpose of training has been to alter the trainee's attitudes towards the job, the court environment, or fellow employees, then the supervisor may be forced to observe the employee's behavior as objectively as possible.

Either of the above evaluation methods for on the job behavior will be reliable only if the supervisor understands and is supportive of the training effort. Consequently, it may be essential that the supervisor be trained in what to look for in employee behavior and how to evaluate and report it.

All of these evaluation methods can be used independently or in conjunction with each other. The method or methods used should be valid and should reflect as accurately as possible the quality and impact of the training session.

Frequently funding bodies request hard facts, such as cost/benefit analysis to determine the worth of training. It is very difficult for anyone to determine accurately whether the benefits of a training program outweigh the costs. Courts and court systems have no control over their case or work loads and relatively limited control over the speed at which a case moves through the court. These aspects of court environment make it difficult to use standard methods of determining work efficiency, such as measuring increased or decreased productivity and of the impact of a training program in this respect. It is far better to rely on the evaluation methods previously discussed rather than to create difficulties through the use of cost/benefit measures to determine training program effectiveness.

NOTES

1. This schedule is taken from the Trial Court Orientation Program offered by the Colorado Judicial System.

9. Discipline and Employees' Rights

EMPLOYEE DISCIPLINE

No matter how carefully the personnel selection system has been established to handle the placement of new personnel, it will not be infallible. There will always be employees who pass through the most carefully designed screening system with personal traits or work patterns which are not fully acceptable to the organization. A well thought-out design in the recruiting and examination process will help to eliminate the chances of inadequate personnel being selected, but cannot be expected to be always successful.

A court administrator must expect and be prepared for the problem of an employee unable to do the job for which he or she was selected, or who, after being selected, acts as a disrupting influence on other employees.

A formalized system for handling problem employees should be established, so that contradictory and disparate penalties for infractions of work rules will be avoided. Depending on the nature of the offense committed by an employee, the action taken by the administrator may range from a simple oral or written reprimand to termination. A short review follows of the types of action which may be taken.

Corrective Actions

Corrective actions are those which are taken by the administrator or supervisor to correct an employee's work habits which are erratic or which deviate from the accepted norm. These actions are not intended to be disciplinary in nature, but are designed to improve the employee's job performance.

Typically, they are taken to correct minor incongruities which, if left unattended, can grow and become serious problems.

An oral action of this nature should be administered in private and should include discussion with the employee as to what action or plan of action the employee should take to correct the problem. Also, the employee should be allowed to explain why he or she has been acting in an unsatisfactory manner. It may be that the unsatisfactory performance is in response to an unusual stimulus and is normal considering the circumstances.

A more formal means of administering a corrective action is through a written complaint to the employee. This should be done after a conference with the employee, and a copy of the complaint should be placed in his or her personnel file.

An oral or written corrective action should state the problem, what the employee must do to correct the problem, and the consequences he or she faces if the problem is not corrected. If, after the written corrective action is administered, the employee's performance improves over a specific period of time, then he or she should be allowed to have it removed from his or her personnel file.

Another form of discipline resulting from a corrective action, and one which is a little more severe, is the reassignment of an employee to other job duties. This is not recommended as it is relatively ineffective in altering an employee's work patterns and habits. It may also serve to move the problem from one area of work to another and, therefore, solve nothing.

Disciplinary Actions

Suspension. The form of disciplinary action (as opposed to corrective action) most often used by governmental agencies is suspension without pay. Employees may be suspended for a limited period for actions which deviate from the accepted norm. This may be administered for a single severe incident or for an accumulation of lesser incidents that may have been dealt with ineffectively through corrective actions. Suspension of an employee without pay must be in writing, should state why the employee is being suspended, and the length of time of the suspension. A suspension should not be for more than thirty days and most frequently is for a shorter period. Suspensions for periods longer than thirty dyas are essentially the same as termination, i.e., if the employee is suspended for six months, he or she has little recourse other than to search for a new job.

If the suspension and discussion of the reasons for it are handled carefully, the employee may return to work with a better attitude and improved work habits.

Demotion. A more severe form of disciplinary action is a reduction in pay or classification. This more or less permanently limits the wage or salary potential of an individual and does little to solve the problem of an employee's performance or attitude. In addition, it has some of the same problems inherent in it as the reassignment of an employee.

Termination. Termination of an employee is the most severe penalty which can be administered. Termination can, contrary to popular belief, be invoked for a single severe instance of unacceptable behavior. It may also be used after a series of corrective or disciplinary actions have been tried. The termination of an employee should be considered seriously before any action is taken. The employer's case for termination must be solid, especially today when a disgruntled terminated employee can and will take an employer to court or before an administrative tribunal for actions which may have been too hasty.

Not only is the immediate penalty of termination felt by an employee, but termination carries with it the stigma of the action on the employee's record for the rest of his work career.

Causes for Corrective or Disciplinary Actions

Causes or reasons for administering a corrective or disciplinary action are not necessarily limited to the following, but these present a guideline which may be used.

(d) Causes for Corrective or Disciplinary Actions

(1) Causes for initiating corrective or disciplinary action shall include, but are not limited to;

(2) Violation of, or failure to comply with, the state constitution or statutes, supreme court rules and regulations, or local court

rules and regulations;

(3) Failure or refusal to comply with a lawful order or to accept a reasonable and proper assignment from an authorized supervisor;

(4) Documented inefficiency, incompetency, negligence, or brutality in the performance of duties;

(5) Under the influence of or unauthorized possession of alcohol, narcotics, or other drugs while on duty;

(6) Medical evidence of physical or mental incapacity to perform duties;

(7) Careless, negligent, or improper use of state property, equipment, or funds;

(8) Use of undue influence to gain, or attempt to gain, promotion, leave, favorable assignment, or other individual benefit or advantage;

(9) Failure to obtain and maintain a current license or certificate as a condition of employment, if required by law, supreme court standards, or these rules;

(10) Conduct unbecoming to a state officer or employee;

(11) Chronic absences or tardiness in reporting to work; or

(12) Taking unauthorized leave.[1]

Other reasons may be used at the discretion of the court administrator. Admittedly, some of the above causes are rather vague, e.g., (d)(10), but they are sufficient to handle most problems which arise.

The important thing to remember at this juncture is that the personnel system under consideration is a merit system incorporating disciplinary rules applied to nonjudicial employees of a court or court system. Many courts and court systems still have no formalized system of discipline. Consequently, many employees have lost their jobs simply because the judge who appointed them has been voted out of office during a political election. In addition, it is likely that discipline for the same or similar infractions of work rules has been treated in a widely disparate manner in many courts.

GRIEVANCES AND APPEALS

As in the private sector, as well as other public agencies, court personnel systems should make it possible for employees to air their grievances and complaints and also to appeal a disciplinary action taken against them by supervisors or judges.

Grievances

For the purpose of definition, a grievance is an action filed by an employee who feels that his supervisor is treating him or her unfairly or who feels that the administration is not following the rules governing personnel policies. Grievances may also be filed over duty assignments, shift assignments, hours worked, working conditions, leave policies, and other similar matters.

Persons who have a right to the grievance procedure vary from system to system. Many executive branch agencies give full rights of the grievance procedure to all employees, except those who are appointed to positions outside the merit system. Grievance procedures are now found in a few judicial systems and individual trial courts, either provided by rule or under a collective bargaining contract.[2]

In a judicial merit system, it is important that employees be allowed access to the grievance procedure. The availability of the system will allow an employee to ventilate the problems which he feels are affecting his performance on the job. In some statewide judicial and trial court personnel systems, some employees are exempted from the grievance procedure. These are usually employees who are directly responsible to a judge or those who are in top professional and administrative positions. This practice protects a judge from being overruled by an administrative tribunal with respect to his confidential employees. In a few systems and courts, the judges have recognized the benefits of a grievance procedure, and it has been expanded to include all employees.

Grievance Procedure Steps. Typical steps for a grievance procedure in a non-union merit system are as follows:

Step 1: An employee who feels he or she has a grievance should discuss the matter first with his or her immediate supervisor. If the immediate supervisor cannot or will not attempt to solve the problem, the employee should be allowed to proceed to Step 2 of the procedure. If the employee's grievance is against his immediate supervisor, then the employee should be allowed to start the grievance procedure at Step 2.

Step 2: An unresolved employee grievance at this level should be handled by a person who is in the middle of the organization structure. In a locally funded court system, this could be a mid-level administrator or supervisor. In a state funded system, this function could be performed by the administrator of the court or judicial district, or by the chief or presiding judge of the court or district. Whoever handles the grievance at the second step should have the option of appointing an impartial review panel or of retaining the services of a hearings officer to make an investigation of the grievance. These options are very important, if there is a possibility of a conflict of interest for the person charged with the grievance responsibility. Decisions reached at the second step level should be in writing. An aggrieved employee who does not receive satisfaction should be allowed to continue to a third and final step in the procedure.

Step 3: As Step 3 is the final step for an unresolved grievance, it should be handled under the auspices of the highest authority available to the system. This could be the chief or presiding judge in a locally funded court or judicial district, or the administrator of the court or district acting for the chief or presiding judge. In a state system, the grievance should go to the chief justice, or to the state court administrator acting for the chief justice. At the third step, it is imperative that an impartial grievance review panel be established and maintained to hear last resort grievances. As Step 3 is the third and final step, great care should be taken to assure that correct procedure is followed and that the decision handed down, in writing, is fair and equitable.

Additional steps may be taken between the first and final steps of the procedure, but they do little other than dilute the process and drag out the time involved in reaching ultimate resolution. On the other hand, the elimination of one or two steps in the three-step procedure places a greater burden on higher level administration personnel, as they will be feeling the weight of a larger number of grievances without the aid of a filtering process at the lower end of the system.

An analogy can be drawn between the grievance procedure and the usual procedure in court systems where a case enters the system in a limited jurisdiction court, is appealed to a general jurisdiction court and, if a litigant or defendant is still not satisfied, may be appealed to an intermediate appellate court or the supreme court. There is one major difference, however. Under the usual grievance procedure, the process from Step 2 to Step 3 is automatic, while in court cases, the ultimate appellate tribunal may have the discretion to decide whether it will hear the matter.

Ideally, most grievances should be filtered out at the first step of the system in a formal or informal manner. Access to a grievance procedure which is formalized and legitimized by rule can straighten out unpleasant working situations that can be detrimental to the over-all working environment.

Appeal Procedure

An appeals, or review, procedure differs from the grievance procedure in that it occurs on motion by an employee who has been reduced in rank or classification, has been suspended from work, or has been terminated from his position in the court. A request for review or appeal is lodged by an employee who has been subject to one of these disciplinary actions when he or she feel wronged by the action or feels that the action was inappropriate or unfair in light of the nature of the alleged wrongdoing.

The appeals/review procedure is formalized procedure for handling employee appeals. It is formalized to the extend that hearings officers may be retained (either on the payroll or by contract) to hear and present findings of law in the cases at hand. In short, it is an administrative procedure which is one step removed from the courtroom. Its purpose is to operate as a check on or safeguard against arbitrary or unfair personnel or administrative practices which place an employee in jeopardy.

The appeals/review procedure may be a one-step affair, with no preliminary procedures. A review board may hear the case after all the documents have been submitted and may make a ruling based on fact. The action by the employee may be denied by the board or the board may find in favor of the employee and order that remedial action be taken.

The process may also have two steps, the first step being a hearing of a concerned employee before a hearing officer, with full or partial evidentiary proceedings. After a determination by the hearing officer is handed down in writing, either party may appeal the decision to the board as a whole. The board must then either affirm the decision of the hearing officer, or overturn his decision and state why it is doing so.³

An appeals procedure is vital for any personnel system which desires to assure that the employees of the system are being treated fairly.

Limitations on the Right of Appeal

Should all employees have a right to the appeals/review procedure as was suggested earlier in this chapter for grievances? While it can be stated idealistically that this is highly desirable, practicality indicates that it is not. There are positions in all personnel systems which should be excluded from the appeals process. These are positions which involve a confidential or close working relationship with the top administrative officials of the organization and usually include senior level professional and administrative staff. It can be argued that employees in these positions should be allowed to appeal a disciplinary action to an administrative tribunal having the power to reinstate an employee over the wishes of the top administrative authority. To do so would serve only to undermine severely the authority of the administrator and to erode further the working relationship between the parties. This is especially true with courts and court administration. The reinstatement of an employee who is directly responsible to a justice or judge, or of a senior level administrative or professional staff member who is responsible to a supreme court, trial judges en banc, or a court administrator would make for difficult or impossible working conditions.

The stated purpose for appeals from disciplinary actions is to protect an employee from irresponsible or irrational actions on the part of a supervisor. In a court setting, judges must interact with those responsible directly to them and must feel comfortable with this interaction. Consequently, those employees (court administrators, chief probation officers, parajudicial personnel, and clerks of court) who work closely with the judges should be denied access to an appeal which is administrative in nature. If this seems harsh, it must be remembered that the disgruntled employee still may have legal avenues to pursue.[4]

In establishing an appeals process, the board composition and the procedures themselves should foster even-handedness. This is necessary to maintain public confidence, as well as employee morale, while at the same time not being too lenient or employee-oriented. If employees who should be terminated are retained, there will be a definite decrease in desired administrative efficiency.

Making the Process Work

The relatively slow pace of some court procedures should be avoided in designing the appeals/review process. Fundamental fairness should be accorded the employee and his rights protected, but the process should be designed to bring the matter to a conclusion as soon as possible. Even if the process is so designed, a disciplinary matter may drag on for an unnecessary period, simply because an administrator or judge(s) may be reluctant to take disciplinary action against an employee who is performing inadequately or is a disruptive influence on other court personnel.

Good personnel management requires that those in authority take action quickly, once justified by the facts, no matter how disagreeable the task may seem. Once that action is taken, the employee may avail himself of the appeals/review procedure or any other action open to him. Some judges and other court personnel may be reluctant to act because they may not enjoy the prospect of being reversed or even having an appeal brought. On the other hand, the employee may feel he faces a difficult situation in having to bring his appeal before a forum composed, at least in part, of peers of the administrator or judge(s) who took the action.

Very seldom is an employee dismissed because of a criminal act or gross negligence. Usually an employee is terminated because he cannot or will not perform at the level expected of him. To be too lenient with an employee who is not doing his job does him a disservice, as well as the court or judicial system which employs him and the public who pays the bills.

The danger is not that employees will be disciplined or terminated without sufficient cause. The appeals/review process, as previously indicated, should safeguard against this happening. Experience in some public personnel systems has shown just the opposite. Undesirable or incompetent employees may remain on the job, because of a combination of administrative inertia and cumbersome appeal procedures.

NOTES

1. Colorado, Supreme Court. <u>Colorado Judicial System Personnel Rules</u> (Denver: Colorado Supreme Court), rule 25(d)(1-12).

2. Grievance procedure rules are discussed in Chapter 10, including the variations among different judicial systems and courts.

3. Appeal procedure rules and the difference among judicial systems and trial courts, both as to procedures and appeal board composition, are discussed in Chapter 10.

4. See Appendix D for decision concerning <u>Hamm v. Scott</u>. See Civil Action No. 76 M 910 United States District Court, Denver, Colorado.

SECTION 3.
SETTING THE FRAMEWORK

10. Personnel Rules

INTRODUCTION

   The judicial system, probably more than any other public institution, operates according to very specific and detailed rules. They govern all facets of practice and procedure in the courts from the filing of a case through the ultimate disposition and even post-judgment actions. Not only are judges and the lawyers who practice before them required to become familiar with the rules, but so are employees of the court who are responsible for case processing, assistance in the courtroom, and related tasks. It is surprising that such a rule-oriented and formalistic institution has been so slow to adopt rules covering all aspects of the employment of court personnel, especially when similar rules have governed employment in the executive branch at national, state, and local levels for better than half a century (and much longer in some instances).
   The reasons it has taken professional personnel management so long to become accepted in a court setting were discussed in Chapter 1. Obviously, professional personnel management and rules of personnel governance go hand in hand. The former requires the latter to assure even-handed treatment for all employees. The latter would not be effective without professional administration. All of which may help explain the delay in adding court personnel to the list of subjects and activities covered by court rules.
   During the past decade, a number of state court systems have adopted personnel rules. Some locally funded trial courts, primarily in urban areas, have also adopted personnel rules. In a number of locations, trial court employees are covered by executive branch personnel rules, although some are ex-

pressly exempt from all or specified provisions, and the judges may have the ultimate authority for hiring and removal.

State Systems

Jurisdictions that have adopted personnel rules which cover employees of all state-funded courts include: Alaska, Alabama, Colorado, Connecticut, Hawaii, Kansas, Kentucky, Maine, New Mexico, North Carolina, South Dakota, and West Virginia.

Nebraska has promulgated personnel rules covering county court personnel, as the county court is the only trial court that is state funded. Virginia has done the same for personnel of the district court (court of limited jurisdiction), which in that state is the only state-funded trial court. Delaware is in the process of making its personnel system and the application of its rules statewide.[1]

Nevada[2] is considering proposed personnel rules which would cover all employees in the state judicial system. A study of trial court personnel, which included proposed personnel rules, was commissioned by the Kansas Legislative Council. Maryland is also having a personnel study made, which will have proposed rules as one of the by-products.

Trial Courts

The number of trial courts in non-state funded jurisdictions with their own personnel systems and rules is not know. Some representative courts are the Superior Court of Los Angeles County (California); Circuit Court of Jackson County (Missouri); Courts of Common Pleas of Cuyahoga and Hamilton Counties (Ohio); and the Circuit Court of Multnomah County (Oregon).

PERSONNEL RULES CONTENT

Court personnel systems, whether they have statewide application, or apply only to an individual trail court, differ in several respects from traditional civil service or merit systems found in the executive branch.[3] These differences usually relate to these matters: 1) exempt or partially exempt employees; 2) testing procedures and employee appointment requirements; 3) grievance and appeal procedures or the lack of same; 4) administrative decentralization; and 5) prescribed or limited employee activities. Each of these will be discussed

in the appropriate sections to follow.
   Generally, court system personnel rules cover the following subjects:
   1) Scope
   2) Administrative Authority and Responsibilities
   3) Definitions
   4) Classification Plan
   5) Compensation
   6) Recruitment, Testing, and Appointment
   7) Employee Evaluation and Discipline
   8) Termination of Employment
   9) Grievances and Appeals
   10) Fringe Benefits and Working Conditions
   11) Special Provisions (i.e., proscribed or limited activities, such as partisan political participation and outside employment)

Rule Format and Organization

   The personnel rule format varies from jurisdiction to jurisdiction, with subject matter organized in different ways. Colorado was the first state to adopt extensive systemwide personnel rules, and the Colorado format has been followed generally by several other jurisdictions, including Delaware, New Mexico, South Dakota, and the proposed Kansas rules. The Colorado Rules are organized as follows:

COLORADO JUDICIAL SYSTEM PERSONNEL RULES

Page

I. CITATION, SCOPE, RESPONSIBILITY AND DEFINITIONS. 1

   Rule 1. Citation 1
   Rule 2. Scope. 1
   Rule 3. Responsibility 1
   Rule 4. Definitions. 2

II. COMPENSATION 5

   Rule 5. Compensation Plan. 5
   Rule 6. Hiring Rates 5
   Rule 7. Salary Computation 6
   Rule 8. Anniversary Increase 7
   Rule 9. Effect of Position Change on Compensation. 9
   Rule 10. Salary Adjustments from Salary Surveys. 10

			Page
	Rule 11.	Salary Computation for Simultaneous Personnel Actions	10
	Rule 12.	Pay Computation for Terminating and Deceased Employees	10
III.	CLASSIFICATION PLAN AND STAFFING PATTERNS		11
	Rule 13.	Classification Plan	11
	Rule 14.	Reclassification of a Filled Position	13
	Rule 15.	Classification Appeals	13
	Rule 16.	Staffing Patterns and Position Allocations	15
IV.	APPOINTMENT OF EMPLOYEES		17
	Rule 17.	Qualifications of New Employees	17
	Rule 18.	Appointing Authority	17
	Rule 19.	Examinations and Qualification Reviews	20
	Rule 20.	Employment Eligibility Lists	24
	Rule 21.	Recruitment and Filling Positions	25
	Rule 22.	Probationary Period	25
	Rule 23.	Trial Service Period	26
V.	EMPLOYEE EVALUATION AND DISCIPLINE		27
	Rule 24.	Performance Evaluation	27
	Rule 25.	Employee Discipline	28
	Rule 26.	Involuntary Termination (Dismissal)	30
	Rule 27.	Layoff Procedures	30
	Rule 28.	Resignations	33
	Rule 29.	Outside Employment	33
	Rule 30.	Political Activity	34
	Rule 31.	Employee Organizations and Representation	34
VI.	LEAVE, HOLIDAYS, RETIREMENT, AND OVERTIME		35
	Rule 32.	Annual Leave	35
	Rule 33.	Sick Leave	36
	Rule 34.	Maternity Leave	37
	Rule 35.	Injury Leave	38
	Rule 36.	Funeral Leave	38
	Rule 37.	Continuing Education	39
	Rule 38.	Leave Without Pay	39
	Rule 39.	Administrative Leave	40

  Page

          Rule 40. Military Leave 40
          Rule 41. Holidays 40
          Rule 42. Retirement 41
          Rule 43. Hours of Work and Overtime   42

VII.   GRIEVANCE AND REVIEW PROCEDURES.   43

          Rule 44. Grievance. 43
          Rule 45. Board of Review.   44
          Rule 46. Review Procedure   45

VIII. APPENDICES   49

          Appendix A-Salary Schedule   49
          Appendix B-Alphabetical Index. . . . .   61[4]

The personnel rules in Maine and West Virginia are organized in a similar fashion. The Main rules cover more subjects and, for that reason, are used here as an example.

                MAINE COURT SYSTEM PERSONNEL POLICIES

          1.0   PURPOSE AND SCOPE OF THE SYSTEM

          1.1   System Purpose
          1.2   System Scope

          2.0   RESPONSIBILITIES OF SYSTEM PARTICIPANTS

          2.1   Responsibilities of the Supreme Judicial
                Court
          2.2   Responsibilities of the State Court
                Administrator
          2.3   Responsibilities of the Regional Court
                Administrators
          2.4   Responsibilities of the Justices and
                Judges
          2.5   Responsibilities of Clerks
          2.6   Responsibilities of all Court System
                Employees

          3.0   COMPENSATION PLAN

          3.1   Compenastion Plan Objectives
          3.2   General Pay Policies
          3.3   Salary Grades
          3.4   Procedures for Determining Individual Pay
          3.5   Implementation Steps

4.0   ADDITIONAL COMPENSATION PROVISIONS

4.1   Overtime Compensation
4.2   Termination Compensation
4.3   Holiday Compensation
4.4   Accumulated Compensatory Time
4.5   Part-time Employees
4.6   Temporary Employees

5.0   HIRING POLICIES AND EMPLOYMENT CONDITIONS

5.1   Selecting Authority
5.2   Hiring Authority
5.3   Applicant Testing
5.4   Probationary Period
5.5   Certification
5.6   Recruitment
5.7   Employee Resignation
5.8   Employment of Relatives
5.9   Outside Employment
5.10   Political Activity
5.11   Practice of Law
5.12   Equal Employment Opportunity
5.13   Promotion

6.0   EMPLOYEE EVALUATION

6.1   Responsibility for Evaluation
6.2   Evaluation Procedures
6.3   Unsatisfactory Evaluation
6.4   Date of Evaluation

7.0   EMPLOYEE DISCIPLINE

7.1   Responsibility for Employee Discipline
7.2   Discipline Procedures
7.3   Right of Appeal

8.0   HOURS OF WORK, LEAVE AND HOLIDAYS

8.1   Hours of Work
8.2   Annual Leave
8.3   Sick Leave
8.4   Leave Without Pay
8.5   Military Leave
8.6   Personal Leave
8.7   Transfer of Leave from other Departments
8.9   Leave Records
8.10   Transfer of Leave on July 1, 1976
8.11   Holidays

9.0   INSURANCE AND RETIREMENT BENEFITS

9.1   Insurance Benefits
9.2   Retirement Benefits
9.3   Mandatory Retirement Age

10.0 GRIEVANCE AND APPEAL PROCEDURES

10.1 Employee Right of Appeal
10.2 Appeal Board
10.3 Appeal Process

APPENDIX A - CLASS DESCRIPTIONS

A.1   Position Classifications
A.2   Class Descriptions

APPENDIX B - COMPENSATION SCALES

B.1   Compensation Scale Structure
B.2   Compensation Scales

APPENDIX C - GRADE ASSIGNMENTS[5]

The format of the Multnomah County Circuit Court (Oregon) personnel rules is one of the best examples of personnel rule organization applicable to an individual trial court.

TABLE OF CONTENTS TO PERSONNEL RULES

	Page
SECTION I INTRODUCTION	
Personnel Plan	1
Allocating Positions/Duties	2
Personnel Selection	4
Compliance with Personnel Rules	6
Rules of Conduct	7
Role of the Court Administrator	9
Role of the General Committee	10
Work Hours, Break Periods, Luncheon Period	11
Definitions	13
SECTION II COMPENSATION	
Compensation	1
Rates of Pay	2
Compensation for Work Out-of-Classification	4
Overtime Compensation	5
Merit Plan	6
Performance Evaluation	11
Promotion	12
Transfer	13
Employee Benefits	14
Retirement Benefits	15

SECTION III ABSENCE AND LEAVES   Page
    Authorized Leaves of Absence With Pay. 1
    Authorized Leaves of Absence Without Pay 3
    Cancellation/Reinstatement of Leave. 5
    Holidays 6
    Inclement Weather. 7
    Maternity Leave. 9
    Personal Holidays. 11
    Sick Leave 12
    Vacation 14
SECTION IV DISCIPLINE
    Disciplinary Action. 1
    Demotion 3
    Dismissal (Administrative Personnel) 5
    Grievance Procedure. 7
    Grievance Board. 9
    Lay Off. 11
    Resignation. 13
    Suspension 14
    Tardiness. 15
SECTION V MISCELLANEOUS
    Court Property 1
    Employee Personnel Records - Confidentiality . . . 2
    Professional Attire and Demeanor 3
    Releases of Information. . . . . 4[6]

There are other examples that might be used, but these three are sufficient to illustrate different ways in which personnel rules might be organized according to subject matter.

Content

Specific rule provisions differ as personnel systems differ, even among jurisdictions using similar format in personnel rule organization. Even though provisions differ, the subject matter covered is much the same.

    <u>Scope</u>. The employees covered by the rules may be specified. Conversely, only those employees who are exempt may be specified, such as the court administrator's office or elected court clerks. Under most court personnel systems, some categories of employees may be partially exempt, i.e., covered by some rules, such as those relating to classification, compensation, fringe benefits, and working conditions, but exempt from grievance and appeal procedures. In this category are usually found top administrative and professional staff and personal or confidential employees of judges, including any or all of the following: secretary, division or courtroom clerk, reporter, law clerk, and bailiff.

It is usually in this portion of the rules that the relationship between the personnel rules, other court rules, and statutory provisions is clarified.

Administrative Authority and Responsibilities. Rules in this category usually set forth the authority and responsibility of judges, administrators, and others in the court or judicial system for administering all or a portion of the personnel rules. For example, West Virginia has six rules dealing with the responsibility of the supreme court of appeals, administrative director, circuit judges, chief circuit judge, magistrates, and judicial employees, respectively.[7]

The Colorado Judicial System Personnel Rules state concisely what some of these responsibilities entail. Rule 3(2)(b) states:

> (b) Scope of Responsibility. (1) appointing authorities, district administrators, and supervisors are responsible in their respective jurisdictions for:
> (2) administration of these rules and compliance with the policies contained herein;
> (3) orientation and on-the-job training of employees;
> (4) review and evaluation of employees' performance in accordance with these rules;
> (5) corrective or disciplinary action when required in accordance with these rules; and
> (6) providing a work environment conducive to employee welfare and safety.[8]

In addition to a specific rule or series of rules on this subject, references to administrative authority and responsibility are usually found throughout the rules in connection with recruitment, hiring, classification, employee discipline, and related matters.

Definitions. As is true with almost every professional specialty, personnel administration has an argot all its own. To make this argot comprehensible, the personnel rules should contain a complete set of definitions with clear explanations. The following composite list of defined words and terms was taken from several sets of court system personnel rules.

Administrative Director
Administrative Authority
Allocation of Positions
Appointing Authority
Appointments
Anniversary Dates

Bumping Rights

Certification
Certified Employee
Class
Class Series
Class Specification
Classified Service
Classification Plan
Compensation Schedule
Conditional Promotion
Confidential Employees
Continuous Service
Current Rate of Pay

Demotion
Director
Dismissal

Eligible
Eligibility List
Exempt Position

Grade
Grievance

Increment
Immediate Family
In-Grade Hiring

Job Description
Judicial Officer

Lay Off
Lead Worker

Non-Exempt Position

Pay Range
Performance Evaluation Report
Permanent Employee
Permanent Full-time Position
Permanent Part-time Position
Position
Position Control Number
Primary Duties
Probationary Period
Promotion
Promotional Transfer

Reallocation
Reclassification
Re-employment
Reinstatement

Selection Process
Staffing Pattern
Step
Step-for-Step
Supervisor

Termination
Temporary Appointment
Temporary Full-time Position
Temporary Part-time Position
Transfer
Trial Service Period

Unclassified Positions

Classification Plan. The rules relating to the classification plan vary among jurisdictions as to content, but generally include the same subjects. First, the rules usually cover the purposes and content of the classification plan, how it is to be developed initially, and how it is to be applied and administered. Maintenance of the classification plan requires periodic review by those who are responsible for personnel administration, and the rules may specify how often certain classes or all classes of positions are to be reexamined. This is necessary because duties may change.

The rules should also provide a procedure for employees to request reclassification and state the basis for position reclassification. In at least two jurisdictions, there is a special process by which an employee can appeal his denial of reclassification or a new classification given to his position. In Colorado, there is a special classification review board consisting of a judge, a staff member from the state court administrator's office, and a trial court administrator.[9] In Maine, the appeal is heard by the same board that hears grievances. The general practice is for an appeal to be taken to the office or staff members who made the decision being appealed. Both Colorado and Maine apparently feel that a separate body would give the matter more impartial consideration. Some court personnel rules do not provide for any appeal of a classification determination.

Administrative authorities, such as presiding judges or trial court administrators in a state system or a department or section head under a trial court personnel system should also have the opportunity to reclassify or reallocate an existing position, whether vacant or filled, and the rules usually provide the procedure and basis for such requests.

Compensation. The compensation plan and its applications receive considerable attention in court system personnel rules. The rules provide for the type of compensation plan to be used, which usually consists of a number of grades and steps within each grade.[10] The rules also provide for the assignment of each position class to a grade.

Another important subject usually covered is initial hiring rates, whether an employee can be hired above the initial step, under what circumstances, and with whose approval.

Provision is made for merit and longevity increases (sometimes called anniversary salary increases) and the relationship of various compensation increases to the employee's hiring or anniversary date. Equally important is a rule explaining the basis for salary computations--monthly, daily, or hourly. Special computation problems are usually dealt with, such as payment to terminating and deceased employees, effect of position changes on compensation, and how to handle two simultaneous personnel actions that relate to compensation.

It is now common for the rules on compensation to provide for an annual review and update of the compensation plan, either based on cost of living increases or a change in prevailing wages for comparable positions. The court or judicial system may make its own survey, or it may use one made by the executive branch.

Recruitment, Testing, and Appointment. Several rules are usually required to cover all facets of employee recruitment, testing, and appointment. The rules usually provide that there will be no discrimination because of race, creed, color, sex, or age (within whatever limits are set--usually legal voting age to mandatory retirement). This has been a standard provision of all public personnel system rules for many years. New provisions in the same vein are designed to foster active recruitment and employment of minorities. They generally involve widespread and out-reach notification of job openings and the use of examinations which are job related but not cultural value oriented.

Personnel administration in state court systems, even with a state-wide personnel program, tends to be decentralized. This means that hiring is done locally, and the central administrative office performs post audits to determine if the chosen applicant meets the requisite qualifications and that the testing or application review process was properly conducted. Because of the number of courts and adjunct judicial agencies involved, the rules are usually quite extensive in detailing who has hiring authority and of what employees. The post audit function is spelled out by rule, with the added provision in some jurisdictions that the position cannot be filled without the prior approval of the central office.

The state court administrator's office also is usually involved in recruitment, including the wide circulation of job announcements and out-of-state recruitment for high level positions.

Testing is not used as extensively in court personnel systems (whether state-wide or local) as is the general practice in executive civil service. Written tests are used only for entry level clerical positions to determine typing, clerical, and stenographic skills. Oral boards are used for professional and administrative positions, but not extensively as yet. Interviews and review of applicants' resumes and applications still constitute the major testing device. Testing in whatever form is covered by rule, as are the establishment of eligibility lists, their application and duration.

In most jurisdictions, the appointing authority may select any qualified applicant. Colorado is one exception; in that state, the appointing authority must select one of the top three candidates, and the rules so provide. Most court personnel rules are silent on this point.

Employee Evaluation and Discipline. All new employees serve a probationary period, usually six months, and, during that time, the protections afforded classified employees under the personnel rules usually do not apply. This means a probationary employee can be dismissed without recourse. Once an employee is certified, the rules specify the acts of commission and omission for which an employee may be disciplined. The possible penalties, such as reprimand, demotion, suspension, or dismissal, and the procedures to be followed are set forth by rule, as well as any appeals that might be exercised by a certified employee.

Employee evaluation involves rules covering performance evaluation procedures, when evaluation is to take place, and the possible alternatives, if an employee receives an unsatisfactory evaluation.

Termination of Employment. This category overlaps to a certain extent the preceding one, because of the penalty of dismissal. Employment termination rules cover much more than dismissal or involuntary termination. They cover voluntary terminations (resignations) and related notice requirements, and also layoff procedures and employee "bumping", and reinstatement rights and procedures. Layoff provisions can become quite complicated, involving seniority, employee status, and possible transfer procedures.

Grievances and Appeals. Grievances generally fall in two major categories, although both may be handled in the same way under court personnel rules. The first category relates primarily to working conditions and on-the-job relationships and practices, as discussed in Chapter 7. The second category pertains to employee disciplinary actions, such as demotion, suspension, and dismissal. (As already mentioned, some jurisdictions also treat reclassification or reallocation appeals as grievances.)

As indicated previously, in some jurisdictions there are employees who are excluded from the grievance procedure, whether in the first or second category. These are usually high level professional and administrative employees and the confidential or personal employees of judges. One exception is Maine, where all employees may avail themselves of the grievance procedure.[11]

Grievances in the first category are handled

generally in the same way in those jurisdictions whose rules provide for some sort of grievance procedure. The first step is for the employee to discuss the matter informally with his or her supervisor. If the grievance is not resolved to the employee's satisfaction, the second step is either for the employee to appeal to the chief judge or his designated representative, as in Colorado, or to appeal to the state court administrator or someone in his office as designated by the personnel rules, usually the personnel officer. In Colorado, appeal to the state court administrator constitutes the third step and may be made by the employee if dissatisfied with the decision of the chief judge or that panel established by him to review the grievance.[12]

The second step in the Multnomah County Circuit Court is referral to the court administrator. The administrator may either attempt to resolve the matter within ten days or refer it to the grievance board.[13]

There is some variation on how a grievance is handled upon appeal to the state level in a statewide judicial personnel system. In Colorado, the state court administrator appoints a three-member appeals board, whose decision is final. The board consists of a trial judge, a district administrator, and the state court administrator or his designee. A separate board is constituted for each grievance, and these boards are different from the body that reviews appeals of demotion, suspension, or dismissal.[14]

The following examples illustrate other variations. In Maine, the appeal is heard by the board that hears all grievances.[15] This is also the situation in Kentucky.[16] In Alaska, the hearing is held informally by the personnel officer, with a formal hearing the ultimate step. The formal hearing is conducted by a board comprising three members of the bar, one chosen by the employee, one by the personnel officer, and the third by the other two.[17] In Multnomah County, the grievance board hears all grievances referred by the court administrator.[18]

In most jurisdictions, the decision made as a result of the ultimate appellate process is final. The one exception found in the personnel rules examined is in Kentucky, where the employee has the right to appeal to the court of proper jurisdiction, if he is dissatisfied with the appeal board decision.[19] In all jurisdictions examined, the employee has the right to appear and to be represented by counsel or some other person of his own choosing.

While grievances in the second category are generally heard by the same body that reviews other grievances, the process is usually different in that the appeal is taken to the review board in the first instance, bypassing the intermediate steps. The elimination of the intermediary steps is a recognition that grievances in this category are much more serious, since they involve suspension, demotion, or dismissal. In some jurisdictions a hearing by the review board is automatic; in others, the board determines whether a hearing is warranted.

Colorado was the only jurisdiction examined where a different board hears grievances concerning suspension, demotion, or dismissal. This board is appointed by the chief justice and consists of a supreme court justice, who serves as chairman; a district judge other than a chief judge; a county judge other than a presiding judge; a district administrator; and a trial court employee. The staff counsel of the state court administrator's office serves as the legal counsel to the administrative authority who instigated the disciplinary action complained of, and the board may appoint a hearing officer, if it determines that a hearing is required.[20]

There is considerable variation in the composition of the ultimate grievance review bodies. Colorado and Alaska have already been covered. In Multnomah County, the presiding judge is the sole appellate review authority, but presumably he could appoint a review board, if he deems it desirable. The rules do not so provide, but he probably could do so under his general authority as presiding judge.

Two other examples illustrate the variations in review board composition. In Maine, the board has seven members appointed by the chief justice of the supreme judicial court. The board has a member of the supreme court, a superior court justice, a district court judge, a regional court administrator, and three judicial system employees.[21] The Kentucky board is also appointed by the chief justice and has five members: a female, a minority race member, an attorney not employed by the judicial system, a non-supervisory employee of the judicial system, and a personnel specialist not employed by the judicial system.[22]

Fringe Benefits and Working Conditions. These rules cover a multitude of related subjects, such as hours of work; overtime provisions, including compensatory time; official holidays; mandatory retirement; shift differentials, if any; and various kinds of leave. The rules in some jurisdictions also cover insurance benefits (health and group life) and retirement benefits. The rules on insurance and retirement benefits are necessary if judicial branch employees are not covered by the same plans applicable to employees of the executive branch.

Rules providing for employee leave usually cover annual leave, sick leave, maternity leave, injury leave, funeral leave, educational leave, administrative leave, and leave without pay. Those relating to annual leave specify maximum accrual, the maximum amount of unused leave for which an employee may be paid upon termination, and the amount of leave that may be transferred from an executive or legislative branch agency upon employment in the judicial branch. In some jurisdictions, the amount of leave which may be accumulated annually, as well as maximum accrual, increases according to length of service.

Rules providing for sick leave also cover annual and maximum accrual limits and the amount of leave that may be transferred in upon employment. In most jurisdictions, terminated employees are not compensated for unused sick leave; Colorado and Maine are exceptions. In Colorado, one-fourth of unused sick leave, up to a maximum of forty-five days, is paid upon termination.[23] In Maine, employees may be compensated for one-half of unused sick leave upon termination.[24]

Generally, judicial branch fringe benefits, whether systemwide or applicable to an individual trial court, parallel those of the executive branch, so that all employees are treated in a similar manner.

Special Provisions. This category covers a variety of provisions found throughout the personnel rules examined relating to employee conduct both on and off the job, nepotism, and other restrictions and limitations. Of the most significance are those rules limiting or proscribing political activity by court employees and those relating to outside employment.

Not all court or judicial system personnel rules deal with both of these subjects. Some jurisdictions cover one and not the other in their rules. Examples of rules limiting employee political activity are found in Alaska, Colorado, Kentucky, and Maine.

Alaska bars employees from being members of any

national, state, or local committee of a political party; nor may any employee take part in the management of a political campaign.[25] No employee or representative of the Alaska court system may require any assessment, subscription, contribution, or service from any other employee for any political candidate, party, or activity, or for any nonpartisan or charitable fund-raising activity.[26]

Colorado judicial system employees are barred from holding any political party office or taking an active part in any political campaign; nor can any employee be granted leave without pay to engage in partisan political activity or serve in an elected office.[27] The prohibition against holding a nonpartisan local government office is designed to avoid a seeming conflict of interest should the local government unit be involved in litigation in the court where the employee is employed. The rule is silent on attendance at political meetings such as party caucuses or making voluntary contributions, so presumably these are not prohibited.

Employees of the Maine judicial system are barred both from holding office or an office in a political party; nor can they take an active part in any political campaign or management of a political party.[28] The Maine rules also specifically bar employees from wearing campaign buttons or distributing campaign literature in the courthouse. Unlike Alaska and Colorado, some employees in the Maine judicial system (above a certain grade) are also barred from participation in public political functions or making contributions.[29]

Kentucky's rule is generally similar to those in Alaska, Colorado, and Maine. Employees, however, are expressly permitted to hold office in a town or school district, if the election or selection is nonpartisan and compensation is limited to per diem payments.[30] Employees are also expressly permitted to make voluntary contributions, be members of a political party or club, and attend political rallies, receptions, and parties.[31]

Unlike Maine, employees may display political stickers on their cars and wear political buttons. They may also work at the polls in nonpartisan statutory positions paid from public funds, such as precinct judge or clerk. In addition, they may work actively in political campaigns not identified with a political party or the courts, such as for or against constitutional amendments, referendums, or municipal ordinances.[32]

The extent to which judicial branch employees

should be permitted to engage in political activity has been subject to considerable debate, especially if the provisions in the judicial system or court personnel rules are more restrictive than those applying to executive branch employees.

On the one hand is the argument that judicial branch employees should not be required to be second class citizens because of their employment. The opposing argument is that judicial branch employees are in very sensitive positions and, for that reason, possible conflicts of interest should be avoided; in fact, there should not be even the appearance of a possible conflict of interest. This point of view has especially prevailed in those jurisdictions where judges are selected under what is known as the Missouri plan or some variation thereof. The reasoning here is that, since judges are barred from political activity or from making contributions, employees should be similarly restricted.

As can be seen from the examples cited above, different jurisdictions have dealt with this problem in somewhat different ways. Others have not dealt with it at all. It is obvious that there is no satisfactory universal solution, and each jurisdiction will either continue to struggle with this problem or resolve it according to the local political environment, tradition, and the degree to which judges, themselves, are removed from the political arena.

The question of conflict of interest arises again in connection with outside employment. The personnel rules in some of the jurisdictions examined deal with this question. Others ignore it completely. Rules were found on this matter in Colorado, Maine, New Mexico, and Multnomah County (Oregon).

Colorado judicial system personnel rules provide that an employee may engage in outside employment if: 1) it does not interfere with job performance; 2) it does not interfere with the interests of the judicial system of the state of Colorado; and 3) it is not the type of employment which could reasonably give rise to criticism or suspicion of conflicting interests or duties. Further, no employee may engage in outside employment without the approval of the administrative authority.[33]

The Maine rules have a similar provision, but also expressly prohibit any employee from engaging in the practice of law.[34] The New Mexico personnel rules are similar, but prohibit fulltime law clerks only from engaging in the practice of law, rather

rather than extending this provision to all employees in the system.35

The Multnomah County (Oregon) personnel rules prohibit an employee from engaging in or accepting outside employment which may reasonably impair or preclude the discharge of official duties.36 Employees may receive honoraria, expenses, and consulting fees for papers, seminars, lectures, and related activities on non-court time. If such activity takes place during working hours, prior approval of the court administrator is required.37

While no jurisdiction attempts to prescribe a dress code by rule, a few specify that employees be neat, clean, and well groomed and also should dress appropriately. This requirement is in addition to those found in all of the court and judicial system personnel rules examined, which describe conduct which could subject employees to disciplinary action.

Several of the jurisdictions examined have rules prohibiting or limiting nepotism. Maine perhaps has the simplest rule on this subject:

> 5.8 Employment of Relatives
> No person will be hired, promoted or transferred to a position where the selecting authority will be a relative of the employee.38

DRAFTING PERSONNEL RULES

Drafting a set of personnel rules for a trial court or a judicial system is no longer the difficult task it once seemed a relatively few years ago. Then there were many executive branch personnel systems to use as models, and there was no dearth of public personnel specialists and textbook and reference material. The problem was that personnel specialists were not familiar with the court environment and its special problems, nor were there any textbooks, reference material, or models directly applying to the courts. Conversely, judges, administrators, and other court personnel were relatively unfamiliar with professional personnel management practices. Not only were they not sure of the need of a formal personnel system and rules, but generally, they were also suspicious of outside experts.

The scene has changed, because there are now judicial systems and individual trial courts which have developed their own expertise in personnel management. Outside consultants and specialists have gained sufficient knowledge about the court environment to be helpful in developing court personnel systems, making classification studies, and drafting rules. Standards on court organization and judicial administration, as well as many conferences and workshops, have emphasized the importance of professional personnel management in court administration. Consequently, judges and court personnel are now much more willing to establish and maintain a formal personnel system and to adopt the personnel rules necessary to make the system function. There are now models available,[39] and reference material is being developed which will be helpful both to individual courts and judicial systems.

Preparing the First Set of Rules

Even with the present more favorable climate and the availability of acceptable specialists (both within and outside the court environment), promulgation of the first set of personnel rules for a judicial system or a court is not without some difficulty. There are still a number of problems which must be resolved, not the least of which is general acceptance of the rules by the judges and court personnel who must operate under them and be governed by them.

In meeting this particular problem, the process used in drafting the rules may be as important as the product itself. In other words, high degree of participation by those whom the rules affect may not always be possible, because drafting and promulgation of personnel rules may be subject to rather severe time limits imposed by constitutional or legislative mandate, such as the initial date of state funding of the judicial system. If the degree of participation is, of necessity, curtailed for this reason, every effort should be made to explain the rules and the reasons for them to judges and employees in the system or court as soon as possible after their adoption.

Adoption of systemwide rules is usually the responsibility of the state supreme court. Personnel rules applying only to a particular trial court are usually promulgated by all of the trial judges en banc. Justices or judges usually do not have the time or the expertise to prepare the initial draft, which means that this task will be performed by staff, outside consultants or specialists, or by a combination of the two. The best situation would be for the staff or outside specialists to have the assistance of a representative committee of judges and court personnel. At the very least, the draft might be reviewed by such a committee for comments and suggestions before submission to the adopting body.

Any tendency to adopt wholesale the personnel rules of another jurisdiction should be strongly guarded against. They can serve as models for format, content, and language, but each judicial system or court has slightly different problems and needs, and should resolve the related policy questions for itself. These policy questions involve, but are certainly not limited to, the following:

1) exempt or partially exempt positions, including provision, if any, for personal or confidential employees of judges;
2) extent to which grievance and appeal procedures apply;
3) content of fringe benefits;
4) recruitment and hiring procedures;
5) limitation or proscription of employee political activity and extracurricular employment;
6) nepotism; and
7) mandatory retirement age for employees.

In considering these and other policy questions, parallel provisions in the executive branch personnel system should be considered, so that necessary departures from them are well thought out and explained, should any questions be raised.

In-House Staff or Consultants. One of the major considerations is determing whether to use in-house capability. Another closely related consideration is who is making the classification study, because the two should go hand in hand. A third major consideration is the time available to draft the rules and have them adopted.

If the judicial system or trial court has in-house staff with personnel management knowledge and rule-drafting capability, the use of in-house staff has certain advantages, such as familiarity with the court or judicial system environment, the key actors, and what are likely to be major policy considerations, as these vary from jurisdiction to jurisdiction. This assumes that the in-house staff assigned to the project has sufficient time and resources available to complete the task within the prescribed limits.

A qualified outside consultant or specialist

usually has sufficient expertise to reduce the time required to prepare an initial draft. It should be recognized that he or she may not become completely knowledgeable about the environment or sensitive to the major policy issues, especially if the time to prepare the draft is limited. This problem can be overcome, or at least substantially minimized, with a representative policy or advisory committee, as described above. If an outside consultant is making the classification study, the addition of the rule drafting task should be strongly considered.

When using an outside consultant, care should be exercised that the rule-drafting product is not "boiler plate," so that many provisions are not applicable. On the other hand, even a "boiler plate" product can provide a solid base for pointing up the policy decisions and the changes that need to be made to make the rules fit the requirements of a particular jurisdiction.

Perhaps the best solution would be a combination of in-house staff and an outside consultant or specialist. The former can provide background information on the judicial system or court environment and will have the understanding of the proposed rules requisite to following through after the consultant leaves. The consultant, on the other hand, can provide the expertise to identify issues quickly and to provide technical assistance, especially in areas which may be less familiar to more generalist in-house staff.

Rule Submission. The draft of the proposed rules finally submitted to the judicial body which has the responsibility for their adoption should be accompanied by sufficient commentary to explain each of the rules, why it is needed, and how it relates to the other rules, as well as how the rules in toto relate to personnel management of the system or court. This is required, because of the time demands on, and probable lack of personnel management expertise and experience of, the justices or judges charged with the responsibility of adopting the rules. If an advisory committee is used, any of its recommendations or suggestions not included in the final draft should also be submitted to the adopting body with commentary as to the reasons why they were suggested and why they were not adopted.

Continued Rule Revision

Once personnel rules are adopted, it should not

be assumed that they are cast in concrete. No matter how carefully the draft has been prepared and reviewed, it is more than likely that something has been overlooked or that conflicting provisions have been adopted. It is often hard to determine how well rules that seem satisfactory on paper will fare in day to day application. It may also be necessary to amend, delete, or add rules to meet changing conditions, to correspond to legislative changes, or to take into account personnel rule revisions in the executive branch.

Consideration of rule revisions should have the same kind of representative participation suggested for original preparation and should be submitted to the adopting body with commentary showing the old rule, the change, and the reason it is needed. This should be a continuing piecemeal process.

Every three to five years, it is desirable to examine the entire set of personnel rules in light of experience and the changing state of the art of personnel management. Since more time should be available than when the rules were first adopted, there should be ample opportunity for input from and review by judges and other court personnel.

NOTES

1. The Delaware Judiciary: Position Classification, Pay, and Equal Employment Opportunity (Chicago: Public Information Service, 1976). This plan is effective statewide, September, 1979.
2. Nevada, State Court Administrator's Office, Draft Prepared by the State Court Administrator's Office (Carson City, Nevada: State Court Administrator's Office, 1977).
3. These differences and the reasons therefor were discussed in Chapter 1.
4. Colorado Supreme Court, Colorado Judicial System Personnel Rules (Denver: Colorado Supreme Court, 1975).
5. Maine Supreme Judicial Court, Maine Court System Personnel Policy and Procedures Manual (Portland, Maine: Supreme Judicial Court, 1976, as amended).
6. Multnomah County, Oregon, Office of the Circuit Court Administrator, Personnel Rules for Employees of the Circuit Court of Multnomah County (Portland, Oregon: Office of the Circuit Court Administrator, 1978).
7. West Virginia, Supreme Court of Appeals,

West Virginia Judicial Personnel System Policy and Procedures Manual (Charleston: West Virginia Supreme Court of Appeals, 1976), rules 2.1-2.6.
    8. Colorado Judicial System Personnel Rules, rule 3(2)(b).
    9. Ibid., rule 15(d).
    10. See Chapter VI, Compensation and Benefits.
    11. Maine Court System Personnel Policy and Procedures Manual, rule 10.1.
    12. Colorado Judicial System Personnel Rules, rule 44.
    13. Multnomah County (Oregon) Personnel Rules, Grievance Procedure, Section IV 2.
    14. Colorado Judicial System Personnel Rules, rule 44(d)(6).
    15. Maine Court System Personnel Policy and Procedures Manual, rules 10.2 & 10.3.
    16. Kentucky, Court of Justice, Administrative Procedures of the Court of Justice (Frankfort, KY: Court of Justice, 1977), rule 5.06(2).
    17. Alaska, Supreme Court, Alaska Court System Personnel Rules (Anchorage: Alaska Supreme Court, 1977), rules 9.04 and 9.05.
    18. Multnomah County (Oregon) Personnel Rules, Grievance Board, Section IV 2.
    19. Kentucky Administrative Procedures of the Court of Justice, rule 5.06(2).
    20. Colorado Judicial System Personnel Rules, rules 41 and 46.
    21. Maine Court System Personnel Policy and Procedures Manual, rule 10.2.
    22. Kentucky Administrative Procedures of the Court of Justice, rule 5.07.
    23. Colorado Judicial System Personnel Rules, rule 33(e).
    24. Maine Court System Personnel Policy and Procedures Manual, rule 83.
    25. Alaska, Supreme Court, Alaska Court System Personnel Rules, rule 10.00.
    26. Ibid., rule 10.03.
    27. Colorado Judicial System Personnel Rules, rule 30.
    28. Maine Court System Personnel Policy and Procedures Manual, rule 5.10.
    29. Ibid.
    30. Kentucky Administrative Procedures of the Court of Justice, rule 6.23.
    31. Ibid.
    32. Ibid.
    33. Colorado Judicial System Personnel Rules, rule 30.

34. *Maine Court System Personnel Policy and Procedures Manual*, rules 5.9 & 5.11.
35. New Mexico, Supreme Court, *New Mexico Judicial System Personnel Plan*, (Santa Fe: New Mexico Supreme Court, 1976).
36. *Multnomah County (Oregon) Personnel Rules*, Rules of Conduct, Section I 2(f).
37. Ibid., 2(d) and (e).
38. *Maine Court System Personnel Policy and Procedures Manual*, rule 5.8.
39. See Appendix F for examples of complete sets of court personnel rules.

11. Administering the Court Personnel System

INTRODUCTION

This chapter focuses on administering the court personnel system as contrasted with managing the personnel within the system.[1] The concern here is with who has, or should have, the authority and responsibility for over-all system administration, as well as the administration of the major personnel functions within the system. Also of concern is the scope and nature of administrative authority and responsibility. To discuss this subject properly, it is necessary to distinguish between statewide judicial personnel systems and those solely within one court, county, circuit, or district.

There are major differences between the administration of a judicial branch personnel system (whether statewide or local) and the administration of an executive branch state or local personnel system. These differences not only relate to the placement and exercise of authority and responsibility, but also to the number of full-time people required for administration of the system in ratio to the number of employees in the system. For example, statewide judicial personnel systems usually have a full-time personnel professional for each 400 to 600 employees in the system.[2] In the executive branch, the ratio is more likely to be one to 200-250.[3]

The major reasons for this difference are: 1) Judicial personnel systems are not as highly structured as those in the executive branch. 2) Central personnel staffs are responsible for fewer functions in judicial systems than they are in executive branch systems, because authority and responsibility are usually more diffused in judicial branch personnel systems than in executive branch systems. 4) The executive branch personnel department is usually not only separate from other executive agencies, but independent of them, even in making policy. In court personnel systems, personnel administration is part of the state court administrator's office and policy may be made by the supreme court.

STATEWIDE SYSTEMS

Over-all Authority and Responsibility

Authority and responsibility for over-all personnel administration is lodged at the state level in statewide judicial branch personnel systems. It may be vested solely in the state court administrator and his staff; it may be vested solely in the chief justice or the supreme court; or it may be distributed among the state court administrator, the chief justice, and the supreme court. This latter pattern is more prevalent, but the distribution of authority and responsibility varies among jurisdictions.

In Colorado, for example, the chief justice and the supreme court have over-all authority and responsibility for operation of the personnel system.[4] The chief justice or the state court administrator may authorize paygrade adjustments under certain circumstances, even though the supreme court adopts the compensation plan after preparation by the state court administrator.[5]

The chief justice and the state court administrator divide the authorization of in-grade hiring, depending on the grade level, and the state court administrator maintains the classification plan and conducts reclassification studies.[6]

The state court administrator reviews the qualifications of all new employees to see if standards have been met and may accept alternate or lesser qualifications in some circumstances.[7] He is required to assist in recruitment[8] and also in the conduct of examinations upon request of the appointing authority. He prescribes examination content subject to the approval of the chief justice.[9] Another responsibility of the state court administrator is the maintenance of personnel records.

In Maine, the supreme judicial court is responsible for establishment of the system, but the state court administrator is responsible for its implementation, maintenance, and operation.[10]

The state court administrator's authority and

responsibility are delineated as follows:

> 2.2.1 Determining that all potential court system employees meet minimum standards as defined in the Classification Plan. Such determination will be made prior to the individual being hired.
>
> 2.2.2 Ensuring that all court system employees are evaluated at least once each year. Actual evaluations, other than for employees of the Administrative Office of the Courts (AOC), are not the responsibility of the SCA.
>
> 2.2.3 Conducting periodic interviews and audits to ensure that the Classification and Compensation Plans are current and accurate.
>
> 2.2.4 Maintenance of personnel records, including payroll records, leave balances and personal histories.[11]

In most judicial branch personnel systems the division of authority and responsibility between the supreme court or chief justice and the state court administrator is generally similar to that outlined above for Colorado and Maine. The Alaska system is somewhat different. The administrative director of the courts has the over-all authority and responsibility for the system, including hiring, but he may delegate this function to hiring supervisors.[12] The director of personnel is designated as the operational head of the personnel system.[13]

Local Authority

Even with over-all administrative authority and responsibility at the state level, chief judges of trial courts and heads of other units in the statewide system usually are given the authority, subject to the personnel rules and regulations, for recruitment, hiring, evaluation, promotion, discipline, and removal. Alaska, as noted above, is an exception.

Actions in some of these areas--particularly evaluation, discipline, and removal--may usually be appealed to a grievance or review board. Others may be subject to post-audit by the state court administrator, and his assistance may be requested or even required in recruitment and testing procedures.

This decentralization of personnel authority and responsibility is not often found in executive agencies, especially to the extent found in the judiciary. It is very understandable that judicial branch personnel systems have taken this approach, given the judicial environment and the relatively short time most judicial branch personnel systems have been in existence. Only a few are more than ten years old and most have been established in the past five years.

Personnel System Adoption

Personnel system adoption usually came in the wake of court reorganization and provision of state funding. Before these major changes took place, trial courts operated as independent entities. Judges usually exercised complete authority over court personnel, except for elected court clerks and their employees. In recognition of this long-standing practice and to gain at least limited acceptance from trial judges, judicial branch personnel systems have been designed to retain some authority at the trial court or circuit level. Doing so has made the transition to a more uniform system easier. Geography and supreme court reluctance to build a large central staff, if some other alternative was possible, were other factors influencing the division of authority and responsibility for personnel.

Experience indicates that this approach to personnel administration in the courts is working as well, if not better, than a more centralized system in most jurisdictions, although it takes central monitoring or post-auditing to assure reasonable compliance with the rules and regulations. During the first two or three years, the new system is usually tested by judges and employees, and exceptions and irregularities are bound to occur. Once judges and employees become familiar with the system, recognize that it is here to stay, and see that it has advantages that outweigh the imposition of rules and regulations, more orderly operation is the likely result. As the system matures, there is greater acceptance, and new judges and employees accept it as a given.

Even though it is a separate personnel system controlled and maintained by the judiciary, it is likely to resemble the executive branch personnel system in some ways. One impetus for similarity between systems in some states is legislation requiring that the personnel system be designed in such a way that employees of all three branches are treated as equally as possible.[14] The compensation plans most often are the same. Not only does this similarity seem to reassure the legislature that there is parity among the branches, but, as explained in Chapter 5, it makes it easier for the judicial branch to apply labor market wage surveys conducted by the executive branch. In small states, the executive branch personnel system can be of assistance in providing specialized services or in making ADP record-keeping systems available for judicial system use.

LOCAL SYSTEMS

Authority and Responsibility

In personnel systems covering only one court, district, or circuit, authority and responsibility for operating the system is likely to be placed in one or a combination of the following: chief or presiding judge, a committee of judges, or the trial court administrator. Policy formulation and rule adoption and amendment is usually the responsibility of judges; in fact, the court en banc may be the rule-making body.

The court administrator is generally responsible for the technical and record-keeping aspects of personnel administration. He may also hire, discipline, and promote employees, although some of his decisions may be subject to judicial review, even without employee appeal. Whatever the administrator's authority, it is not likely to extend to confidential or personal employees of judges. It certainly does not extend to employees of elected court clerks.

Responsibility of Trial Court Administrator

The trial court administrator usually does not have any professional position devoted exclusively to personnel administration, unless he or she is in a large, multi-judge trial court with several hundred employees. In fact, there may not be any professional administrative staff positions besides his own. If there are any professional assistants, personnel administration is just one of many functions shared with them by the administrator. Because of staff limitations, the trial court administrator may make use of staff services provided by the county or municipal personnel department, such as classification studies, design and maintenance of personnel records, preparation of job descriptions, wage surveys, etc. As is true of state-wide systems, the individual trial court system probably resembles the executive branch system at least as to compensation plan design and fringe benefits, for the same reasons as do state-wide systems.

STAFFING THE PERSONNEL UNIT

Staff Size

While a specific professional staff position (or positions) for personnel administration is the exception in trial court personnel systems, it is the usual rule in state-wide judicial branch personnel systems. Staff size and the skills required depend on several factors:

1) A major consideration is the number and kinds of employees in the system. As previously indicated, the ratio of personnel professionals to employees is one to 400-600 in most judicial branch state-wide systems.

2) Very important in determining staff size is the division of authority and responsibility between the supreme court and the state court administrator's office at the state level, and the trial courts or court services units. For example, if recruitment, hiring, evaluation, and discipline are primarily local functions, then the size of central staff can be smaller.

3) Other functions to be performed also affect central staff size. For example, if labor market wage surveys are performed by the state executive branch personnel department, that department also maintains personnel records for the judicial branch, and if that department or consultants are engaged for major reclassification studies, then not as many central staff positions will be needed. If training is a direct personnel central unit responsibility, an additional staff member may be required.

4) The kinds of court services under the judicial system and how these services are centrally administered or coordinated will have a bearing on personnel staff size. Judicial systems in some jurisdictions have court services administrators or coordinators, e.g., Connecticut, Kansas, New Mexico, and South Dakota. These administrators or coordinators may have as part of their duties some responsibilities for the court services personnel function,

usually in collaboration with the personnel officer.

5) Another consideration is whether the personnel function is to be combined with some other professional activity such as management analysis, as was once done in the Colorado judicial system. A combination of functions such as this affects both staff size and staff qualifications.

As a minimum, a personnel officer will be required. Depending on the duties to be performed and the number of employees in the system, one or more personnel technicians may be needed. As indicated above, these may be a combination of personnel and management analysts.

A strong argument can be made that all aspects of employee training, from orientation to various kinds of in-service and supervisory programs, should be the responsibility of the personnel unit. A training officer should be employed for this purpose, even if a court services administrator or coordinator shares this responsibility for probation counselors and similar personnel categories.

Personnel Staff Qualifications

Personnel Director. Even if the personnel unit staff's prime responsibility is administering the personnel function, state court administrative staffs are usually small enough so that personnel professionals may become involved in other activities from time to time. Management analysis has already been mentioned in this chapter. Other closely related functions are planning, budgeting, and fiscal administration.[15] These considerations mean that the personnel officer and director should have education and experience in judicial administration or public administration, in addition to specialization in personnel administration. This is true even if the job description doesn't refer to it specifically. A background in judicial administration may be preferable, because of the peculiarities of the judicial environment.

At the time that personnel and management analysis were combined in the Colorado state court administrator's office, the qualifications for personnel and management director were set forth as follows:

DESIRABLE KNOWLEDGE, ABILITIES, AND SKILLS

Thorough knowledge of public personnel and management principles and techniques and their practical application.

Thorough knowledge of procedures analysis, budgeting, work simplification, forms and records control and staff utilization.

Considerable knowledge of the principles and methods of administration and supervision.

Ability to prepare charts, layouts, forms, handbooks, memoranda, and other media of information and instruction.

Ability to prepare comprehensive reports and to present facts clearly and concisely, orally and in writing.

DESIRABLE EDUCATION AND EXPERIENCE

Graduation from an accredited four-year college or university with a Master's degree in business administration, personnel management, or a closely related field; and thorough experience in personnel administration, management analysis, or a related field.[16]

Colorado changed from the combination of personnel administration and management analysis, because staff expansion made it possible to have a greater degree of specialization. Nevertheless, the personnel staff is still involved in management studies from time to time. This combination remains a useful approach for smaller offices. The new job description for personnel director contains many of the qualifications and experience requirements of the formerly combined position, emphasizing the desirability of a broad background.

An example of a desirable background for a judicial system personnel officer is found in the job description for this position in the Kansas judicial system:

DESIRABLE EDUCATION AND EXPERIENCE

Graduation from an accredited four-year college or university supplemented by a Master's degree in judicial administration, business administration, public administration, personnel management, or a closely related field; and thorough experience in personnel administration, management analysis, or a related field, or any equivalent combination of education and experience which provides the following knowledge, abilities, and skills:

Thorough knowledge of public personnel and management principles and techniques and their practical application.

Knowledge of tests and measurements theory and methods.

Knowledge of position classification service rating techniques and procedures.

Considerable knowledge of the principles and methods of administration and supervision.

Ability to prepare charts, layouts, forms, handbooks, memoranda, and other media of information and instruction.

Ability to prepare comprehensive reports and to present facts clearly and concisely, orally and in writing.[17]

Personnel Technician. The requirement for personnel technician are somewhat similar to those of personnel officer or director, although less experience, education, and knowledge are required as shown by the following (also taken from the Kansas judicial system job description):

DESIRABLE EDUCATION AND EXPERIENCE

Graduation from an accredited four-year college or university with major course work in the social sciences, and experience in the field of personnel administration or closely related field, or any equivalent combination of education and experience which provides the following knowledge, abilities, and skills:

Knowledge of a wide variety of occupational categories and the qualifications required in such work.

Knowledge of the general rules and regulations of the judicial personnel system.

Knowledge of the principles and practices of modern personnel management as they apply to recruitment and examination, classification and compensation, and employee training and development.

Ability to obtain, analyze, and place in testing form the knowledge, abilities, and skills needed to perform work in a variety of classes or positions.

Ability to analyze classification pay problems and needs and make effective recommendations.

Ability to express ideas effectively, orally and in writing.[18]

Training Specialist. The training specialist needs to have the following knowledge, abilities, and skills:

1) thorough knowledge of the principles, practices, and techniques of employee training;

2) considerable knowledge of the basic principles of teaching methods and of learning processes;

3) considerable knowledge of literature, developments, and trends in employee training;

4) considerable knowledge of the principles and practices of public administration and personnel management;

5) ability to plan, organize, and administer agency-wide training programs; and

6) ability to express oneself, clearly and effectively, orally and in writing.

At least a bachelor's degree and considerable employee training experience are desirable qualifications. It would be helpful if the training specialist has an understanding of and experience in the court or legal environment. Court or legal environment knowledge and experience are extremely helpful if training administration is combined for judges and nonjudicial personnel.

In some jurisdictions where these are combined, the training function may be separate from and independent of personnel administration. Employee training should be a personnel function, but judicial training--rightly or wrongly--is usually perceived as being separate and apart from employee training. For this reason, the two, perhaps, should be kept separate, even though this may not be feasible in smaller states.

Personnel Staff Compensation

The importance of the personnel function requires a well-qualified and experienced director. For this reason, his salary should be at the same level as other senior professionals and division heads, such as budget director, planning director, and director of research and statistics.

Personnel technicians should usually be hired at the entry level for professional employees and advanced to the professional journeyman level after two or three years' experience, with demonstrated competence and ability.

Training specialists and intermediate personnel positions requiring special skills such as classification, negotiations, etc., should be compensated at or above the journeyman level, depending on labor market competition for these skills.

PERSONNEL RECORD KEEPING AND INFORMATION SYSTEMS

All bureaucratic functions, including personnel administration, generate their own sets of paperwork to establish a permanent record of the different transactions which take place.

Generally, it can be stated that a system which uses only necessary basic records has the best chance of expediting personnel actions with a minimum amount of fuss and bother. Unfortunately, most court systems, with their penchant for collecting and saving all types of records, are prone to collecting and saving every scrap of personnel information whether it is necessary or not.

Basic Personnel Form Content

The personnel record-keeping function need not be cluttered, but there is certain information which must be gathered if the system is to run at all. The most rudimentary and basic personnel form should contain the employee's name, address, social security number, birth date, service date, the location where the person works, the employee's position number, the employee's rate of pay, the position classification, the date of the employee's next scheduled evaluation or merit increase, and basic information concerning the employee's sick and annual leave. In addition, it is prudent to have information concerning the employee's ethnicity and sex (for E.E.O. purposes) and the employee's marital status (for tax purposes). In essence, this is all that is needed for the personnel file.

Fiscal Information Requirements

More is required than basic personnel information. The budget and fiscal staffs usually want to add a variety of information which will enable them to do their jobs better. Some of this information may include the employee's marital status (again); the number of exemptions; state and local tax information; health insurance information; retirement or social security information; overtime; other pay-rate information, including basic pay, any deductions from the employee's check; and virtually anything else which has a fiscal impact.

In addition to this fiscal information, those responsible for budget preparation are going to want and need other data concerning the employee's position. This information will probably include pay rate, the amount budgeted for the position, whether the position is full time or part time, the position number, where the position is located, and any information concerning what the position does, e.g., case processing, judicial support, or administration.

As can be seen from the foregoing, there is some information which is required by two or even three divisions, and some information which is unique to each. Consequently, each division should have its own form, with all three forms complementing the others to establish a personnel/payroll system. These forms provide the means by which information is generated for the over-all system.

Personnel Reports

There are many reports which can be developed from this information to enhance the personnel function. The extent to which reports are used will depend to a great extent on whether records are automated. If they are, a system of any size can generate almost any number and type of reports. In smaller jurisdictions, which cannot justify the added expense of data processing, some rudimentary but effective reports can be developed to aid the court administrator or presiding judge in management.

Personnel and related information serves as a basis for a personnel management reporting system. Almost any report can be developed which will array any collected information which is of help to management. The more sophisticated, complex reports are not truly adaptable to a manual system, but data processing applications can handle the relatively complex almost as easily as the simple. The availability of ADP makes it possible for those responsible for management of the judicial system or a trial court to request whatever reports they consider necessary.

The larger systems (more than 100 employees) are, of course, more cost efficient when data processing is used. Some of the reports which are of use are: an alphabetical name index; a social security number index; a filled position by location report; a vacant position by location report (the two foregoing are valuable in multi-location jurisdictions); a filled position by type of classification report; a vacant position by type of classification report; potential retirement report; terminations by type and location report; sick and annual leave report; evaluation due report; and ethnicity, age, and sex reports by class and location.

Smaller systems (fewer than 100 employees) are encouraged to participate in a data processing system only if participation is cost beneficial. Frequently, a court, or small court system, can participate in the larger county, city, or state data processing program for a minimal cost.

If participation by a smaller system in data processing is not possible, a manual system can be purchased in a prepackaged form, or can be developed either in house or through the assistance of a consultant. The prepackaged format is valuable in that it is a common shelf item and generally carries a smaller price tag. The custom-built aystem, although costing more, should be of more use.

The personnel reporting system should be timed and coupled with the payroll system. Reports generated by the system should not be produced more often than once a month, as storage will be a problem, and the information will generally not be significantly different if produced more frequently.

If up-to-date information is desired, or necessary, a system can be set up which uses a cathode ray tube (CRT) coupled with a keyboard input system through which the entire system can be updated daily. The various reports desired can be called up on the screen when desired, and, if a printer is coupled with the CRT, a screen image can be printed out. The disadvantages of a system of this nature are its expense (both initial and ongoing) and the lack of permanent hard copy.

All personnel systems have a problem with the storage of computer reports. One way around this problem is to have the computer tape which generates the reports sent to an independent company to have the reports printed on micro-fiche rather than paper. In this way, several years' records can be stored in the same space required for one month of computer print outs.

DETERMINING PERSONNEL NEEDS

The determination of personnel needs in the courts, as in other public agencies, requires a combination of skills in addition to personnel management, including fiscal analysis, management analysis, research and data collection, and planning and forecasting. In most state funded court systems and some large trial courts, each of these skills is represented by one or more staff members, and a team or task force approach can be used for needs determination. In the smaller state-funded systems and in most trial courts, this combination of skills--if present at all--will be found in one or two staff members. These small staffs usually have enough on-going duties that it may not be possible to find the time to make a needs analysis, even if the requisite skills are present. In this instance, consideration should be given to hiring outside consultants.

Factors Affecting Needs Assessment Methodology

There are a number of approaches that may be taken to determine staff needs, ranging from very simple analyses to very complicated and sophisticated ones. The approach or approaches used will depend on a number of generally interrelated factors, in addition to staff capability and resources already mentioned:

1) size, complexity, and diversity of the system and the functions performed, e.g., urban and rural courts or central and branch court locations;

2) time available to develop needs assessment formulae and validate them;

3) availability and timeliness of relevant data and the degree of difficulty in updating this information;

4) degree of difficulty and complexity involved in updating formulae and their application;

5) extent and variety of mechanization and the frequency of technological innovation;

6) kind and degree of documentation required by the funding agency; and

7) purposes for which the formulae will be used.

Most of these factors are interrelated as the

discussion shows:

1) **System Size and Diversity**. Judicial systems and even individual trial courts encompass a number of different functions and activities, especially if court services are involved, such as probation or juvenile detention. There is a significant difference in staffing needs between urban and rural courts, as well as the way in which personnel are assigned duties. There is also a significant difference between metropolitan courts and medium size urban ones. These differences also appear between large central urban or metropolitan courts and branch or satellite courts.

In larger courts, employees are usually departmentalized and perform discrete functions. Those in the clerk's office are not likely to be involved in jury management, or in maintaining the law library, for example. In rural courts, employees may perform a combination of tasks which are separated in large urban courts. Again, jury management and law library maintenance are good examples. Staff ratios developed to document and forecast personnel needs must account for these differences in employee use to be accurate and effective. There are several ways to do this, as explained in subsequent sections.

The measures needed to determine need for court service agency professionals, such as probation officers, are entirely different from those used for court clerical personnel, even if the principle used is the same. Further, consideration should be given to travel requirements in multi-county rural circuits or districts.

These are but a few examples of the impact of size, complexity, and diversity on deciding the methodology to be used to determine staff needs.

2) **Time Limitations**. It is obvious that the less time available to develop a personnel needs assessment formula or formulae, the less likely is the methodology to be sophisticated or complicated, unless outside consultants are used. Even if a simple formula is used, such as cases filed or pending per employee, it should be designed so that it is as adaptable as possible to more sophisticated analysis at a later date. It is desirable to have continuity even with subsequent revision.

3) **Data Availability and Timeliness**. The successful use of sophisticated techniques to determine personnel needs depends on the availability of adequate and timely relevant data. These data should also be automatically updated at given times--per-

haps monthly or quarterly. In other words, without an adequate management information system, the personnel needs assessment methods that can be used successfully are greatly limited. If the decision is made to make an extensive field study (either in house or by consultants), a mechanism should be built in for automatically updating the information used. Otherwise, the measures will lose their validity and another expensive and time-consuming field study will be needed to determine validity of the formula or formulae and update the components.

    4) <u>Updating Difficulty</u>. Even if there is sufficient information available or which can be gathered through a field study, it may be better to stick with a simple personnel needs formula, if it is going to be difficult to update and validate on an on-going basis. The comments in the preceding paragraph apply here as well.

    5) <u>Technology</u>. On-line computer terminals, complex microfilm programs, and mag card typewriters, for example, are usually found only in large courts or court units, because volume determines cost effectiveness; court employees usually can handle more work than those in smaller courts because of specialization, location, concentration, and economics of scale. Technology increases this disparity, and it must be taken into consideration in developing personnel needs assessment formulae.

This is an on-going problem in courts and judicial systems which are innovative and try to use technology to reduce labor intensity. It may be an on-going problem in presently less innovative judicial systems and trial courts, because judicial systems and courts cannot expect to add personnel at the same rate as in the past to cope with increasing caseloads. Of necessity, this will force courts in the direction of examining, adopting, and adapting every useful technological innovation whether it be mag card typewriters, microfilming, or introduction or expansion of automated data processing. Manual procedures will be streamlined as well, aimed at increasing employee productivity.

    6) <u>Funding Agency Requirements</u>. Appropriation bodies expect courts to justify expenditures for hardware and new systems by showing offsetting savings through a reduction in new personnel or even in present personnel, despite projected caseload increases. This means it will be necessary for courts and appropriation bodies to agree on some kind of productivity or workload formulae to have an acceptable basis both for justifying new personnel and

for determining savings through greater productivity and elimination of employees.

Personnel needs justification becomes more important as appropriation bodies become more tightfisted in response to anti tax and spending referenda and proposed referenda. The courts will probably have to tailor personnel needs assessment methodology to what the funding body is likely to accept as justification.

7) <u>Formulae Use</u>. If the intent is only to develop formulae that may be acceptable to the funding authority in documenting personnel needs, the simpler the better. If more extensive use is to be made--for internal management assessments, decisions, and planning--as well as for budget justification--simple ratios may not be sufficient.

As on-going management information system is required which will include the elements needed for developing continuing measurements of changing productivity. This system can be fairly complicated, depending on the number of measures to be used, how they are to be integrated, and to whom they are to be applied.

Accounting for Court Employment Diversity

There is no universal fool-proof methodology or magic formula for determining immediate personnel needs and forecasting future ones. In some jurisdictions, especially small ones, it may be possible to use a very simple formula using cases filed, cases pending, or cases closed per employee to establish personnel needs. Such a formula may be sufficient for limited management purposes and may even be acceptable to the funding authority.

Larger trial courts and state systems should take into account the diversity of court employment. Whether this can be done successfully and with minimal difficulty will depend on the budgeting, accounting, and management information systems. Following is an example of one way in which trial court employees may be categorized according to tasks performed and their purposes. The authors do not opt for this approach, which is generally similar to that used for budget purposes in Colorado; rather, it is set forth here to illustrate different kinds of trial court employee activity.[19]

In this example, trial court personnel are divided into several broad categories related to functions that are required in all trial courts:
1) administration; 2) case disposition; 3) direct

judicial support; 4) indirect judicial support; 5) jury administration; 6) law library mainenance; and 7) ancillary, auxiliary, and miscellaneous services and functions. A number of positions and functions are included in each of these categories.

1) <u>Administration</u>. This category includes personnel involved in the over-all administration of the court, including budget and fiscal management, personnel administration, facility maintenance, purchasing, etc. Typically, the court administrator, his secretary, and any other assistants would fall into this category. In a small court, probably only a portion of the time of one or two employees could be ascribed to these functions.

2) <u>Case Disposition</u>. This category includes masters, referees, and hearing officers--personnel other than judges who hear and dispose of cases. These parajudges usually hear certain kinds of juvenile matters, non-contested domestic relations cases and temporary orders, minor civil and traffic cases, or small claims, depending on the court and its jurisdiction. Parajudges are paid less than judges, require only a small hearing room rather than a courtroom, and the assistance, usually, of only one employee, who serves as secretary, clerk, and operator of the electronic equipment used to record the proceedings.

3) <u>Direct Judicial Support</u>. Supporting staff for judges and parajudges are in this category, including court reporters, division or courtroom clerks, private secretaries, bailiffs, law clerks, and any other personnel whose duties are generally confined to serving one judge or parajudge. In courts of limited jurisdiction, the record is usually made by electronic recording equipment, with a machine monitor rather than a reporter. There may also be a separate central transcribing pool. Electronic equipment use is increasing in courts of general jurisdiction, especially for relatively uncomplex and minor cases.

Law clerks are usually found only in the larger trial courts of general jurisdiction. In some places, this function is combined with that of bailiff, and second or third year law students are employed. In some jurisdictions, bailiffs are employees of the sheriff's office or another law enforcement agency, as in New Jersey. Consequently, the court has no control over their recruitment, compensation, or work assignments.

4) <u>Indirect Judicial Support</u>. The clerk of court and his or her staff make up the major portion

of this category. These employees are responsible for all case files and records; issuance of process; collection and disbursement of fines, fees, and court registry funds; recording of judgments; issuing copies of documents; etc. In courts with probate jurisdiction, functions may include estate auditing and examination. Employees involved in the calendaring process also fall in this category.

In rural areas, it is not unusual for the clerk's office staff to serve as court room clerks as required by judges who travel around the district or circuit accompanied by a reporter but not a clerk. This divided assignment places these employees partially in the direct judicial support category.

5) <u>Jury Administration</u>. The jury commissioner and any assistance are in this category. The number of employees will depend on the size of the court, the number of jurors summoned, and the extent to which the process is automated. Management of the jury lounge or assembly area is also a responsibility under this category, along with summoning and assigning jurors, and paying them.

In some jurisdictions, especially in smaller courts, the jury commissioner may also be the clerk of court or an employee in the clerk's office so designated. It is also possible that the jury commissioner could be comeone other than a direct court employee and who is selected by the county governing body.

6) <u>Law Library Maintenance</u>. The size of trial court libraries usually depends on the size of the court and the practicing bar and the proximity to state or university law libraries. The law librarian may be a professional, with a degree in library science in a large trial court library and have one or two assistants. Paraprofessional or clerical employees (some on a part-time basis) usually provide minimal staff services in smaller law libraries. Courts of limited or special jurisdiction are not likely to have libraries and may share in the use of the one in the court of general jurisdiction.

7) <u>Ancillary, Auxiliary, and Miscellaneous Services and Functions</u>. This group includes all court personnel and activities that cannot be otherwise categorized.

a) Many courts employ marriage counselors who provide this service upon order of the court in domestic relations matters. These counselors are professionally trained, usually with graduate degrees in social work, and are assisted by secretarial/clerical personnel.

b) It is not unusual for courts, especially those exercising juvenile jurisdiction, to have court-employed psychologists and psychiatric social workers to conduct evaluations and even take part in court-ordered treatment programs. Part-time psychiatric services are usually purchased under contract. Secretarial and clerical support is required for professional staff providing these services.

c) Bail bonding should be recognized as a distinct activity to the extent that employees are assigned exclusively to this function or a special night and weekend staff is required. In most medium-sized and small courts, employees handling bail bonding may do so as part of their regular clerical activities, but in large courts, a separate unit may be required, although the employee's qualifications and skills are comparable to those of clerk's office personnel.

In many jurisdictions, the personal recognizance release program is also a judicial responsibility rather than that of the district attorney or probation department (assuming the latter is part of the executive branch rather than under the judiciary). This activity involves investigations and interviews to provide reports and recommendations to the court. Personnel engaged in this activity may have the same professional training and qualifications as probation officers, or they may be paraprofessionals. In either case, clerical support is required.

d) Probation services in some jurisdictions are under the judicial branch, e.g., Colorado, Connecticut, Hawaii, and Kansas. In some states, (New Mexico, for example) the judiciary has the responsibility for probation and related services for juveniles, while adult probation services are provided by the executive branch. Sometimes, probation services for misdemeanants are a judicial responsibility, while similar services for felons are under the executive branch. One other variation is worth noting: In some jurisdictions, where probation services are not in the judicial branch, the courts, nontheless, have staffs of investigators to conduct pre-sentence investigations and may even have counselors to supervise offenders released under deferred sentence or deferred prosecution programs.

e) Juvenile detention facilities in several jurisdictions are the responsibility of the court exercising juvenile jurisdiction, whether it is a separate court or a division of the trial court of general jurisdiction. This responsibility extends judicial system personnel requirements even further to encompass cooks, maintenance staff, unit counselors, nurses, and perhaps, teachers.

Deciding on and Applying Measures

Identify Available Data. Identifying already available pertinent information is the first step in deciding which methodology or formulae to use to determine personnel needs. This information falls in two major categories: basic and derived. Examples of basic data are: 1) number of cases filed, pending, and closed (preferably by court and type of case); 2) number of judges and parajudges (preferably by court and assignment; and 3) number of employees (preferably by court and position classification or work assignment).

Examples of derived data are: 1) number of employees per judge (preferably by court and position classification or assignment); 2) number of cases per employee (preferably by type of case and employee classification or work assignment); and 3) medians and means for 1) and 2) (preferably by court groupings).

In deriving employee-caseload ratios, cases filed, pending, or closed may be used. In fact, all three and combinations thereof may be tried to determine which is most pertinent. Court groupings should reflect size (number of judges and employees), volume (caseload and caseflow), and degree of mechanization.

Besides identifying already available information, it is necessary to ascertain how long comparable data have been collected; several years' data provide a much better base than one or two years. Assuming that there has been no change in court organization or jurisdiction, several years' data should show significant trends and be an aid in determining the most appropriate unit of measure.

Once available information is identified, the next step is to decide what else is needed and how difficult it will be to collect it, update it, and back date it. If very little pertinent and timely information is available or easily updated, design of an expanded information system is indicated. This may be necessary, even if a very simple formula is to be used, such as total cases filed per employee. Information system expansion should take into account other data requirements besides personnel needs determination.

Formulae Alternatives. Assuming that adequate data are available or can be obtained, without undue difficulty or cost, there are several formulae alternatives that may be chosen to determine personnel needs. In deciding which to use, consideration should be given to the factors listed and discussed on pages 185 and 188. Attention should also be paid to court employees' work assignment diversity. Several formulae might be tried, and, if they all produce about the same result, the one selected should be the easiest to understand, verify, and update. This selection assumes acceptance by the funding body.

In addition to total cases filed per employee, cases terminated or pending might be used. Cases terminated plus cases pending may provide a more accurate measure of work performed by clerk's office personnel in the direct support category. Jury days served is an appropriate measure to determine jury administration personnel needs.

There are several possible problems in using multiple measures.

1) The formulae may be too complicated to apply or understand, especially if several variations are used to differentiate between urban and rural courts, multi-county and single-county districts, or high and low volume courts.

2) It is difficult to develop units of measure for some court support activities, such as administration. Consequently, employees in this category may have to be subjectively divided into measureable activities, thereby affecting the formulae ratios.

3) In smaller courts, employees may be assigned two or more measurable activities. Accurate apportionment among tasks is not possible without a sophisticated accounting and information system. Such a system may not be worth the time and expense required, unless it is used for purposes besides employee needs projection.

There is problem, as well, in using existing employee-productivity ratios or averages. Such use implies that existing staffing patterns are sufficient to do the job and that the formula or formulae developed are designed to meet anticipated workload increases and decreases at the same level of results. This is a difficult assumption to justify without at least three years of historical data. It also assumes that present procedures, forms, records, etc., provide maximum productivity and are uniform throughout the court or judicial system.

Even with adequate historical information, it may still be desirable to conduct some field studies--especially if some courts are automated to a considerable extent and others are not.

What is suggested here is that under the best conditions: adequate and timely information, generally efficient operation of court support activities, and uniform records, forms, and procedures, a generally accurate system of forecasting personnel needs can be developed and updated. Even if all these conditions are not present, a rudimentary system can be established which will provide general measures of need. The creation of even a simple system will provide a basis for greater sophistication and refinement at a later date.

<u>Weighted Caseloads</u>. Weighted caseloads have been used in some jurisdictions to predict personnel needs with greater accuracy. This involves an extensive field study and time measurements of activities in different size courts. A study of this kind was conducted by outside consultants for the clerks' offices in the reorganized Kentucky court system.[18]

Figure 11.1 shows the average minutes per case by clerk's office personnel according to case type, with separate calculations made for the largest circuit courts.[19]

The minutes for each type of case were multiplied by the number of filings in that category and divided by the amount of available clerk's minutes per year to determine the number of clerks needed. The amount of clerk minutes per year was determined as follows:

Days Available Per Year

Total Days Per Year		365
less weekends	104 leaving	261
less holidays	12 leaving	249
less vacation	11 leaving	234
less sick leave, workshops, institutes and travel	8, leaving	226
Total workday		7.5
less breaks and personal time (15 percent of work time)		.98
TOTAL		6.52 hours/day

FIGURE 11.1

(Average Minutes Per Filing[a])

District Court

Case Type	Non-Judicial
Felony Preliminary	177
Misdemeanor/City Ordinance	69
Serious Traffic	97
Other Non-Parking Traffic	30
Parking	8
Probate	227
Juvenile	146
Civil	75

Circuit Court

	Non-Judicial	
Case Type	Jefferson Kenton Fayette	Other Counties
Criminal	979	1,855
Domestic Relations	379	244
Other Civil	559	781
Lower Court Appeals	88	135

a. Filings for the following case types are based upon the number of persons accused: Criminal, felony, preliminary, misdemeanor/city ordinance, serious traffic, and other non-parking traffic.

Clerk-Year Calculation

6.52 hours x 226 days x 60 minutes = 88,440 minutes per year[20]

Case weighting systems are useful, but require updating whenever procedural or form changes are made, technological change takes place, or new laws are passed affecting court support activities. It is also necessary to make certain that all measureable activities are included and properly grouped.
If a case weighting system is used, a more

simplified formula as explained previously, might be applied as a parallel system. If the results are similar, it might be wiser to use the less complicated system, because it is easier to understand and update. It is unfortunate that jurisdictions that develop case weighting formulae usually do not make the parallel test suggested here to see if the case weighting system is worth the effort and expense.

An example of another approach to determining needs is set forth in Appendix F. It combines costs and caseload data and was developed by the Colorado Judicial System.

Summary

There are several ways to determine court personnel needs. There is no perfect method, and all have some shortcomings. Despite the difficulties and imperfections, ratios and formulae provide a basis for planning and budgeting for needs, and funding bodies usually require documentation for budget requests. Whatever formulae are used, accurate caseload projection is necessary to provide validity for the projected personnel needs.

BUDGETING FOR PERSONNEL NEEDS: AN EXAMPLE

Once a method of projecting personnel needs is adopted, it is necessary to translate these needs into number of employees (FTE's) and the amount required to fund them.

Position Costs

New position requests are made routinely once a year to the funding body. In developing the cost of each new position requested, several different factors must be taken into consideration.

It is a rather simple matter to state that an administrative assistant's salary is $10,000 per year; however, the associated costs bring the total to a level which is significantly higher than the base salary.

Most jurisdictions have either a retirement plan or social security, or a combination of the two. In addition there are frequently health insurance plans and life insurance plans and other benefits associated.[21] In addition, a new position must have a desk or work station available, and an adjustment should be made to cover any travel that the new employee will be making, or any Xerox paper and other supplies which will be needed.

The $10,000 salary cited above is just the base, as can be seen below:

Base Salary	$10,000	
Retirement Contribution 10.5%	1,050	
Health Ins. at $50/month	600	
Life Ins. at $5/month	60	
Personnel Total	$11,710	$11,710
Desk	$ 375	
File Cabinet	150	
Chair	100	
Bookcase	150	
Equipment Total	$ 775	775
Travel and subsistence		500
Supplies and operating		250
	TOTAL	$13,235

All but the $775 in capital outlay will be ongoing costs associated with the position. Consequently, it can be seen that there is considerably more to budgeting personnel than salary alone.

Future Year Costs. In addition to the basic salary and costs for a new position, there are other associated costs which will be added over the years. The example above shows a basic $12,460 cost (plus $775 for equipment) for the position during the first year. If there is the usual allowance for 5 percent merit increase for satisfactory or better performance by the employee after one year of service, this will affect second year costs. If in addition, state law allows for a cost of living increase once per year to help employees' salaries keep up with inflation, this will also affect costs.

The total second year cost of the position (assuming satisfactory performance by the employee and a 5.9 percent cost of living adjustment) would be:

Base Salary	$10,000
5 percent merit increase	500
5.9 percent cost of living	618

Retirement on base salary
and adjustments at 10.5
percent $ 1,167
Health Ins. at $50/month   600
Life Ins. at $5/month   60

Personnel Total $12,945 $12,945

Travel and subsistence   500
Supplies and operating   250

                         TOTAL $13,695

    The personnel cost has risen 10.6 percent due to built-in system benefits. This is a direct payroll cost and must be taken into consideration when building the budget. Please note that the retirement contribution is not calculated until all costs have been built into the base salary.

    It is not unlikely that an occupant of an entry level position will request that his position be reclassified. If such a request is approved (from Administrative Assistant I to Administrative Assistant II) it would result in a 10 percent increase. The third year's cost includes this assumption as well as a 4.75 percent adjustment for cost of living and a 5 percent merit increase:

2nd year base cost $11,118
Reclassification   1,112
5 percent merit increase   612
4.75 percent cost of
  living   610
Retirement on base salary
and adjustments at 10.5
percent   1,412
Health Ins. at $50/month   600
Life Ins. at $5/month   60

Personnel Total $15,524 $15,524

Travel and subsistence   500
Supplies and operating   250

                         TOTAL $16,274

    The third year costs of the position are 20 percent greater than the second year cost and 32.6 percent greater than the first year cost.

    Personnel costs such as those shown in the example are not at all unusual and are directly associated with the concept of hiring and retaining the most competent employees possible. This discussion shows the need for taking long-range impact into account in budgeting for personnel needs. It is especially important to do this for public bodies as labor intensive as courts, where approximately 85 percent of the costs are personnel related.

NOTES

1. See Appendix A for a bibliography on managing personnel in public agencies.
2. Examples are Colorado, Kansas, and South Dakota.
3. Winston W. Crouch, editor, Local Government Personnel Administration (Chicago: International City Management Association, 1976) p. 30.
4. Colorado Supreme Court, Colorado Judicial System Personnel Rules (Denver, Colorado: Supreme Court, 1975, as amended) rule 2.
5. Ibid., rule 5.
6. Ibid., rules 6, 13 and 14.
7. Ibid., rule 17.
8. Ibid., rule 21(a).
9. Ibid., rule 19.
10. Maine Supreme Judicial Court, Maine Court System Personnel Policy and Procedures Manual (Portland, Maine: Supreme Judicial Court, 1977, as amended), rules 2.1 and 2.2.
11. Ibid.
12. Alaska Court System Personnel Rules (Anchorage, Alaska: 1974, revised 1977), rule 1.03.
13. Ibid., rule 1.04.
14. As an example, see model legislation proposed by Advisory Commission on Intergovernmental Relations, Court Reform, (Washington, D.C.: Advisory Commission on Intergovernmental Relations, 1971) Title XX p. 20.
15. See Chapter 1, p. 4 for a discussion of the relationship of personnel administration and these activities.
16. Public Administration Service, A Report on Position Classification and Pay Plan, Colorado State Judicial Department (Public Administration Service: Chicago, Ill., 1973), Class 2201.
17. Institute for Advanced Studies in Justice, Criminal Courts Technical Assistance Project, Implementation of State Funding for Court and Probation Personnel by the Kansas Supreme Court (Washington, D.C.: The American University Law School, 1978) Appendix A.

18. Ibid.
19. Arthur Young & Co., *Guidelines: Number of 1978 Non-Judicial Personnel, Circuit and District Courts,* (Frankfurt, Kentucky: Arthur Young & Co., 1976).
20. Ibid.
21. This discussion does not cover cost determination of sick, annual, and holiday leave, but it should be remembered that these are a factor.

12. Collective Bargaining

INTRODUCTION

Taft-Hartley Act

Collective bargaining in the United States derives its definition from the Taft-Hartley Act, Section 8(d):[1]

> For the purpose of this section, to bargain collectively is the performance of the mutual obligation of the employer and the representative of the employees to meet at reasonable times and confer in good faith with respect to wages, hours, and other terms and conditions of employment, or the negotiation of an agreement, or any question arising thereunder, and the execution of a written contract incorporating any agreement reached if requested by either party, but such obligation does not compel either party to agree to a proposal or require the making of a concession.[2]

Taft-Hartley established five requirements:

1) designation of management and the exclusive representatives of the employees, with mutual legal obligations;

2) meeting and conferring in good faith;

3) bargaining on wages, hours, terms, and conditions of employment;

4) agreement to be embodied in a written contract; and

5) bilateral administration, interpretation, and enforcement of the agreement.[3]

Up until the Taft-Hartley Act (1947), collective bargaining occurred largely in the private sector. In an estimated 100 or more cities in the United States, municipal officials conducted negotiations with unions and their employees.[4] By 1965, 44.6 percent of municipalities with populations of more than 10,000 reported some employees belonging to national unions or associations.[5]

Public Employee Collective Bargaining

Collective bargaining experience in the executive branch has been varied. Six states have the limited right to strike: Alaska, Hawaii, Montana, Oregon, Pennsylvania, and Vermont (local employees only); fifteen states have authorized a union shop or agency shop, by law in Hawaii, Minnesota, Rhode Island (state employees), while eleven states make this negotiable: Alaska, California (teachers only), Kentucky (firefighters only), Maine (university employees only), Massachusetts, Michigan, Montana, Oregon, Vermont (local employees only), Washington, and Wisconsin. Pennsylvania provides for maintenance of membership.[6]

Twenty-four states have comprehensive bargaining laws for public employees, both state and local: Alaska, California, Connecticut, Delaware, Florida, Hawaii, Iowa, Kansas, Maine, Massachusetts, Minnesota, Montana, Nebraska, New Hampshire, New Jersey, New York, North Dakota, Oregon, Pennsylvania, Rhode Island, South Dakota, Vermont, Washington, and Wisconsin.[7]

Federal Employees. Although unionization of federal employees had been permitted for many years, the federal government had no stated policy respecting dealings with unions until Executive Order No. 10988, January 17, 1962, which directed federal agencies (except the FBI and CIA) to recognize and enter into agreements with employee organizations, under specified conditions. The pace of unionization has slowed down in private employment, whereas it has picked up greatly in governmental service. It is estimated that during the period 1947-1967, the number of unionized government employees has doubled, while private sector unionization remained stable or declined.[8]

For some time it was believed that were the government to enter into a collective bargaining agreement with an employee organization, it would yield its sovereignty.[9] Since legislative bodies determined terms of employment, it was argued to be illegal if such authority was delegated to an executive agency which in turn signed labor contracts. This line of reasoning appears later in the Michigan court decisions affecting collective bargaining between employees and the courts. Certain judges, for example, believed that binding arbitration, were it to come about, would result in the government binding itself to decisions of private parties (the arbitrators).[10] A New York court said in 1943:

> To tolerate or recognize any combination of Civil Service employees of the government as a labor organization or union is not only incompatible with the spirit of democracy, but inconsistent with every principle upon which our Government is founded. Nothing is more dangerous to public welfare than to admit that hired servants of the state can dictate to the Government the hours, the wages, and conditions under which they will carry on essential services vital for the welfare, safety, and security of the citizen. To admit as true that Government employees have power to halt or check the functions of Government, unless their demands are satisfied, is to transfer to them all legislative, executive, and judicial power. Nothing would be more ridiculous.[11]

Collective Bargaining in the Judicial Branch. Ridiculous or not, the courts found themselves entering into labor contracts, for example, in Michigan in 1971.[12] It has generally been agreed in Michigan that courts are employers and must be represented separately at the bargaining table, but, in addition, that the funding body, normally the county commissioners, must also be represented. The Michigan Public Employees Relation Act (PERA)[13] requires a public employer, now including the courts, to bargain with the representatives of its employees with respect to wages, hours, and other terms and conditions of employment.

Other states have joined Michigan in full or

partial collective bargaining as follows: California, Connecticut, Hawaii, Massachusetts, Minnesota, Missouri, New Jersey, New Mexico, New York, Oregon, Pennsylvania, Rhode Island, Washington, and Wisconsin. Closer inspection of these states reveals that only in Connecticut, Hawaii, Massachusetts, Michigan, New Jersey, New York, Pennsylvania, and Washington is there any specific written official reference to court employed personnel as opposed to executive branch personnel working in the courts, primarily probation officers and the clerk's office. The remainder have limited the courts' involvement with negotiation to that of court reporters (New Mexico and Rhode Island) or have yielded to the executive branch, i.e., the counties, to negotiate on their behalf (California, Minnesota, Oregon, and Wisconsin).

Not every state has accepted collective bargaining in good faith for the courts. Pennsylvania recently decided against the trial courts following multiple litigation and empassioned briefs. In a group of companion cases[14] the Supreme Court upheld the constitutionality of applying the state's Public Employee Relations Act (Act 195)[15] to the judiciary (for nonjudicial employees); designated the county (Pennsylvania courts are largely funded by the counties) as the "managerial representatives" and, in effect, determined that the court and the county are joint public employers. <u>Ellenbogen</u> sums up the court's holding:

> With respect to representation proceedings before the Pennsylvania Labor Relations Board or collective bargaining negotiations involving any or all employees paid from the county treasury, the board of county commissioners shall have the sole power and responsibility to represent judges of the court of common pleas, the county and all elected or appointed county officers having any employment powers over the affected employees. The exercise of such responsibilities by the county commissioners shall in no way affect the hiring, discharging and supervising rights and obligations with respect to such employees as may be vested in the judges or other county officers.[16]

Thus, the judges had maintained their management rights but had to negotiate regarding monetary matters through the county. The judges had argued eloquently against having to negotiate at all.

The initial issue raised in Pennsylvania was whether the court was the sole employer of judicial employees (which in Pennsylvania means a locally funded court), whether the local government body was the sole employer, or whether each was a co-employer. The judges argued that if they were not the sole employer, the Pennsylvania Public Employees Act (Act 195) was unconstitutional.[17] The Pennsylvania Supreme Court resolved the employer question similar to the way it was resolved in Michigan, Washington, and New Jersey. Each of these states funds its trial courts locally. Each recognizes a dual interest: the court's need to hire, fire, administer, and discipline its employees; and the funding body's obligation to satisfy the terms of contract negotiations as to wages, hours, terms, and conditions of employment.

Certain states have directed the employer question toward the state level, essentially those court systems which are unified and which have unitary budgeting.[18] One state, Hawaii, permits the executive branch (the Governor through his chief labor negotiator) to bargain on behalf of judicial employers.[19] Massachusetts has designated the chief justice as the employer of judicial employees, leaving open the question of the funding body's role, in this case the state legislature. New York is similarly situated. Should the state legislature balk at funding negotiated agreements, a dilemma would ensue. There is no particular reason to believe that this would occur though collective bargaining in New York, particularly New York City, is no sport for the short winded.[20]

ISSUES

Who is the Employer?

As discussed earlier, the court may be the sole employer of judicial employees, as it is by statute in Massachusetts; the executive branch may be the sole employer of employees working in the courts, as it is in California, Minnesota, Oregon, and Wisconsin;[21] or, the court and the executive branch may be co-employers, the prime examples of which are Michigan, New Jersey, Pennsylvania and Washington. In each case raising the question of whether or not the court was the sole employer, the judges have lost.[22] Underlying the challenge, in the first place, was frequently, if not always, the desire on the part of the court to assert its independence as an employer and, therefore, its exclusion from a state public employee relations act, were one to exist.

The court did not believe that the executive branch typically denoted as the employer in PERA's as the state, county, or any political subdivision of the state should or could, constitutionally, interfere with the administration of judicial employees. State supreme courts, when called upon to resolve this issue[23] acknowledged a dual role: the court would hire, fire, discipline, and administer; the funding body would negotiate with respect to wages, hours, terms and conditions of employment. Noticeably, this decision has only occurred in states having local funding of the courts (Michigan, New Jersey and Washington). In New York, the decision was made prior to unitary budgeting.

Management Rights

This and other issues are somewhat in their infancy among court-union contracts. Further challenges can be expected. It is through the management rights clause that the courts have been allocated their share of the employer's rights: the authority to hire, fire, discipline, and administer. Management rights clauses have followed the language typically found in other public sector contracts.

> The employer reserves and retains, solely and exclusively, all management rights, powers, and authority, including the right of management to manage, control, and direct its work forces and operations except those as may be modified under this agreement.[24]

If court contracts follow the pattern of other public sector contracts future negotiations may make reference to work standards, allocations and scheduling as has occurred in teaching, fire, and police. Probation caseloads, court reporter transcripts, and cases filed might inevitably appear as topics for employee-employer negotiation. Management has typically viewed such provisions as invasions of management rights.[25] Connecticut left very little to the imagination in its quite lengthy management rights clause:

Such rights include but are not limited to establishing standards of productivity and performance of its employees, including establishing qualifications for ability to perform work in classes and/or ratings; determining its budget, its mission, and the methods, means, and personnel necessary to fulfill that mission, including the contracting out, or the discontinuation of services, positions, or programs in whole or in part; the determination of the content of job classifications; the appointment, promotion, assignment, direction and transfer of personnel; the suspension, demotion, discharge or any other disciplinary action against its employees; the relief from duty of its employees because of lack of work or other legitimate reasons as stated in Article XV; to determine the hours, days when, and locations where the courts will be in operation; to enforce existing rules and regulations for the governance of the Department and to add to, eliminate, or modify such rules or regulations as it deems appropriate..."[26]

Civil Service

Both state and local governments have maintained merit or civil service systems as parallels with collective bargaining systems. The advent of contract negotiations has shifted the role of the merit system to that of recruitment, examining, and employee appeals. Fears that the resolution of grievances would be affected by two opportunities for review do not appear to have materialized.[27] Either contract language prohibits such tactics or practice brought about the same result. Presumably employees would opt for the contract grievance procedure. If unsuccessful, it is unlikely that a civil service appeal would promise to yield a more favorable result (i.e., to be more "pro-employee").

The State of Hawaii has engaged in collective bargaining since 1968.[28] On July 1, 1977, the legislature added several sections[29] essentially establishing a merit system for the judicial branch apart from that of the executive branch. Thus, though the governor of Hawaii acts as "employer for the judicial as well as the executive branch" for purposes of collective bargaining[30] the chief justice and administrative director of the courts may now administer their own personnel system.[31] This change recognizes the need for the courts effectively to carry out their management rights.

STRIKES

The debate regarding strikes bought by public employees rests, for the moment, on a legal base. In the absence of specific legislative authority permitting strikes by public employees the courts have held there is no right to strike.[32] That is not to say that public employees don't strike with or without legislative authority.[33] The issue has been somewhat academic concerning unionized court employees, since, until recently, no example presented itself.

Judges, of course, have warned of the untenable situation which might exist were a strike to occur. Contract language, accordingly, tends to preclude strikes and lockouts and provides for contract disputes to be resolved through fact finding, mediation, and arbitration.

Wayne County Strike

The first challenge of the status quo occurred in Wayne County, Michigan, in the Third Judicial Circuit Court. On February 7, 1979, approximately 4,000 employees in Wayne County (Detroit area) went out on strike affecting numerous county functions and including court operations.[34]

The Wayne County strike lasted five days, two days of which were Saturday and Sunday. The settlement granted county workers a 4 percent raise retroactive to October 1, 1978; a 2 percent increase on July 1, 1979; and a 3 percent raise on December 1, 1979. A 50 percent cost of living increase would be added on January 1, 1980.

Court Employee Union Coverage. Most Third Judicial Circuit Court employees were covered by union agreements. Only management and confidential employees were excluded. Primary groups of employees include clerical employees, court reporters, probation officers, and friend of the court. As early as November, 1978, a strike by county employees became imminent. This prompted the chief judge of the court to warn his judges that it might be their responsibility to maintain a record of courtroom activities. Though it was expected that certain employees would participate in the strike, the court prepared to assign its confidential employees, certain supervisors, and friend of the court (represented by a separate bargaining unit) to court activities.

Contingency Plan. The court administrator proposed a contingency plan which the court adopted. The contingency plan allowed for the following assignments:
1) All judicial secretaries, research law clerks, supervisors and marriage counselors would be assigned to criminal courtrooms, the Assignment Clerk's Office and other departments as needed.
2) Court reporters would be expected to remain on the job since their contract did not expire until July 1, 1979 (with a separate bargaining unit).
3) Deputy Sheriffs would be expected to remain on the job (separate contract).
4) Friend of the Court would be expected to remain on the job (separate contract).[35]

Employees of the Third Judicial Circuit were notified by memorandum from the chief judge of the prohibition against strikes embodied in Act 379 of the Public Acts of 1965 and that disciplinary action might be forthcoming.[36] In addition, the chief judge notified attorneys that, in the event of a strike, all matters except emergency matters and criminal matters would be cancelled.[37]

The Wayne County strike did not seriously hamper courtroom activities primarily due to the implementation of the contingency plan and the strike's short duration. Had the strike continued, it is likely that support functions such as probation and Friend of the Court would have been affected. It may be surmised that ultimately courtroom activities would be curtailed.

The Wayne County situation need not signal the advent of strikes by court employees nor should it induce complacency. In fact, this strike between Wayne County and Council 25 of the American Federation of State, County and Municipal Employees was the first in county history. Detroit and Wayne County, like other major metropolitan centers, are experiencing declining tax bases, rising costs, demands for lower taxes, calls for reduction in government personnel, and political opportunism.

While it is popular to espouse reduced government spending, the public employee is caught in an inflationary economy, as is the employer. In a state such as Michigan public employees watch contract awards in the private sector carefully. City and county officials look longingly at the state to bail out services, particularly those mandated by the state constitution or statute. The courts, naturally, are state mandated. Whether state funding will be applied to the courts in Michigan (as it has totally or to a significant extent in twenty-two states) remains to be seen. The evidence, to date, does not suggest that strike or no strike, employees and judges are willing to drive a wedge between themselves.[38]

COLLECTIVE BARGAINING EXPERIENCE AND DEVELOPMENTS

Overview

In some fifteen states, court employees have entered into collective bargaining agreements. In certain states, agreements are negotiated under the authority of a Public Employment Relations Act (PERA): Connecticut, Hawaii, Michigan, Minnesota, Missouri, New York, Oregon, Pennsylvania, Rhode Island and Wisconsin. New Jersey and Washington negotiate under authority of the court and PERA.[40] California negotiates with its executive branch employees through municipal and county ordinances; Massachusetts authorizes collective bargaining with court employees by statute;[41] New Mexico negotiates under authority of the court.

Individual States

The heaviest court involvement in collective bargaining occurs in Hawaii, Michigan, New Jersey, and New York.

Hawaii. Hawaii has a unified court system with a unitary budget. Though the court is the employer, the negotiator for collective bargaining purposes is the executive branch. The courts formerly were part of the executive branch merit system, but a separate judicial branch personnel system went into effect on July 1, 1977.

The Hawaii PERA grants state employees the right to form and join employee organizations, to bargain collectively on wages, hours, and other terms and conditions of employment. Management rights are established to insure that the employer may direct, hire, assign, discipline, transfer, and lay off employees; to determine employee qualifications; and the methods to conduct agency operations.

Court employees are represented by five different collective bargaining units as follows: Unit 1: nonsupervisory blue collar workers; Unit 3: nonsupervisory white collar workers; Unit 4: supervisory white collar workers; Unit 10: nonprofessional hospital and institutional workers; and Unit 13: professional and scientific workers.[42]

Collective bargaining agreements are quite comprehensive. The agreement between the state of Hawaii[43] and United Public Workers, Local 646, American Federation of State, County, and Municipal Employees, AFL-CIO,[44] includes all matters relating to wages, hours, and terms and conditions of employment. A no-strike or lockout provision is included.[45] In addition, disciplinary actions require notice to the union[46] which must follow a specific step by step grievance procedure.[47] Fringe benefits are included.[48]

Michigan. In 1977, the Michigan court administrator's office reported that, in the following courts at least, some of the employees were represented by a collective bargaining agent:[49]

Circuit Court (Court of General Jurisdiction)	22 of 48 = 45 percent
Probate Court	31 of 79 = 39 percent
District Court (Court of Limited Jurisdiction)	34 of 85 = 40 percent

Provisions of Michigan contracts include cost of living plans, vacation policies, holiday policies, sick leave policies, health insurance, life insurance, retirement, longevity, and, of course, classification, wages, and hours. A provision is made for grievance arbitration, mediation, and fact-finding by the governor.

The Wayne County circuit court (Detroit) is perhaps the prime example of Michigan developments in judicial employee collective bargaining. The Court has contracts with two locals of AFSCME (300 clerical and fifty probation officers); the Wayne County Bar Association (thirty-five attorneys, referees, and friends of court); a local Supervisors'

Association (twenty-five first-line supervisors and marriage counselors); and, a special section of the clerical local of AFSCME for thirty-six court reporters. Contract periods vary from one to three years.

Bargaining in Michigan is established on the principle of "good faith bargaining" rather than "meet and confer." This principle mades the employer liable for unfair labor practices. The primary negotiator for the courts is the county labor relations negotiator. The courts have a representative present at these negotiations. Contracts affecting the courts are ratified by the court administrative committee.

Wayne County Circuit Court has an agency shop agreement with its primary bargaining units.[50] A bargaining agent is exclusive for that unit and is, after proper election, certified by the Michigan Employment Relations Commission (MERC). A bargaining unit consists of employees located in similar job classifications, e.g., clerical employees, court reporters, probation officers, etc. A supervisor of any of these groups would belong to a separate bargaining unit.

Wayne County has agreed to voluntary arbitration on grievances and contract violations. Contract negotiations, were they to break down, would be subject to fact-finding and mediation. The board of arbitration consists of one member representing the court, one member representing the union, and a third member, mutually selected by the two, acts as chairperson. Should the two fail to agree on a third member, the grieving party requests the American Arbitration Association to appoint a third member.[51]

New Jersey. The New Jersey courts have collective bargaining only in probation. Of the twenty-one counties, twenty have agreements with one of the following bargaining agents: Probation Officers' Association, AFSCME, Teamsters, PPO Association and the Supervisors' Union.

Probation officer agreements include such items as: supper allowance, mileage rate, insurance reimbursement, cash educational award (for M.A. and Ph.D), promotional increase, tuition reimbursement, longevity, grievance procedures, holidays, vacation, health and welfare benefits, management rights statement, residency provisions, seniority provisions, compensatory time, sick leave, and leaves of absence.

New Jersey probation officers, unlike those in

New York, serve in the judicial branch. Consequently, union agreements are with the judges. Article 1, Sec. A, of the Morris County Probation Officers' Agreement (1976) is instructive:

> The judges recognize the Union (New Jersey Council 52 and its affiliated Local 2654, Morris County Probation Officers, American Federal of State, County, and Municipal Employees, AFL-CIO) as the sole and exclusive bargaining agent for the purpose of establishing salaries, wages, and other conditions of employment as falls within their purview and the administration of grievances arising therewith...

The agreement excluded probation officers acting as supervisors, the definition for which is included in the Public Employment Relations Act. The Management Rights section is defined in Art. 2, Sec. A. It primarily asserts that "The Court hereby reserves and retains unto itself, as employer, all the powers, rights, authority, duties and responsibilities conferred upon or vested in it by law prior to the signing of this agreement..." In New Jersey most nonjudicial court employees are funded by the county.

Despite collective bargaining for probation officers in the trial courts, the New Jersey Supreme Court does not favor the practice:

> Can the control of probation officers and of the whole statewide system of probation, seemingly entrusted to the Judiciary by the terms of the Constitution be in any way diluted or modified by legislation [The Employer-Employee Relations Act]... We think it clear that it cannot.[52]

As noted earlier, the Passaic dissent adknowledges collective bargaining. The dissent states further:

> I am convinced...that the Judiciary as a state employer must tolerate such incidental inconvenience in administration as attends affording Judiciary employees their rights under the labor relations act...[53]

New York. New York State has 10,000 nonjudicial court employees under collective bargaining agreements, 5,000 of whom are in New York City. In New York City alone, eleven unions represent court reporters, law assistants, librarians, administrators, identification officers, court assistants, court clerks, and others, amounting to a total of fifty-one job classifications.

Negotiations in New York City affect employees of the following agencies: mayor's office, health and hospital corporation (with exceptions), administration board of the judicial conference, off-track betting corporation, New York City housing authority (with limitations), and several others, including the district attorneys. Each classification covered has one union as the sole bargaining representative. A typical contract includes provisions for working hours, shift differential and holiday premium, overtime, annual leave, sick leave, leave of absence, holidays, compensatory time, terminal leave pay, meal allowances, health insurance, car allowances, personnel and pay practices, personal security, employee evaluation, career development, training trust fund, union rights, dues check-off, welfare funds (health and security), adjustment of disputes, and no-strike clause.

New York's PERA, the so-called Taylor Law, was submitted to that state's high court to determine whether "provisions of the Act prohibiting strikes by public employees is applicable to nonjudicial employees of the unified system."[54] The court held that the Taylor Act apparently applied, issuing a mild warning that inherent powers might become more than an academic issue. The court said:

> The subjection of the Board [Administrative Board of the Judicial Conference which administers the state court system] to certain legislative action, such as the Taylor Law, does not derogate its basic administrative control over the court system, but rather, only requires the Board to be subject to certain reasonable limitations in the exercise of this power. It may be that some future legislative action would so deeply cut at the basic fibre of administrative power as to be violative of Article VI, Sec. 28, of the Constitution. The application of the Taylor Law, however, is not such a case.[55]

SUMMARY

Collective bargaining agreements covering court employees are found in several states where private and public sector bargaining has been well established. Connecticut, Hawaii, Massachusetts, Michigan, Minnesota, New Jersey, New York, Oregon, Pennsylvania, Rhode Island, Washington, and Wisconsin are examples. For the most part, these states have a PERA, and court employees are included either explicitly or by approbation of the state's high court. New Jersey and Washington used administrative authority to extend the reasoning of their high courts.

New Mexico extends bargaining only to court reporters by administrative authority, while California limits coverage to executive branch employees as provided by municipal and county ordinances.

Courts may bargain exclusively with one bargaining agent, may be involved in an agency shop, and may or may not have a formal role at the bargaining table with the funding unit. For the moment, both the unions and the courts seem willing to recognize a sphere of influence for each. Unions bargain for strength on wages, hours, and terms and conditions of employment. The courts retain management's right to hire, administer, discipline, and remove their employees. The funding bodies remain somewhere in the middle.

NOTES

1. This section is paraphrased from Chet Newland's, "Collective Bargaining Concepts: Applications in Governments," which appeared in a special issue on collective bargaining, "A Symposium: Collective Negotiations in the Public Services," Public Administration Review 28 (March/April, 1968), hereafter referred to as Symposium. A full discussion of the American labor movement is beyond the scope of this book. A quick listing of historical labor events may be found in Wendell French, The Personnel Management Process: Human Resources Administration, 2nd ed. (Boston: Houghton Mifflin, 1970), pp. 609-23.
2. Labor Management Relations (Taft-Hartley) Act, §141 et seq., 29 U.S.C. (1970).
3. Ibid.
4. Symposium, p. 111.

5. Ibid.
6. A. Lawrence Chickering, ed., Public Employee Unions: A Study of the Crisis in Public Sector Labor Relations (San Francisco: Institute for Contemporary Studies, 1976), p. 167.
7. Ibid.
8. Symposium, p. 112.
9. Ibid., p. 138.
10. Ibid.
11. Railway Mail Association v. Murphy, 44 N.Y. Supp. (2) 601.
12. See Wayne Circuit Judges v. Wayne County, 386 Mich. 1 (1971); Judges v. Bay County, 385 Mich. 710 (1971); Livingston County v. Livingston Circuit Judges, 393 Mich. 265 (1975); and Michigan Supreme Court Administrative Order, 1971-6.
13. 1965 Mich. Pub. Acts 379; Mich. Comp. Laws Ann. §423.01, et seq.
14. Ellenbogen v. Alleghany County, 7/14/78, 388 A 2d 736, Comm. ex rel. Bradley v. Pennsylvania Labor Relations Board, 7/14/78, 388 A 2d 736; Sweet v. Pennsylvania Labor Relations Board, 7/14/78, 388 A 2d 740.
15. Pa. Stat. Ann. Tit. 43§1101.101 et seq. (Purdon).
16. Ellenbogen, op.cit.
17. The judges referred to County of Washington v. P.L.R.B., 26 Commonwealth Ct. 135, 365, A. 2d 519 (1976); Sweet v. P.L.R.B., No. 76, March Term, 1977, Ellenbogen v. County of Alleghany, No. 117, March Term 1977; Board of Judges of Bucks County v. Bucks County Commissioners, Bradley v. P.L.R.B., No. 366, January Term, 1977.
18. Unitary budgeting refers to total, or nearly total, state funding of the unified court system.
19. Act 159, Sec. 1, Hawaii State Legislature (1977) "The governor is considered the employer for the judicial as well as the executive branch in order to avoid potential conflict of interest."
20. See Sam Zagoria (ed.), Public Workers and Public Unions, (Englewood Cliffs, N.J.: Prentice Hall, Inc., 1972).
21. All states in which the courts are locally funded and in which the employees or a significant number of them are in county personnel systems.
22. 461 Pa. 494, 337 A 2d 262 (1975).
23. Only in Hawaii and Massachusetts was this decision prescribed by statute.
24. Unit 3 agreement between Hawaii Government Employees' Association, AFSCME, Local 152, AFL-CIO and State of Hawaii, City and County of Honolulu,

County of Hawaii, County of Maui, County of Kauai, July 1, 1977 to June 30, 1979.

25. See Sam Zagoria (ed.), Public Workers and Public Unions, (Englewood Cliffs, N.J.: Prentice Hall, Inc., 1972).

26. Judicial Units Contract Between the State of Connecticut Judicial Department and Connecticut State Employees Association, June 30, 1978 through June 28, 1979.

27. Presumably one could pursue a grievance through civil service and if unsuccessful, turn to the contract grievance procedure.

28. Hawaii State Constitution, Article XII, Sec. 2.

29. Several chapters of the Hawaii Revised Statutes were affected as embodied in Act 159, Relating to Personnel of the Judicial Branch.

30. Ibid.

31. Hawaii has a unified court with unitary budgeting.

32. See for example, United Federation of Postal Clerks v. Blount, 325 F. Supp. 879 (D.D.C.) Aff'd 404 U.S. 802 (1971).

33. The 1979 strike by New Orleans police serves as an example.

34. The authors are indebted to L. M. Jacobs, IV, Court Administrator, Third Judicial Circuit Court, for providing us with factual information surrounding the strike.

35. Memorandum from L. M. Jacobs, IV, November 1, 1978.

36. Memorandum to all Wayne County Circuit Court Employees, November 1, 1978.

37. Notice to attorneys, November 2, 1978.

38. California took care of the problem by saying that a strike takes more than one form (In re Webb, 80 LC 72,576):

> while public employees do not have the right to strike in California, several court clerks and a court reporter could not be held in contempt for their failure to work in a county's superior court during a union strike against the county. The employees effectively terminated their employment when they withdrew their labor by engaging in a strike. Therefore, they could not be ordered to perform the duties incident to their former employment because having elected to exercise their constitutional right to withhold their services, they were no longer employees of the county.

At least the court was saying that the contempt action was improper. Lacking an injunction against the employees the court had to resort to its own rules. But these rules apparently did not affect employees who had withdrawn their services.

39. Our findings coincide with those of the Futures Group, Glastonbury, Connecticut. See George F. Cole and John R. Wadsworth, "Unionization of State Court Employees: A Growing Movement," Judicature, 61 (1978), 262-70.

40. In Passaic County Probation Officers' Association v. County of Passaic, 73 N.J. 245, 374 A. 2d 449 (1977), the court basically concluded the PERA, a legislative act, could not "dilute" the control of the court system over its employees (in N.J., probation officers only). The dissent, however, found application of PERA to judicial employees would not "pose any substantial threat to the proper and efficient administration of judicial organization by this court and the Chief Justice."

41. Judicial Employees Collective Bargaining Act (Chap. 378), 1977 Mass. Acts.

42. Hawaii Judiciary, Employee Handbook (Honolulu: Hawaii Judiciary, 1977).

43. Included, as well, are the City and County of Honolulu, County of Hawaii, County of Maui, and County of Kauai.

44. Agreement of State of Hawaii and the United Public Workers, Local 646, AFSCME, July 1, 1977 - June 30, 1979.

45. Ibid., Sec. 10.
46. Ibid., Sec. 11.
47. Ibid., Sec. 15.
48. Ibid., Secs. 36-42, 47.
49. Michigan, State Court Administrative Office, Personnel Dept., 1977 Court Employee Compensation Survey (Lansing: Michigan State Court Administrative Office, 1977).

50. Under an agency shop agreement, employees must pay union dues and join the union or pay a service fee and be represented by the union whether or not they join.

51. These paragraphs regarding Wayne County need to be read in concert with the earlier discussion regarding a strike in the court.

52. Passaic County Probation Officers' Association v. County of Passaic, 73 N.J. 247, 374 A.2d 449 (1977).

53. Ibid.
54. McCoy v. Selby, 28 N.Y. 2d 790 (Ct. of Appeals, 1971), 321 N.Y.S. 2d. 902.
55. Ibid.

Appendixes

Appendix A: Bibliography

Byers, Kenneth T., ed., <u>Employee Training and Development in the Public Service,</u> Chicago: Public Personnel Association, 1970.

Charlesworthy, James C., <u>Government Administration</u>, New York: Harper, 1951.

Chickering, A. Lawrence, ed., <u>Public Employee Unions, A Study of the Crises in Public Sector Labor Relations,</u> San Francisco: Institute for Contemporary Studies, 1976.

Cohen, Michael, "The Personnel Policy-Making System," in Robert T. Golembiewski and Michael Cohen, eds., <u>People in Public Service</u>, Itasca, Ill., F. E. Peacock, 1970.

Collett, Merrill J., <u>Streamlining Personnel Communications</u>, Chicago, International Personnel Management Association, 1969.

Crouch, Winston, W., ed., <u>Local Government Personnel Administration</u>, 7th ed., Washington, D.C., International City Management Association, 1976.

Fomularo, Joseph J., ed., <u>Handbook of Modern Personnel Administration,</u> New York: McGraw-Hill Book Company, 1972.

Golembiewski, Robert T. and Michael Cohen, eds., <u>People in Public Service: A Reader in Public Personnel Administration</u>, Itaska, Ill.: F. E. Peacock Publishers, 1970.

Greenlaw, Paul S., and Robert D. Smith, eds., <u>Personnel Management: A Man-Science Approach</u>, Scranton, Pa., International Textbook, 1970.

Harvey, Donald R., <u>The Civil Service Commission</u>, New York, Praeger, 1970.

Institute for Court Management, <u>Courts and Personnel Systems</u>, Denver, 1975.

Lang, Theodore H., *Public Personnel Councils*, Personnel Report No. 583, Chicago, International Personnel Management Association, 1958.

Lewpawsky, Albert, ed., *Administration, The Art and Science of Organization and Management*, New York: Knopf, 1952.

Newland, Chester A., et al., *MBO and Productivity Bargaining in the Public Sector*, Chicago, International Personnel Management Association, 1973.

Nigro, Felix A. and Lloyd G. Nigro, *The New Public Personnel Administration*, Itasca, Ill.: F. E. Peacock Publishers, Inc., 1976.

Odiorne, George S., *Personnel Administration by Objectives*, Homewood, Ill., Richard D. Irwin, Inc., 1971.

Page, Tom, ed., *The Public Personnel Agency and the Chief Executive: A Symposium*, Personnel Report No. 601, Chicago, International Personnel Management Association, 1960.

Powell, Norman, *Personnel Administration in Government*, Englewood Cliffs, N.J.: Prentice Hall, 1956.

Sayles, Leonard R. and George Strauss, *Human Behavior in Organizations*, Englewood Cliffs, N.J.: Prentice-Hall, 1966.

Shafritz, Jerry M., Walter L. Balk, Albert C. Hyde, David H. Rosenbloom, *Personnel Management in Government: Politics and Process*, New York, N.Y.: Marcel Deklser, Inc., 1978.

Stahl, O. Glenn, *The Personnel Job of Government Managers*, Chicago: Public Personnel Association, 1971.

Stahl, O. Glenn, *Public Personnel Administration*, 5th, 6th, and 7th eds., New York: Harper & Rowe Publishers, 1961, 1971, and 1976.

Warner, Kenneth O. and J. J. Donovan, eds., *Practical Guidelines to Public Pay Administration*, Vol. 1, 1963; Vol. 2, 1965, Chicago: Public Personnel Association.

Appendix B-1:
Court Clerk II Job Description

                                                    4102
                    COURT CLERK II

DEFINITION OF WORK

   This is technical clerical work in a court of the Colorado state court system.
   Work involves performing a variety of technical clerical functions which may require the application of independent judgment and the interpretation of routine policies and regulations on the basis of training and knowledge gained through experience on the job. Work is reviewed by a supervisor through observation of operations, and advice and assistance are available when unusual or difficult matters arise.

EXAMPLES OF WORK PERFORMED   (Any one position may not include all of the duties listed, nor do the examples cover all the duties which may be performed.)

   Reviews stipulations, writs of restitution, bindovers, dismissal under rule, and similar documents for completeness, adequacy, and accuracy; determines processing required and takes necessary action in accordance with court rules or refers difficult matters to superiors.
   Issues summons, notices, subpoenas duces tecum, and similar processes; computes applicable dates for service and return of service, affixes court seal, and authenticates documents as an officer of the court.
   Assures completeness and accuracy of records

leaving the court's jurisdiction pursuant to change of venue, outgoing reciprocals, and similar matters.

Makes certain bondsman's license is in order as a means of evaluating the acceptability of surety bonds; enters required information on permanent various records by hand, typewriter, or photocopy process; and prepares appropriate indices for ready reference.

Answers inquiries and furnishes information by reviewing court records.

Performs related work as required.

DESIRABLE KNOWLEDGES, ABILITIES, AND SKILLS

Knowledge of court procedures and policies, legal documents, laws and legal factors pertaining to the court.

Knowledge of the organization operations, functions and scope of authority of the court or activity to which assigned.

Knowledge of modern office practices and procedures.

Ability to understand and follow oral and written instructions.

Ability to make work decisions in accordance with laws, regulations and departmental policies and procedures.

Ability to maintain a variety of complex records and prepare reports from such records.

DESIRABLE EDUCATION AND EXPERIENCE

Graduation from high school, supplemented by completion of courses in business or legal training; and experience in work, including familiarity with procedures, policies, laws and operations of the court of assignment.

4/73

Appendix B-2:
Judicial District Administrator I
Job Description

JUDICIAL DISTRICT ADMINISTRATOR I   1231

DEFINITION OF WORK

    This is highly responsible administrative and supervisory work in directing the administrative activities of a small judicial district.
    Work involves responsibility for organizing, directing, coordinating, and supervising directly or through the use of intermediate supervisors the activities of subordinates engaged in processing all district and county court cases in a multi-county judicial district. Work is performed under the general direction of the Chief Judge of the appropriate judicial district and is reviewed through conferences and reports and on the basis of results obtained.

EXAMPLES OF WORK PERFORMED (Any one position may not include all of the duties listed, nor do the examples cover all the duties which may be performed.)

    Plans and organizes administrative services; determines organizational requirements and plans office layout, space utilization, and work flow of court administrative activities.
    Assigns personnel to administrative and clerical functions; develops and establishes procedures for operating and maintaining required administrative systems; procures equipment and supplies to perform administrative services of the court; disseminates information to court personnel.
    Directs administrative services; directs budgeting, accounting, personnel, statistics, purchasing,

financial reporting, jury management, property management, and other major staff services; directs personnel in the preparation, reproduction, and distribution of court orders, directives, administrative publications, communications and reports; directs personnel in the identification and evaluation of court record material and in the application of proper filing and disposition procedures; directs the record management activities of the judicial district.

Directs and evaluates the effectiveness of personnel and administrative programs to determine requirements for program modification and personnel training, promotion, or reassignment; establishes training program for court clerical personnel.

Monitors budget and controls expenditures for the judicial district probation department.

Maintains contact with various court locations within the district by means of periodic visits and other communications.

Confers with judges, attorneys, public and private agencies and criminal justice system participants to insure adequate communication, administrative services, and provide for changing or unusual demands.

Performs related work as required.

DESIRABLE KNOWLEDGES, ABILITIES, AND SKILLS

Thorough knowledge of modern principles and practices of public administration.

Thorough knowledge of court procedures, legal documents, laws, and legal factors pertaining to the court.

Thorough knowledge of the organization, functions, responsibilities, and procedures of the courts.

Ability to organize, direct, and coordinate the administrative activities of a small judicial district in a manner conducive to full performance and high morale.

Ability to express ideas on technical subjects clearly and concisely, orally and in writing.

DESIRABLE EDUCATION AND EXPERIENCE

Graduation from an accredited four-year college or university with major course work in public administration, business administration, or a related field; and experience in an administrative capacity, including some experience in court or related administrative or professional work.

2/77

Appendix C: Instructions and Suggestions for Filling Out Position Classification Questionnaire

Do Not Attempt To Fill Out Questionnaire Until You Have Read These Instructions

WHAT THE CLASSIFICATION SURVEY IS

This is a job inventory. It is not concerned with your ability on the job or with your qualifications. The kind of work you do and the responsibilities of your position are the things to be shown on the classification questionnaire.

This survey is simply an analysis of the duties and responsibilities of positions in order to develop a classification plan. This plan will consist of a grouping together of all positions having substantially similar duties and responsibilities and requiring like abilities and skills for successful performance.

The classification plan is used as the basis for sound practices in selection, promotion, and transfer, and for uniform and equitable compensation standards. It is essential that the plan be accurate and fair. Therefore, detailed and exact information about the duties and responsibilities of each position is necessary.

You are the best person to provide complete information about your job. You know the exact duties you perform and your responsibilities. Consequently, you are asked to fill in the classification questionnaire. Use great care in doing this, so that a clear and complete understanding of your job can be obtained from your answers. The information provided through questionnaires will be supplemented by information obtained by discussions of the work of individual positions with supervisors and the employees themselves in a number of cases. However, the information provided by you on your classification questionnaire will be very important in determining in what class your position belongs. Your statements will not be changed by your supervisor.

Do not copy other people's answers even though their work is the same as your own. We want your own statement of your work—not the ideas of others about your work. Ask your supervisor to explain questions you do not understand, but use your own words in answering all questions. If you are new on your job, ask your supervisor what duties you will have in addition to those with which you have already become familiar.

PART I — TO THE EMPLOYEE

Read these instructions carefully. Write your answers on one copy of the questionnaire. See that they are correct and complete. Then type your answers on the other two sheets. Sign and return the two typewritten forms to your supervisor within five days. Keep your work copy of the questionnaire.

If you cannot type yourself, write your answers on one sheet and return the forms to your supervisor for copying within five days. He will return the forms to you for review, dating, and signature. Then return the typewritten copies to him and keep the sheet which you filled out originally.

The following explanation will help you to understand just what information is wanted. Read the explanation for each item just before answering each question.

ITEM 1 — Give your last name first, then your first name, then your middle initial. Indicate whether Mr., Mrs., or Miss by crossing out the two designations which do *not* apply.

ITEM 2 — Give your present official title as carried on the payroll. If you do not know, ask your supervisor. Under "Usual Working Title of Position," write the title you and your fellow workers customarily use for your job.

ITEM 3 — Indicate your regularly established work schedule, showing your regular starting and stopping times for each day, the length of your regularly established lunch period, and the total number of hours in your regularly established work week. If your official work schedule varies from week to week, show the average number of hours you work in the space for "Total Hrs. per Wk." If you are subject to rotating shifts, explain the system of rotation as it affects you, indicating whether you change shifts at weekly or monthly intervals and what shifts you rotate through. If your job requires that you be available at a specified location a fixed period each week for emergency service as required, in addition to your regular work time, indicate the average number of hours per week involved in this "on-call" or "stand-by" time.

ITEM 4 — Enter the name of the major branch of the jurisdiction in which you are employed, giving the name of the department, board, or commission in which you work.

ITEM 5 — Enter the name of that division or other principal subdivision of the department in which you work.

ITEM 6 — Enter the name of that section or other unit of the division or institution in which you are employed.

ITEM 7 — Enter the room number, building name or street location of building, and name of the city in which you work, as Room 182, Memorial Hospital, Capital City. If you work out of doors or on projects at different locations, as in a highway district or on institutional premises, give the room number, building name, or street location of building, and city in which your headquarters are located—that is, the place where you report for instructions, etc.

ITEM 8 — Indicate by checking the appropriate box whether your job is full-time or part-time, and whether it is of a year-round character or whether you are employed only, for example, for the summer months or for some other limited period. If you work part-time, indicate whether you work half-time, three-quarters time, five hours a week, or otherwise show what proportion of full-time employment is involved in your job. If you work seasonally or on a temporary basis, indicate for how long a period your employment is expected to continue during the year.

ITEM 9 — If you receive maintenance in the form of meals, lodging, laundry, or the like, either for yourself or for both yourself and your family, *in addition to your cash salary,* check the "Yes" box. Maintenance, as used here, does *not* refer to reimbursement for travel and transportation expenses incurred in the course of official travel.

ITEM 10 — This, the most important question on the form, is where you tell in detail what you do. Each kind of work that you do should be carefully explained. The task which you consider most important should be given first, followed by the less important work, until the least important is described. If your work varies from season to season or at specific times, duties should be grouped together according to such periods. Give your complete work assignments over a long enough period of time to picture your job as a whole. If one kind of work takes one-half your time, say so. If another kind takes one day a month, say that. You may prefer to show the time spent on different duties as percentages or fractions, as 75% of your time, or one-third of the year. Use whatever method you think will give a clear understanding of how you spend your working time, but be sure to show how much time is used for each type of work. Do not state it is impossible to estimate the time spent on various tasks; it may be difficult, but you are in a better position to do this than anyone else.

If you are performing duties other than those of your usual position, describe both. In describing the temporary position, you should give the name of the person you are replacing, how long you have been filling in for him, how long you expect to continue doing so, and the reason, such as vacation, sick leave, etc.

If necessary for a full explanation of your job, attach copies of forms used, being careful to explain how each is used and what entries you make, but do not attach copies unless you feel they are needed to describe your work.

Make your description so clear that anyone who reads your answer, even if he knows nothing about your job, will understand what you do. Be specific; do not use general phrases.

Examples of work in different fields are given below as a guide to the kind of statements wanted. Do not copy *these* examples—use your own words. Ordinarily it will take all the space provided on the questionnaire to tell what you do. *If you do not have enough space, attach additional sheets.*

EXAMPLES IN THE LABOR FIELD (Skilled and Unskilled)

2 months:	I dig trenches with pick and shovel. Mr. Brown, my boss, tells me where to dig and when to stop.
1 month:	I fill wheel barrows with sand or gravel and take it to the concrete mixer. I tamp concrete after it is poured into forms.
1 month: Etc.	I ride a ten-ton flat-bed truck and help load and unload bags of cement, heavy rock, reinforcing steel........etc. We generally haul from the warehouse yards to maintenance or construction jobs. I wash the truck . . . etc.

3 months:	I operate a tractor on construction work as follows:..
1 month:	Hoisting work with a two- or three-drum hoist. (Vacation relief.)
2 months:	Pile driving for retaining walls, excavations, and foundations. Sometimes I . . . etc.

EXAMPLES IN THE CLERICAL AND RELATED FIELDS

Average 4 hrs. per day:	I type vouchers in duplicate to accompany invoices, after they have been approved by Mr. Jones and extensions checked by Miss Smith.
2 hrs.:	I type reports from rough pencil copy.
1 hr.: Etc.	I also . . . etc.

2 days:	I file purchase orders chronologically and by department and vendor.
1 day: Etc.	I sort and distribute letters.

10%:	I take dictation from Mr. Brown, including letters, memoranda, and drafts of speeches, but Miss White takes all his engineering dictation.
5%: Etc.	I file . . . etc.

EXAMPLES IN THE ENGINEERING FIELD

6 months:	I lay out and trace plan-profile sheets for street improvements. I reduce survey notes, balance traverses, and plot maps from the field books brought in by the field survey parties, also plot cross-sections and planimeter for cut and fill areas.
2 months: Etc.	I draft . . . etc.

EXAMPLES IN THE ACCOUNTING FIELD

10%:	I supervise three clerks assigned to the cost accounting system for road construction and maintenance.
10%:	I assemble job record reports, post to summary sheets, and do other routine work.
5%:	I tabulate and prove material for weekly, monthly, and annual reports.
2%: Etc:	I compile . . . etc.

EXAMPLES IN THE CUSTODIAL FIELD

1/2 day:	Washing floors, walls, windows, and woodwork by hand.
1/3 day:	Polishing metal; waxing and polishing floors with a polishing machine.

ITEM 11 — Give the name and title of your actual immediate supervisor—the crew chief, section leader or similar person to whom you look for orders, advice or decisions and who probably works very closely and directly with you.

ITEM 12 — If you have five or fewer persons under your supervision, give their names and payroll titles. If more than five, give their payroll titles and give the number of employees under each title. If you supervise no employees, write "none."

ITEM 13 — List here any major items of equipment, machines, or office appliances which you use in your work and the approximate percentage of your working time which you spend in the operation of each.

ITEM 14 — What instructions or directions do your superiors give you in relation to the work you do? How detailed are instructions about what you are to do and how you are to do it? You may have had instructions only when you were new on the job. You may get special instructions with each new task. Describe the nature and extent of the instructions you receive.

ITEM 15 — Describe the check or review that is made of your work. Are there any automatic checks by other offices, or are there procedures which would catch any errors you might make? How final are the decisions you make about your work? Describe such features as these.

ITEM 16 — Explain the nature and purpose of important contacts you have with people other than your fellow workers. Is the purpose to obtain or give information, to persuade others, or to obtain cooperation? What problems and difficulties are involved?

PART II—INSTRUCTIONS TO GENERAL SUPERVISORS AND DEPARTMENTAL OFFICIALS
Method of Distributing and Reviewing the Classification Questionnaires

You will be supplied with a complete set of three Classification Questionnaires and a copy of these Instructions for each employee under your supervision.

Give each employee a set of Classification Questionnaires and Instructions. Ask employees who have access to typewriters to work out their answers on one copy, and then type them on the other two copies, and return the two signed typewritten copies to you within five days.

Ask those employees who cannot type their own questionnaires to write their answers on one sheet and return the complete set to you within five days, for typing. When typed, return all three copies to the employees. Have the two typewritten copies reviewed, dated, signed, and returned to you.

Go over each employee's questionnaire carefully to see that it is accurate and complete. Then fill out Items 17 to 22, inclusive. The general supervisor should fill out Items 17 to 20 on the questionnaire forms of only those employees whom he supervises. A department head should not fill in these items for employees whom he directs through a sub-executive but only for those to whom he assigns work directly. In all instances, the director or other administrative officer, or a representative designated by him, should look over both the employees' and their supervisors' statements and indicate under Item 22 any inaccuracies found. Neither the general supervisor nor the administrative officer, however, should make any alteration or change in the statements made by a subordinate.

If there is a regular position under you which is temporarily vacant, or if an employee is not available to fill out the questionnaire, please supply a form for that position, made out as accurately as is possible. The fact that an employee did not fill out the form and the reason should be clearly indicated. If the employee returns, he should fill out and submit his own questionnaire.

Suggestions for Filling Out Items 17 through 22

ITEM 17 — Do not change the employee's statements. Read them through and then give your opinion of their accuracy and completeness. Is it a good description of the position? Has he neglected to give a full picture of his duties and responsibilities? Has he overstated them? Has he put emphasis on the wrong points? Either comment generally on his statements or refer to specific items.

If you have a number of positions under you which are practically identical, it will be sufficient to answer Items 18 to 21 fully for one such position only, and then refer to such answers on the other questionnaires. You can merely state, "Same as John Doe."

ITEM 18 — Sum up what you consider to be the distinguishing aspects of the employee's job. What are the most important functions carried on in this position? What operations in the job contribute most to your organization? Is the position a beginning or an advanced one?

ITEMS 19 and 20 — If the job involves any typing or shorthand, even if merely incidental, answer these items completely. If not, check "No."

ITEM 21 — With full consideration of the duties and responsibilites of this position, tell what are the basic qualifications of a person you would choose for the position if it were to become vacant. What must he know? Of what basic subjects, procedures, principles, laws, or regulations must he have a knowledge? Must the knowledge be thorough or is a general knowledge or familiarity sufficient?

What abilities or skills must a successful employee possess? How much formal education is necessary? What course or subjects are required? Which are desirable but not essential? Is previous experience necessary? If so, how much experience, and in what type of work? What degree of physical strength, agility, or endurance is necessary? For what purpose is it used, e.g., for walking, lifting, etc.? Please be as specific and complete as you can in answering these questions.

Indicate, wherever possible, both the basic qualifications required to fill the position and the desirable qualifications which you would like to have in a new employee.

ITEM 22 — The comments made here by the department head or other administrative officer should follow the procedure suggested for the general supervisor in Items 17 and 18 to the extent that additional comment is needed.

Return of Completed Questionnaires

One copy of the questionnaire signed by employee, general supervisor, and administrative officer—the original of the typewritten copies—should be submitted for each employee in the department within no more than two weeks of the date of distribution of the questionnaires to employees. The carbon copy of the completed typewritten form is for departmental files.

POSITION CLASSIFICATION QUESTIONNAIRE

Soc. Sec. Number ☐☐☐-☐☐-☐☐☐☐

| 1. Mr. Mrs. Miss | Last Name | First | Middle Initial |

4. Commission, Board, or Department

2. Official Title of Position

5. Division or Institution

Usual Working Title of Position

6. Section or Other Unit of Division or Institution

3. Regular Schedule of Hours of Work

	From	To
Mon.		
Tues.		
Wed.		
Thur.		
Fri.		
Sat.		
Sun.		

Length of Lunch Period _____

Total Hrs. per Wk. _____
Explain rotation of shifts, if any: _____

Hrs. of "On-Call" Time per Wk. _____

7. Place of Work or Headquarters

8. Is your work ☐ Full-Time? ☐ Part-Time? ☐ Year-round?
   ☐ Seasonal? ☐ Temporary?
   If work is *seasonal, temporary, or part-time*, indicate part of year or proportion of full-time: _____

9. Do you receive any maintenance (room, meals, laundry, etc.) in addition to your cash salary? ☐ Yes ☐ No

10. Describe below in detail the work you do. Use your own words, and make your description so clear that persons unfamiliar with your work can understand what you do. Attach additional sheets if necessary.

TIME	WORK PERFORMED	LEAVE BLANK

11. Name and Title of Your Immediate Supervisor:

12. Give the names and payroll titles of employees you supervise, if five or fewer. If you supervise more than five employees, give the number under each title. If you supervise no employees, write "none." _____

13. Machines or equipment used regularly in your work. Give per cent of time spent in operation of each:

	%		%
	%		%
	%		%

14. What are the nature and extent of instructions you receive regarding your work?

15. What are nature and extent of the check or review of your work?

16. Describe your contacts with departments other than your own, with outside organizations, and with the general public.

CERTIFICATION: I certify that the above answers are my own and are accurate and complete.

Date_____ Employee's Signature_____

STATEMENT OF GENERAL SUPERVISOR

17. Comment on statements of employee. Indicate any exceptions or additions.

18. What do you consider the most important duties of this position?

19. Does this position involve typing?
   ☐ No
   ☐ Yes — Give % of time spent in typing ____%

20. Does this position involve shorthand?
   ☐ No
   ☐ Yes — Give % of time spent in taking shorthand.

Date_____ General Supervisor's Signature_____

STATEMENT OF DEPARTMENT HEAD OR OTHER ADMINISTRATIVE OFFICER

21. Indicate the qualifications which you think should be required in filling a future vacancy in this position. Keep the position itself in mind rather than the qualifications of the individual who now occupies it.

	Basic Qualifications	Additional Desirable Qualifications
Education, general:		
Education, special or professional:		
Experience, length in years and kind:		
Licenses, certificates, or registration:		
Special knowledges, abilities, and skills:		

22. Comment on the above statements of the employee and the supervisor. Indicate any inaccuracies or statement with which you disagree.

Date_____ Department Head's Signature_____

Appendix D:
Civil Action 76 M 910

IN THE UNITED STATES DISTRICT COURT
FOR THE DISTRICT OF COLORADO

Civil Action No. 76 M 910

ROBERT D. HAMM,)
        Plaintiff,)
)
v.)
)
REX H. SCOTT, individually and as Chief)
Judge of the 20th Judicial District of)
the State of Colorado; and Hon. Paul V.)
Hodges, Hon. Marcus O. Shivers, Jr.,)
Hon. John R. Tracey, Mary M. Connell)
and Beverly J. Estrada, as members of)
the Judicial System Personnel Board of)
Review of the Judicial Department of)
the State of Colorado,)
        Defendants)

    Mr. James R. Gilsdorf, 1390 Logan Street, Suite 200, Denver, Colorado 80203 and Mr. Robert F. Moreland, 75 Manhattan Drive, Suite 203, P.O. Box 3185, Boulder, Colorado 80303, attorneys for the plaintiff. Ms. Janice L. Burnett, First Assistant Attorney General, Litigation Section, 1525 Sherman Street, 3rd Floor, Denver, Colorado 80203 and Mr. David R. Broughan, Yegge, Hall & Evans, 1340 Denver Club Building, Denver, Colorado 80202, attorneys for the defendants

FINDINGS, CONCLUSIONS AND ORDER

MATSCH, Judge

Robert D. Hamm seeks relief under the limited jurisdiction granted by 28 U.S.C. § 1343(3) and (4) and 42 U.S.C. § 1983 upon the claim that the termination of his employment as chief juvenile probation officer for the 20th Judicial District of the State of Colorado was a deprivation of his property without due process of law, in violation of the protection given by the Fourteenth Amendment to the Constitution of the United States. The evidence taken at a hearing on the plaintiff's motion for preliminary injunction established the facts upon which the claim is based.

After service as a student volunteer, Robert D. Hamm was appointed as a probation officer for the 20th Judicial District in October, 1967, and four years later he was named the chief juvenile probation officer for that court. During the time of his employment, Mr. Hamm was working under the direction and supervision of Judge Horace Holmes, the district judge assigned to juvenile matters. The official duties of a chief probation officer as set out in the applicable job description include the following:

> Maintains cooperative relationship with state and local welfare and social service agencies, institutions, and law enforcement agencies, and relates the activities of the department to their services; participates in coordinating councils, committees, and other groups interested in probation or crime prevention.

The Honorable Rex H. Scott became a judge of the 20th Judicial District on July 1, 1970, and he was named chief judge of that district in January, 1975. On May 4, 1976, Judge Scott was in possession of copies of correspondence and memoranda concerning the conduct of Mr. Hamm in his official capacity and his relationship with several social service agencies. This correspondence included an exchange of letters with a high school principal in March, 1976. Judge Scott took copies of these documents to Judge Holmes on the morning of May 4, 1976 with a request that Judge Holmes obtain Mr. Hamm's resignation or terminate his employment. Judge Holmes declined to take that action, and Judge Scott then asked Judge Holmes to give the copies to the plaintiff.

When he was informed that Judge Scott wanted a resignation or termination of employment, Mr. Hamm asked to see Judge Scott and, at about 11:30 A.M., they met in Judge Scott's chambers. At that meeting, Mr. Hamm denied the accusations in the letters. Judge Scott told the plaintiff that he should submit his resignation or be discharged by 4 P.M. that day. Mr. Hamm asked for more time, and he asked for an opportunity to bring in agency directors and other persons to make statements on his behalf. Judge Scott adhered to the 4 P.M. deadline. Mr. Hamm did return to Judge Scott's chambers at 4 P.M. on that same day and submitted a handwritten statement which generally denied all accusations and in which Mr. Hamm refused resignation. After reading that document, Judge Scott told Mr. Hamm that he was dismissed, and a letter of termination, signed by Judge Scott, was given to the plaintiff. In that letter, Judge Scott set forth the following reasons for termination.

1. Failure to comply with a reasonable and proper assignment from an authorized supervisor.

2. Documented inefficiency, incompetency, in the performance of duties, i.e. that you have been a negative and alienating force with the youth serving agencies.

3. Conduct unbecoming a state judicial department employee.

Article VI, Section 5(2) of the Colorado Constitution provides that the chief justice is the "executive head" of the judicial system of that state. Section 5(4) of the same article provides that the chief judge of each district shall be appointed by and serve at the pleasure of the chief justice and that each chief judge shall have such administrative powers as shall be delegated to him by the chief justice. On August 27, 1971, Chief Justice Edward E. Pringle executed a written delegation of authority to all chief judges. That delegation was a very broad grant of administrative power, including the authority to appoint and remove personnel, excepting confidential employees of a judge.

The terms and conditions of employment of the employees of the executive branch of Colorado's government are established by a merit personnel system under Article XII, Section 13 of the state's constitution. Those provisions do not apply to those who work in the judicial department. Subparagraph (3) of Section 13 provides:

> (3) Officers and employees within the judicial department, other than judges and justices, may be included within the personnel system of the state upon determination by the supreme court, sitting en banc, that such would be in the best interests of the state.

The Colorado General Assembly has, by statute, provided for the establishment of a personnel classification and compensation plan for all courts pursuant to rules adopted by the Supreme Court of Colorado. 1973 C.R.S. § 13-3-105. Subsection (4) of that section reads as follows:

> (4) To the end that all state employees are treated generally in a similar manner, the supreme court, in promulgating rules as set forth in this section, shall take into consideration the compensation and classification plans, vacation and sick leave provisions, and other conditions of employment applicable to employees of the executive and legislative departments.

The Colorado Supreme Court did adopt personnel rules in 1970. Under those rules, there was no right of review of any personnel decision affecting supervisory positions. The plaintiff here was placed in a supervisory position in 1971.

The rules were rewritten and readopted by the Supreme Court with an effective date of January 1, 1975, and designated Colorado Judicial System Personnel Rules (CJSPR). The plaintiff here was a "certified employee" under those rules, and under Rule 26(a) such an employee may be dismissed for any of the reasons enumerated in Rule 25(d). That rule enumerates grounds which include those set forth in the termination letter issued by Chief Judge Scott.

Rule 45 establishes a Board of Review having jurisdiction over requests for review of discharges and other personnel actions. Rule 46 describes the right of review given to certified employees, and subsection (b)(2) expressly excludes a number of positions from that right of review. Chief probation officers are among those excluded positions.

Mr. Hamm sought to obtain a hearing before the Board of Review. A review board hearing was denied with the approval of Chief Justice Pringle upon the basis of the exclusion in Rule 46.

Mr. Hamm had no written contract of employment and there is nothing in evidence to support a finding of any express oral agreement or promise of any term or tenure.

I.

The plaintiff's principal contention here is that the personnel rules created an objective expectation of tenure which should be characterized as a property interest subject to due process protection on the authority of Board of Regents v. Roth, 408 U.S. 564 (1972); Perry v. Sindermann, 408 U.S. 593 (1972); and Arnett v. Kennedy, 416 U.S. 134 (1974).

In Roth, an assistant professor of political science at a public university had been hired for a one-year fixed term of employment pursuant to a written contract. He had no tenure and there were no statutory or administrative standards of eligibility for reemployment. After he had been openly critical of the school administration, the teacher was notified that he would not be employed for the following academic year. He sued, alleging that he had been punished for his criticism in denial of his First Amendment freedom, and he asserted a right to procedural due process. The district court ordered a partial summary judgment for the plaintiff on the claim of entitlement to procedural due process, which, the court held, required a statement of reasons for non-hiring and an opportunity for a hearing on those reasons. Roth v. Board of Regents, 310 F. Supp. 972 (W.D. Wis. 1970). That result was affirmed in Roth v. Board of Regents, 446 F. 2d 806 (7th Cir. 1971).

A majority of the Supreme Court reversed the order on summary judgment, observing that the only question presented was whether the teacher had a constitutional right to a statement of reasons and a hearing on the decision not to rehire him for another year. In holding that he did not, Justice Stewart concluded that a determination of the nature or character of the teacher's interest was controlling of whether it came within the Fourteenth Amendment's protection of liberty and property. Because the district court had stayed any development of the issues on the claim of retaliation for the exercise of freedom of speech, that allegation was not before the Supreme Court. The Supreme Court's holding in Roth was that a teacher who had not been rehired for one year at one public university had no protectable interest in reemployment without proof of something more.

The Sindermann case came to the Supreme Court differently. There, the district court granted a summary judgment for the defendants, regents of a public junior college, who had failed to renew the plaintiff's one-year employment contract, and who had issued a press release containing allegations of insubordination on which there had been no hearing or factual determination.

The teacher had been employed with the same institution for four successive years under a series of one-year contracts, and he had taught an additional six years at other schools within the state college system. He had been involved in public disagreements with the defendant regents. Without taking evidence, the trial judge dismissed the plaintiff's claim that the failure to renew his contract was a retaliation for his public criticism and the claim that the failure to provide him with a statement of reasons and an opportunity to challenge those reasons resulted in a denial of procedural due process.

The Fifth Circuit had reversed this ruling, Sindermann v. Perry, 430 F. 2d 939 (5th Cir. 1970), for the obvious reason that the plaintiff had not been given an opportunity to develop evidence of his contentions that the defendants withheld renewal of his contract on the impermissible basis of reprisal for the exercise of rights protected by the First Amendment. Having decided to remand, the Fifth Circuit apparently felt obliged to offer direction to the district court with regard to plaintiff's claim of entitlement to a hearing. In considering what academic procedures should be made available, the court said that a determination had to be made as to whether the teacher had "an expectancy of reemployment under the policies and practices of the institution." 430 F. 2d at 943.

Whether such an expectancy existed would

determine whether a pretermination hearing was necessary (with the regents having the burden of establishing cause) because the requirement of cause as a condition to a failure to renew was a part of the contractual expectancy of reemployment. However, if no such expectancy were established by the evidence, the teacher would have the burden of showing that the decision was wrongful and the administrative hearing should be so conducted by the academic authorities. In making that distinction, the court said at page 944:

> On the other hand, if the court resolves that Sindermann did not have an expectancy of reemployment which would require the college to show cause for the decision not to renew his contract, a different procedure would be indicated. In such a situation, upon receipt of notice that a new contract will not be offered, the teacher must bear the burden both of initiating the proceedings and of proving that a wrong has been done by the collegiate action in not rehiring him. It is incumbent upon such a teacher, not the college, to shoulder these responsibilities because the college may base its decision not to reemploy a teacher without tenure or a contractual expectancy of reemployment upon any reason or upon no reason at all.

A majority of the Supreme Court affirmed the circuit. The first question considered was whether the

> . . . lack of a contractual or tenure right to reemployment, taken alone, defeats his claim that the nonrenewal of his contract violated the First and Fourteenth Amendments. (408 U.S. 593, 596)

In holding that the claim was not so disqualified, the Supreme Court applied the well-developed principle that government may not act on any basis which infringes a constitutionally protected individual interest, particularly freedom of speech and association. Accordingly, any claim of contract right was considered to be irrelevant to the freedom of speech claim, and the teacher should have been given the right to develop the factual basis for his claim of infringement.

The Court then considered the separate claim of entitlement to some kind of hearing as a part of the non-renewal decision. It was noted that the teacher had not been given an opportunity to introduce evidence to establish the existence of an interest which would warrant due process protection. The holding was that the allegations of the complaint were sufficient to state a claim of a protectable interest. The majority said at page 600-601:

> In particular, the respondent alleged that the college had a de facto tenure program, and that he had tenure under that program. He claimed that he and others legitimately relied upon an unusual provision that had been in the college's official Faculty Guide for many years:
>
>> "Teacher Tenure: Odessa College has no tenure system. The Administration of the College wishes the faculty member to feel that he has permanent tenure as long as his teaching services are satisfactory and as long as he displays a cooperative attitude toward his co-workers and his superiors, and as long as he is happy in his work."
>
> Moreover, the respondent claimed legitimate reliance upon guidelines promulgated by the Coordinating Board of the Texas College and University System that provided that a person, like himself, who had been employed as a teacher in the state college and university

> system for seven years or more has some form of job tenure. [footnote omitted] Thus, the respondent offered to prove that a teacher with his long period of service at this particular State College had no less a "property" interest in continued employment than a formally tenured teacher at other colleges, and had no less a procedural due process right to a statement of reasons and a hearing before college officials upon their decision not to retain him.

The Court then referred to the concept of implied contract, citing 3 A. Corbin on Contracts §§561-572A (1960), and paraphrased the doctrine of promissory estoppel. Finally, Mr. Justice Stewart wrote:

> We disagree with the Court of Appeals insofar as it held that a mere subjective "expectancy" is protected by procedural due process, but we agree that the respondent must be given an opportunity to prove the legitimacy of his claim of such entitlement in light of "the policies and practices of the institution." 430 F. 2d at 943. Proof of such a property interest would not, of course, entitle him to reinstatement. But such proof would obligate college officials to grant a hearing at his request where he could be informed of the grounds for his nonretention and challenge their sufficiency. (408 U.S. 593, 603)

I most respectfully suggest that much of the apparent confusion and difficulty experienced in the trial and appellate courts since Roth and Sindermann result from a failure to stay within traditional definitions of property interests. Contrary to Mr. Justice Stewart's suggestion, the Fifth Circuit did not indicate any view that a mere subjective expectancy of reemployment entitles one to procedural due process protection. The "contractual expectancy" language in the Fifth Circuit opinion is nothing more than an abbreviated statement of the well-recognized law of implied contract and promissory estoppel. The pretermination hearing with the burden on the college to establish cause was not considered to be a requirement of procedural due process; it was simply one of the terms and conditions of the implied employment contract. As the circuit court noted, if no such contract existed, then the protection of academic freedom required some other form of procedural due process hearing before termination became final.

In Bishop v. Wood, 44 U.S.L.W. 4820 (U.S. June 10, 1976), a majority of the Supreme Court affirmed a summary judgment dismissing the due process claims of a police officer who had been a permanent employee of Marion, North Carolina. The city manager terminated the plaintiff's employment without a hearing to determine any cause for discharge, despite a city ordinance which appeared to require cause. Writing for the majority, Mr. Justice Stevens observed that property interests are created and defined by state law and that the trial court's decision that the ordinance did not create a property interest such as to require constitutional protection was not subject to independent examination by the Supreme Court.[1]

Three Justices agreed with the dissent by Mr. Justice White, who viewed the denial of the existence of a property interest as inconsistent with the views of a majority of the Court in Arnett v. Kennedy, 416 U.S. 134 (1974). In that case, a federal civil service employee was removed from his job as a field representative in a regional office of the Office of Economic Opportunity, pursuant to the procedures established by federal statute and regulations. Written administrative charges were made and upheld by the OEO regional director. The employee failed to avail himself of the right to

---

[1] The only indication of any infringement of a liberty interest was the possible stigmatic effect of the firing. Because the reasons for the discharge had not been communicated to the public, there could be no impact on the plaintiff's reputation and, accordingly, no deprivation of any recognizable liberty interest.

reply to these charges, and he failed to appeal to the Civil Service Commission. He then sued, contending that the statutory standards and procedures were not sufficient protection of his interest to be considered due process of law and that there was an unwarranted interference with freedom of expression.

Mr. Justice Rehnquist, writing for three Justices, found that the statutory procedures for termination and post-termination review were limitations on any property right conferred by the civil service statutes. He stated succinctly at page 155:

> Here the property interest which appellee had in his employment was itself conditioned by the procedural limitations which had accompanied the grant of that interest.

The administrative appeal and review procedures were held to be a sufficient protection of the First Amendment right.

Mr. Justice Powell, joined by Mr. Justice Blackmun, concurred in the result but used different reasoning. The disagreement derived from Mr. Justice Powell's perception of the earlier opinions in Roth and Sindermann as holding that whenever a property interest is found to exist, it is constitutionally protected by the due process clause. He then proceeded to determine what procedure would be adequate for due process by balancing the government's interest in expeditious removal of an unsatisfactory employee against the interests of the employee in continued employment. The conclusion reached by these two Justices was that the procedure established by the federal act and regulations was sufficient to meet the constitutional requirements. Mr. Justice White's concurring and dissenting opinion used the same balancing process with different weights, concluding that due process required a pretermination hearing by an impartial decision-maker, but that the trial type of hearing could be reserved for review.

Read together, these cases offer only the broadest and most generalized guidance for the trial courts in resolving the kind of dispute presented here. The difficulty is compounded because prior to Roth and Sindermann we could presume that employment would not differ from any other form of contract-created property interest; consequently, it could be adequately protected, upon breach or repudiation, by a common law action in damages or by appropriate equitable relief. Does the fact that one of the contracting parties is a governmental entity alter the property characteristics of the agreement? It does so only in the sense that it involves state action, to which the prohibitions of the Fourteenth Amendment apply. Yet, there is nothing to suggest that all state contracts come within the protection of the due process clause. We have not yet seen any case holding that a road builder or supplier of materials must receive notice, a statement of reasons and an opportunity to be heard before the state refuses payment. Absent a statute or specific contractual provision, those parties are, presumably, still required to pursue their remedy in court after a breach has occurred.

Additional confusion results from a recognition of the mutability of the due process doctrine. The Supreme Court has found adequate protection in a great range of procedures, varying them according to the vitality and perceived importance of the interest being protected. For example, where a loss of welfare benefits is threatened, minimal due process has been held to require a pretermination hearing, replete with notice and an opportunity to present oral argument, to obtain counsel, and to confront and cross-examine adverse witnesses. Goldberg v. Kelly, 397 U.S. 254 (1970). The profound deprivation of liberty occasioned by parole revocation is similarly viewed as requiring relatively stringent procedures for due process to be satisfied. The parolee must be afforded the opportunity to present witnesses and documentary evidence before a 'neutral and detached' hearing body, and is entitled to a written statement of facts relied upon in the event parole is revoked. Morrissey v. Brewer, 408 U.S. 471 (1972). Most recently, the Court has determined that public school students may not suffer temporary, short-term suspensions absent procedural due process. Goss v. Lopez, 419 U.S. 565 (1975). In this context, however, the due process clause is satisfied if the student is given "an opportunity to explain his version of the facts" at an informal meeting with the disciplinarian, after having been told of the basis for the accusation. 419 U.S. at 582.[2]

---

2. For a comprehensive discussion of this variable nature of due process protection, see Friendly, "Some Kind of Hearing", 123 U.Pa.L.Rev. 1267 (1975).

Are all public employment contracts to be given some form of pretermination protection by the due process clause? The Supreme Court has not answered that question. It seems significant that <u>Roth</u> and <u>Sindermann</u> involved the employment of teachers. The courts have long been concerned with attempts to articulate academic freedom. The many cases which have arisen on the subject of teacher conduct, curriculum control, retaliation for speech or conduct and parental objections to assignments all reveal the enormous difficulty in the balancing of interests involved in public education. I suggest that this same difficulty has been present in the teacher employment cases and that the concern for procedural protections for such employment is more a reflection of the vital interests in affording fairness and freedom in the public classroom than an elevation of claims of injury to contract and property interests to matters of constitutional moment. As Mr. Justice Douglas fully recognized in <u>Roth</u>, "In the case of teachers whose contracts are not renewed, tenure is not the critical issue." 408 U.S. at 582 (dissenting opinion). Rather, as one might expect, the vast number of teacher employment cases prior to <u>Roth</u> and <u>Sindermann</u> presented the critical issue as one of academic freedom or First Amendment rights, not one of Fourteenth Amendment protection afforded a property interest in continued employment. See, for example, <u>Keyishian v. Board of Regents</u>, 385 U.S. 589 (1967); <u>Shelton v. Tucker</u>, 364 U.S. 479 (1960); and <u>Wieman v. Updegraff</u>, 344 U.S. 183 (1952). While the claims of academic freedom or infringement of First Amendment rights were not directly before the Supreme Court in <u>Roth</u> or <u>Sindermann</u>, such claims were within the pleadings.

In the many opinions coming from the federal courts citing <u>Roth</u> and <u>Sindermann</u>, there are frequent discussions of the expanding notion of property interests, and it has become commonplace to refer to <u>Goldberg v. Kelly</u>, for example, as evidencing such expansion. The failure to distinguish among interests with differing values causes a failure to bring the issues into an appropriate focus. <u>Goldberg v. Kelly</u> was based on the perception that an unfair termination of welfare benefits would create a condition of brutal need. While a casual reference to the possibility of regarding such entitlement as property was mentioned in a footnote, the distinguishing characteristics and the recognition of the importance of pretermination protection were clearly stated in the following language:

> Thus the crucial factor in this context--a factor not present in the case of the blacklisted government contractor, <u>the discharged government employee</u>, the taxpayer denied a tax exemption, or virtually anyone else whose governmental entitlements are ended--is that termination of aid pending resolution of a controversy over eligibility may deprive an <u>eligible</u> recipient of the very means by which to live while he waits. Since he lacks independent resources, his situation becomes immediately desperate. His need to concentrate upon finding the means for daily subsistence, in turn, adversely affects his ability to seek redress from the welfare bureaucracy. [footnote omitted] (397 U.S. 254, 264) [first emphasis added]

I have no quarrel with the holding and reasoning in <u>Goldberg v. Kelly</u>. It reflects a profound concern for protecting the interests of the individual against wrongful or arbitrary action in the ever-increasing areas of impact by governmental authority. That concern is the root philosophy of the constitution. Repudiation of the right-privilege dichotomy is but a recognition that there is a growing dependency upon governmental programs to provide an ability to cope with the conditions of modern living, and a corresponding increase in the danger of destruction of vital individual interests by those in authority acting without fundamental fairness. I had no difficulty in following <u>Goldberg v. Kelly</u> in reaching my decision in <u>Ryan v. Shea</u>, 394 F. Supp. 894 (1974), <u>aff'd</u>. 525 <u>F. 2d 268 (19</u>75).

But to reach these results it is not necessary to distort the principles of property law. It is not necessary to clothe teachers with court-created concepts of property to protect them from governmental actions which interfere with the freedom to practice the teaching profession in a manner which affects the public interest. It would be enough simply to recognize that issues involved in the employment of public school teachers are but a part of the larger area of special concern for public education and its particularized problems of balancing state, public and private interests. That area has long involved the courts and the constitution.[3]

The Tenth Circuit Court of Appeals has recognized that the Supreme Court has differentiated among types of property interests in its concern for constitutional protection. In Abeyta v. Town of Taos, 499 F. 2d 323 (10th Cir. 1974), the circuit court, speaking through Judge Hill, said at page 327:

> The types of property protected by the due process clause vary widely and what may be required by that clause in dealing with one set of interests may not be required in dealing with another set of interests.

In that case, the appellate court affirmed the trial judge's findings and conclusions that police officers in Taos, New Mexico had no contract and that their employment was terminable at will. Accordingly, there was no property interest subject to protection.

Bertot v. School District No. 1, Albany County, Wyo., 522 F. 2d 1171 (10th Cir. 1975) involved the failure to renew the annual contracts of teachers without tenure. The plaintiffs sought relief under Sindermann by claiming an objective expectancy of continued employment because, in the hiring interviews, the school principal was interested in the plaintiffs' intention to become permanent residents of the area; the school board had never failed to reemploy a teacher since 1966; and the expressed hiring philosophy of the school district was the renewal of probationary teachers whose performance was satisfactory. Again, the circuit court affirmed the trial judge's finding and conclusion that these facts did not establish a property interest subject to protection by the Fourteenth Amendment. Judge Holloway analyzed the case in traditional contract terms. He said at page 1176 of the opinion:

> Agreements may be implied though

---

3. For a broad overview of education law, see Education and the Law: State Interests and Individual Rights, 74 Mich.L.Rev. 1373 (1976).

> not formalized, and explicit contractual provisions may be supplemented by other agreements implied from a promisor's words and conduct in the light of the surrounding circumstances.

Again at page 1177 of the opinion:

> Moreover the defendants' conduct and the statements made to the plaintiffs cannot be equated to promissory representations or to words, conduct and usage importing an agreement.

A similar analysis was made in another teacher case, Weathers v. West Yuma County School District, 530 F. 2d 1335 (10th Cir. 1976).

In Mitchell v. King, 537 F. 2d 385 (10th Cir. 1976), the Governor of New Mexico removed the plaintiff as Regent of the Museum of New Mexico without notice or hearing. The New Mexico Constitution gave the governor appointing authority over that position. The court of appeals affirmed the district court's dismissal for failure to state a claim for relief upon the conclusion that there was no protectable property interest. In arriving at that result, Judge Barrett emphasized the state constitutional power given to the governor and the importance of absolute authority to remove policy-making officials when their conduct and acts in office are not in harmony with the views and wishes of an official who is accountable to the people.

These Tenth Circuit cases are a helpful clarification of the language used by the various Supreme Court Justices who have written opinions on the subject of public employment. Thus, it seems now to be clear that the notion of "expectancy" or "Objective expectancy" is not a new doctrine in the law of property. It is nothing more than a paraphrase of the traditional principles of implied contract and promissory estoppel. Consequently, if, under the law of a particular state, implied contracts are not enforceable or promissory estoppel is not recognized or state law holds that such a doctrine as applied to particular types of public employment would be against public policy, then it would follow that no property right can be given constitutional protection for such public employees of that state.

Under the learning of the cases which I have

discussed herein, a proper analysis of the facts involved in the Fourteenth Amendment property claims of state employees requires that four questions be answered:

1. <u>Is there a recognizable contractual or other property interest under state law?</u> Recognizing that new concepts of property interests have and will continue to emerge through legislation and common law development, it is important to be able to identify the existence of such an interest by a definition available from some source other than a broad claim of a need for protection. Thus, the property interest must be subject to recognition in the law of the state. Such property interests include express contracts, contracts implied in fact, contracts implied in law (promissory estoppel), statutory grants and licenses.

2. <u>Is the enforcement of the claimed contractual or other property interest contrary to the expressed public policy of that state?</u> It is familiar learning that courts will not enforce contracts which are illegal because they are in violation of criminal or regulatory laws or because they contravene established public policy. 6 A. Corbin on Contracts, Part VIII (1962). Likewise, the ownership or possession of narcotics, illegal weapons and many kinds of contraband are recognized limitations on property rights.

3. <u>Is the recognized enforceable property interest worthy of the protection of procedural due process under the Fourteenth Amendment?</u> Stated differently, does the affected property interest contain some extra dimension which would warrant the additional protection of procedural due process? If not, the status of the employment property interest would be comparable to that of a commercial contract with the state, and the aggrieved party must resort to a common law remedy for its preservation. The perhaps singular nature of teacher employment--imbued with the precious and precarious notion of academic freedom--provides such an extra dimension deserving of procedural due process safeguards. It would be inappropriate at this time to speculate on what other positions of employment might qualify under this standard.

4. <u>How much protection is required?</u> Due process is an elastic concept; the amount of process due in any given situation varies according to the perceived weight of the interest involved and the context in which it arises. Determination of procedural requirements for the protection of a

property interest in public employment calls for a balancing of the individual's interest with the public interest.

II.

In determining the subject case, each of these four questions will be considered, even though the answer to any one of them may make further inquiry superfluous.

1. Is there a recognizable contractual or other property interest under state law?

Robert Hamm has presented no evidence which would suggest, let alone support, a finding of an express or implied contract. There is nothing to indicate any agreement or meeting of the minds on any term of employment as chief probation officer. There is nothing to show that in accepting appointment as chief probation officer he was relying upon any promise of any term or condition. Rather, the facts compel a finding that Mr. Hamm was aware that he was serving at the pleasure of the chief judge of the district court.

The plaintiff's primary contention is that he has a protectable property interest because Rules 25 and 26 of the CJSPR prescribe reasons for which permanent employees of the judicial department may be discharged, and that is said to be analogous to the position of the federal civil service employee plaintiff in Arnett v. Kennedy, supra. The cases are not comparable. 5 U.S.C. § 7501(a) clearly provides that "[a]n individual in the competitive service may be removed or suspended without pay only for such cause as will promote the efficiency of the service." Congress then provided the procedures for discharge determinations. In four of the five opinions expressing the varying views of the Justices, it was assumed that the requirement of cause conferred a substantive property right. The differences expressed were disagreements about the amount of protection required by the Fifth Amendment. Viewing Arnett from the perspective of my suggested four-step analysis, the property interest arose because the federal statute was the functional equivalent of an express contract of employment which was clear and unequivocal in its terms.

CJSPR cannot be so considered by Mr. Hamm. Rules 25 and 26 must be read in the context of all of the other rules, including Rule 46 prohibiting any review of a discharge. Read in a light most favorable to the plaintiff, there are so many ambiguities and inconsistencies contained in these rules that it is impossible to characterize them as an expression of a mutual agreement. Upon the record before me, I find that the plaintiff had no recognizable interest in his employment.

2. Is the enforcement of the claimed contractual or other property interest contrary to the expressed public policy of that state?

Even if the language of personnel Rules 25 and 26 could be read to create a contractual right to continued employment, the plaintiff here still could not prevail because the recognition of such a contract would violate the expressed public policy of the State of Colorado.

Application of the proposed analysis to Bishop v. Wood, supra, provides a good illustration of this point. There, the fact that the Marion ordinance conditioned petitioner's dismissal on cause could be regarded as having created for him a recognizable property interest based on implied contract. [Step 1]. But by the district court's reading of Still v. Lance, 275 N.C. 254, 182 S.E. 2d 403 (1971), the Supreme Court of North Carolina had expressly negated the existence of such an interest in public employment absent explicit statutory or contractual guarantees. Thus, the expressed public policy of the state had extinguished, as unenforceable, that which otherwise might have constituted a validly claimed protectable property interest. [Step 2].[4]

As previously noted, the Colorado Constitution gives absolute authority over the judicial department to the Supreme Court of Colorado, with administrative control vested in the chief justice. Rule 46 of CJSPR, adopted by the Supreme Court, is unequivocal in excluding chief probation officers from

---

4. Utilization of this two-step approach has the advantage of overcoming the seeming inconsistency between Bishop and its immediate predecessor, Arnett v. Kennedy, supra. In Arnett, six Justices were of the view that an employee necessarily had a property interest if his discharge was conditioned on cause. [See, footnote 8, Bishop v. Wood, supra.] By breaking down the analysis into two discrete steps, Arnett and Bishop can be reconciled to mean that a cause requirement may be sufficient to create a protectable property interest, if, and only if, such a grant is not contrary to the expressed public policy of the state.

any right of review of the termination of their employment. While the Colorado General Assembly has suggested that the court adopt personnel rules which compare to those applicable to the employees covered by the merit system in the Constitution, the Colorado Supreme Court has quite clearly excluded specific types of judicial employees from any protection against arbitrary action by the appointing authority.

It must be recognized that, in Colorado, all of the justices and judges of the judicial department are accountable to the people. They can be removed from office by the Colorado Supreme Court after investigation by a commission on judicial qualifications, pursuant to Article VI, Section 23 of the Colorado Constitution, and they are dependent upon an affirmative vote of the electorate for serving succeeding terms of office under Section 25 of Article VI.

Those who serve the judges and justices in the exercise of their sensitive duties, which certainly include chief probation officers, are made wholly accountable to those who are, in turn, responsible to the public for the performance of their courts. Thus, there is a direct comparability between this position of chief probation officer and that of the regent in Mitchell v. King, supra.

3. Is the recognized enforceable property interest worthy of the protection of procedural due process under the Fourteenth Amendment?

Following the suggested four-step analysis, if it were to be assumed that the plaintiff did have a recognizable property interest which would not be contrary to express public policy, would that interest require the protection of procedural due process under the Fourteenth Amendment? In my view it would not. Again, the nature of the position does not present a need for protecting freedom of action by the employee. Indeed, assistance to the judges in the exercise of their sentencing power is a function which requires subordination of the individual's views and efforts to the authority of the decision-maker. Under any balancing of interests approach, the weight of the public interest in performance is much heavier than the individual's claim to the benefits of employment. Accordingly, the Fourteenth Amendment affords no protection to this plaintiff in this case, other than the ordinary protections that would be afforded in a court of law on a breach of contract suit.

4. How much protection is required?

Finally, assuming that some process were due to

him, how much protection must be given? The Plaintiff here asks that this court order a review board hearing for him in the same manner as that which is provided for permanent employees of the judicial department who are not excluded from review by Rule 46. That would be more than the United States Constitution would require. Again, the amount of protection to be given must be determined by a balancing of the public and private interests and, again, the public interest predominates. In my view, the minimum opportunity to learn of the reasons for the action and a chance to address the decision-maker, as was held to constitute adequate protection in Goss v. Lopez, supra, is all that would be required here. That was done by Chief Judge Scott. While it could be contended that his approach to the plaintiff was authoritarian, his action did meet the kind of minimal standards which the Supreme Court has, at times, recognized as due process. I reach that conclusion with considerable personal regret, because I am reluctant to follow the view that the sturdy shield protecting the individual against government action, which was formerly recognized to require an opportunity for the clash of adversary interests at trial, has been so abraded as to permit the courts to characterize this type of hearing as due process of law.

The plaintiff here also claimed an infringement of a liberty interest. That claim was essentially withdrawn at the preliminary injunction hearing. It is also clear that the plaintiff has no evidence that there was any stigmatic effect upon him or his reputation resulting from the discharge. Accordingly, there is no support for a claim of infringement of a protected liberty interest.

Upon the foregoing findings of fact and conclusions of law, it is

ORDERED that the plaintiff's complaint and this civil action are dismissed.

Dated: January 25, 1977.

BY THE COURT:

Richard P. Matsch, Judge
United States District Court

Appendix E-1

COLORADO JUDICIAL SYSTEM

PERSONNEL RULES

Effective January 1, 1975

PROMULGATED BY THE COLORADO SUPREME COURT

PERSONNEL RULES
COLORADO JUDICIAL SYSTEM

PART I. CITATION, SCOPE, RESPONSIBILITY, AND DEFINITIONS

Rule 1. Citation

These rules shall be known and may be cited as the Colorado Judicial System Personnel Rules or C.J.S.P.R.

Rule 2. Scope

These rules shall apply to the supreme court, court of appeals, office of the state court administrator, all trial courts, and court services covered by C.R.S. 37-11-6, as amended, and all employees thereof, including the confidential employees of a justice or judge.

Rule 3. Responsibility

(a) Responsibility of Administrative Authorities. (1) Administrative authorities shall be responsible to the chief justice and the supreme court for the supervision and administration of all personnel within their respective jurisdictions.
    (2) This authority may be delegated in writing by the administrative authority, if not otherwise prohibited by these rules.
(b) Scope of Responsibility. (1) Appointing authorities, district administrators, and supervisors in their respective jurisdiction for:
    (2) Administration of these rules and compliance with the policies contained herein;
    (3) Orientation and on-the-job training of employees;
    (4) Review and evaluation of employees' performance; in accordance with these rules;
    (5) Corrective or disciplinary action when required in accordance with these rules; and

(6) Providing a work environment conducive to employee welfare and safety.

Rule 4. Definitions

(a) Definitions. (1) <u>Administrative Authority</u>. The official or officials with the primary administrative responsibility for a judicial agency, location, or judicial service, as delegated by the chief justice or specified in these rules.

(2) <u>Anniversary Date</u>. The date on which an employee is eligible for advancement to the next salary step in his pay grade.

(3) <u>Anniversary Increase</u>. The increment to which an employee is entitled on his anniversary date for satisfactory performance.

(4) <u>Appointing Authority</u>. The person or persons vested by these rules with the authority to appoint employees to positions, subject to approval of the appropriate administrative authority, as specified in rule 18.

(5) (i) <u>Appointment</u> - The act of an appointing authority by which a position is filled. Type of appointments include:

(ii) <u>Certified Appointment</u> - The permanent appointment of an employee to a position following successful completion of a probationary period;

(iii) <u>Probationary Appointment</u> - The initial appointment of an individual from outside the judicial system to a permanent position for a probationary period not to exceed six months or for a training period, whichever is longer.

(iv) <u>Reinstatement</u> - The right of rehire within one year vested in certified employees who were involuntarily terminated because of lack of work, lack of funds, reorganization, or exhaustion of paid leave;

(v) <u>Re-employment</u> - The privilege of rehire within one year with retention of certification, which may be granted to a former certified employee of the judicial system who terminated his employment in good standing; and

(vi) <u>Temporary Appointment</u> - An appointment for twelve months or less to a nonpermanent position or to one in which the incumbent is on leave without pay. Temporary appointments convey none of the rights or benefits accrued by permanent employees, except coverage under workmen's compensation.

(vii) <u>Temporary Emergency Appointment</u> -

A limited term appointment without examination for a period not to exceed four months in a twelve month period. Appointments of this nature are subject to the approval of the State Court Administrator.

(6) Bumping Rights. The rights of an employee to another position in the Colorado judicial system as provided in rule 27.

(7) Certified Employee. An employee who has successfully completed his probationary period.

(8) (i) Class - A group of positions sufficiently similar in duties, authority, and responsibilities that:

(ii) The same descriptive title may be used;

(iii) The same qualifications for entrance may be required;

(iv) The same apptitude or proficiency tests may be used; and

(v) The same pay grade may be applied with equity.

(9) Class Series. A sequence of classes that are alike in kind but not in level, starting with an entry level position and advancing upward in duties, complexity, authority, and responsibility.

(10) Class Specification. The official written job description of a class of work which defines the class, lists some of the more typical tasks of the class, and the training, education, and experience standards required for the class.

(11) Classified Service. The aggregate of all non-judicial positions under the judicial system.

(12) Compensation Schedule. The array of pay grades applying to the judicial system classified service.

(13) Conditional Promotion. The promotion of a certified employee to a position for a period not to exceed twelve months.

(14) Confidential Employee. An employee appointed by and directly responsible to a justice or a judge, as provided in rule 18.

(15) Continuous Service. Service in the judicial system which is unbroken by leave or leave without pay as authorized by these rules.

(16) Demotion. Moving an employee from one class to another at a lower pay grade.

(17) Dismissal. The discharge of an employee.

(18) Eligibility List. A roster of persons who have been found qualified for appointment or promotion to positions in the judicial system.

(19) **Exempt Position.** A professional, administrative or executive position in the Colorado judicial system which is exempt from the provisions of the Federal Fair Labor Standards Act.

(20) **Grade.** One of the official ranges of pay at which positions in the judicial system classified service are paid.

(21) **Grievance.** Any complaint filed by an employee in accordance with rule 44 pertaining to employment conditions or personnel practices in the judicial system.

(22) **Job Description.** The written summary of the duties and responsibilities assigned to a position.

(23) **Layoff.** The involuntary separation of an employee due to abolition of a position because of lack of work, lack of funds, or reorganization.

(24) **Non-exempt Position.** A position in the Colorado judicial system which falls within the provisions of the Federal Fair Labor Standards Act.

(25) **Permanent Full-time Position.** A position scheduled for full-time work, i.e., thirty-seven and one-half hours per week, and carried on the staffing pattern. A federally funded position shall be considered permanent only for the duration of the grant or grants unless subsequently state funded.

(26) **Permanent Part-time Positions.** A position scheduled for less than full-time work, i.e., less than thirty-seven and one-half hours per week and carried in the staffing pattern. A federally funded position shall be considered permanent only during the duration of the grant or grants unless subsequently state funded.

(27) **Position.** An individual job within the classified service.

(28) **Primary Duties.** The principle tasks which are assigned to a position.

(29) **Probationary Period.** The designated period following probationary appointment or the trial period following an unsatisfactory performance evaluation.

(30) **Promotion.** Moving an employee from one class to another class at a higher pay grade within the same district.

(31) **Promotional Transfer.** Moving an employee from one class and district to a different class in another district at a higher pay grade.

(32) **Reclassification.** The assignment of a position from one class of work to another.

(33) __Staffing Pattern__. A document showing the number of positions authorized for each location, the grade and title of each position, and other related information, as prescribed in rule 16.
(34) __Step__. Incremental pay increases within a grade.
(35) __Step-for-Step__. A salary adjustment, either up or down, which results in the employee being moved to the same step within his new grade as he was in his former grade.
(36) __Supervisor__. An individual who directs and coordinates the activities of other employees.
(37) __Temporary Full-time Position__. A position scheduled for full-time work which is established for one year or less.
(38) __Temporary Part-time Position__. A position scheduled for less than full-time work which is established for one year or less.
(39) __Terminal Leave__. Accrued leave which an employee is entitled to take or be compensated for at the time of his departure from the judicial system.
(40) __Trainee Position__. An entry level job established to provide on-the-job training.
(41) __Transfer__. Changing an employee from one position to another at the same pay grade, or changing an employee to a different jurisdiction at the same pay grade.
(42) __Trial Service Period__. The four month period following the promotion of a certified employee to a permanent position to evaluate his performance to certification to the position.
(43) __Unclassified Position__. A contract employee, on-call employee, or any position so designated by the supreme court.
(b) __Use of specific pay grade__. Whenever a specific pay grade is cited in these rules, it means the pay grade in effect on July 1, 1973. Even if the pay grade changes, these rules shall be interpreted as though the pay grade, and the positions to which it applies, as of July 1, 1973, is still in effect.

PART II.   COMPENSATION

Rule 5.   Compensation Plan

(a) __Authority__. The supreme court hereby establishes a compensation plan in which each class shall be assigned to a salary range based upon relative responsibilities of work, comparability to prevailing rates, and other pertinent salary and economic data.

(b) Adjustments. (1)(i) Effective July 1 of each year, adjustments in the compensation plan shall be made as a result of salary surveys and relationship studies by the Colorado state department of personnel, except that the chief justice or the state court administrator, if so delegated, may authorize pay grade adjustments prior to any July 1, if:

(ii) Such adjustments are necessitated by the creation of new positions or classes, authorized reorganization, or change in work; and

(iii) The proposed changes do not require expenditures greater than those for which appropriation or approved transfer of funds has been made.

(2) Any employee may request review of the salary range or relationship assigned to his class. Such request shall be submitted to the administrative authority.

(3) An administrative authority may request review of the pay grades or relationships assigned to positions within his jurisdiction.

(4) All requests for review shall be submitted in writing by the administrative authority to the state court administrator.

Rule 6. Hiring Rates

(a) New Employees. Beginning employees shall be compensated at the first step of the pay grade assigned to the class to which they are appointed, except as provided in sections (b) through (e) of this rule.

(b) In-grade Hiring. When recommended and justified by the appointing authority and the administrative authority and approved by the state court administrator, and if funds are available, the new employees at grade 43 and below may be hired at the second or third step in the range because of unusual personal qualifications or other unusual conditions. For the same reasons, but with the approval of the chief justice, new employees at grade 44 and above may be appointed at any step in the grade, up to and including step six.

(c) Re-employed Personnel. Re-employed personnel shall be appointed at the initial hiring step of the class, unless otherwise recommended and justified by the appointing authority and administrative authority and approved by the state court administrator as delegated by the chief justice.

(d) Unclassified Position Brought Under Classified Service. When an occupied unclassified position is brought under the classified service, the salary of the incumbent shall be established at the closest step at or above his present salary, except that if his salary exceeds the maximum rate for the class, the maximum rate shall be assigned.

(e) Change in Position. (1) When an employee is moved to a class other than that to which he is currently appointed, his salary shall be established:

(2) As though he were transferred, if the class is at the same level;

(3) As though he were promoted, if the class is at a higher level; or

(4) As though he were demoted, if the class is at a lower level.

Rule 7. Salary Computation

(a) Application of Compensation Schedule. All employees in the classified service shall be compensated at one of the rates, or at a proportion of one of the monthly rates, established in the salary schedule set forth in appendix A to these rules.

(b) Monthly Work Days - Compensation. (1) In computing the number of work days in a month, holidays which occur on work days during the month shall be counted as work days.

(2) Permanent full-time employees who work or are on paid leave on all scheduled work days of a month shall be compensated at the appropriate monthly rate.

(3) Permanent full-time employees who work less than a full month, including paid leave, shall be compensated at a computed daily rate for each day worked. Payment for holidays shall be determined as prescribed by rule 41. The applicable daily or hourly rate shall be taken from appendix A to these rules.

(4) Permanent part-time employees who work an irregular or intermittent schedule shall be compensated for time actually worked at the appropriate rate established in the salary as prescribed in subsection (b)(3) for time actually worked. Such employees shall not be compensated for holidays, except for holidays actually worked.

(5) Permanent part-time employees who work a regular part-time monthly schedule shall be compensated on a prorated monthly rate. Those

employees whose work schedule is less than a full month shall be compensated in the same manner as regular full-time employees who work less than a full month, as prescribed in subsection (b)(3) of this rule.

(6) Temporary employees hired to work a full month or more shall be compensated in the same manner as regular employees, except that the administrative authority may compensate such employees at the hourly or daily rate as prescribed in appendix A to these rules, rather than the monthly rate.

(7) Temporary employees hired to work less than a full month shall be compensated at either the hourly or daily rate established in appendix A to these rules.

(c) Monthly Work Days - Number. The standard number of work days in a month for judicial system employees shall be twenty-two.

Rule 8. Anniversary Increase

(a) Determination of Anniversary Date. (1) For employees in grade 16, step 2 and above, the anniversary date shall be the first of the month following the date he was appointed, unless the appointment date is the first working day of the month, in which case the first of that month shall be the anniversary date.

(2) For employees appointed to step 1 in grade 16 or below, the anniversary date shall be the first of the month following certification.

(3) When an unclassified employee is brought under the classified service, the date of appointment and the anniversary date shall be established as prescribed in subsection (a)(1).

(b) Pay Step Advancement. (1) (i) Any employee whose job performance is rated satisfactory or superior shall be advanced within the steps in his assigned grade, as follows:

(ii) From step 1 to step 2. Employees in grade 16 and below, after six months of satisfactory service at step 1; employees in all grades above grade 16, after one year of satisfactory service at step 1.

(iii) From step 2 through step 6. Employees in all grades shall be advanced to the next higher step after one year of satisfactory service.

(iv) For advancement from step 6 to 7. Employees in all grades shall be advanced to step 7 only after five years of satisfactory service at step 6.

(2) Permanent part-time employees shall be granted anniversary increases in the same way as regular full-time employees.

(3) Anniversary increases shall not be granted to terminating employees whose anniversary date occurs during the leave period after their last working day on the job.

(c) (1) Withholding Anniversary Increase for Unsatisfactory Service. Any employee whose job performance is unsatisfactory shall not be advanced to the next step in grade.

(2) The administrative authority shall determine whether the employee's performance has been unsatisfactory and whether, on the basis of his performance, the employee should not be advanced.

(3) A performance determination shall be made and the employee notified at least 30 days prior to the employee's anniversary date on the basis of the performance evaluation.

(4) After consultation with one or more persons who supervise the work of the employee and after giving the employee an opportunity to respond to any reported deficiencies made with respect to his performance, the performance determination shall become final on the anniversary date.

(5) At the end of the ninety day probationary period prescribed in rule (24)(e), the administrative authority may advance the employee to the next higher step if the employee has corrected the deficiencies in his performance. The anniversary date shall be adjusted to the first of the month following the end of the probationary period.

(d) (1) When the pay of an employee is adjusted to a different step in his pay grade, he shall be assigned a new anniversary date, which shall be the first of the month following the date of adjustment, unless that date is the first working day of the month, in which case the first of that month shall be the anniversary date.

(2) When an employee is reinstated or re-employed, his date of appointment and the anniversary date shall be determined as prescribed in subsection (a) of this rule.

(3) When an employee returns from educational leave or leave without pay, his anniversary date shall be advanced one month for each month of such leave.

Rule 9. Effect of Position Change on Compensation.

(a) _Transfer at Same Pay Grade_. When an employee is transferred to a class at the same pay grade, his grade, step, salary, and anniversary date shall not change.

(b) _Promotion or Reclassification to a Higher Class_. (1) When an employee is promoted to or reclassified to a class which is not more than six pay grades higher, his salary may be adjusted step-for-step upon recommendation of the administrative authority and approval of the state court administrator. The anniversary date shall not change.

(2) When an employee is promoted to or reclassified to a class which is more than six pay grades higher, he shall be limited to a salary increase of fifteen percent. The anniversary date shall not change. In no event shall he be paid less than the rate assigned to Step 1 of the class to which he has been promoted or reclassified.

(3) When an employee is given a promotional transfer, his compensation shall be governed by this rule.

(c) _Demotion_. (1) When an employee is demoted, his pay shall be adjusted downward step-for-step, except as follows:

(2) _Voluntary Demotion_. If an employee is demoted voluntarily for non-disciplinary reasons, his salary in the new grade shall be the salary closest to his salary prior to demotion, but shall not exceed step 7 of his new grade.

(3) _Classification Actions_. (i) If an employee is downgraded as a result of a position classification study, his salary in the new grade shall be the salary closest to his salary prior to downgrading or shall be frozen at his current salary, if it exceeds step 7 of his new grade.

(ii) If his salary prior to downgrading is within the lower grade, an employee is entitled to regular anniversary increases.

(iii) When an employee's salary has been frozen, he shall become eligible for anniversary increases on his regular anniversary date when the annual wage survey results in his frozen rate of pay falling within the new pay scale for his grade.

(4) _Disciplinary Demotion_. When an employee is demoted for disciplinary reasons, his pay may be adjusted to any step in the new grade at the discretion of the administrative authority, but he shall not be demoted to a step higher than his step

before the demotion.

(d) <u>Probationary Employees</u>. When a probationary employee is demoted or accepts appointment in a lower class, his pay shall be determined as though he were originally appointed in the lower class.

Rule 10. Salary Adjustments from
Salary Surveys

(a) <u>Effect of Pay Grade Change</u>. (1) When the pay grade assigned a class is changed because of salary studies or wage surveys, the pay of all employees in the class shall be changed step-for-step to the new grade, and anniversary dates shall not be changed.

(2) When an employee's salary has been frozen, he shall become eligible for anniversary increases on his regular anniversary date when the annual wage survey results in his salary falling with the new pay scale for his grade.

Rule 11. Salary Computation for Simultaneous
Personnel Actions

(a) <u>Effect of Two or more Actions</u>. (1) When two or more actions affecting pay occur on the same effective date, the new grade, step, and rate shall be computed in the following sequence, as applicable:

(2) If the action occurs on the employee's anniversary date, the anniversary increase for the class from which the employee is being promoted, demoted, or transferred shall also apply.

(3) If the employee is promoted or demoted, the step-for-step promotional or demotional increase or decrease shall apply along with any pay grade adjustments effective the same date, but the anniversary date remains unchanged.

Rule 12. Pay Computation for Terminating
and Deceased Employees

(a) <u>Unused Annual and Holiday Leave</u>. Employees who are terminated, retire, or resign and survivors of deceased employees shall be compensated for unused annual, sick, and holiday leave as prescribed in rules 32, 33, and 40, but not for compensatory time.

(b) <u>Holidays during Terminal Leave</u>. (1) Employees who retire or resign in good standing and survivors of deceased employees shall be credited for a day of work for each legal holiday that occurs on a work day during the paid terminal leave.

(2) Dismissed employees shall not be compensated or credited with holiday leave for holidays occurring on a work day during the terminal leave.

(c) Temporary Employees. Temporary employees accrue no leave and shall not be paid for any time after their last day of work.

(d) Termination Date. The termination date shall be an employee's last day on the job, even though payment is made for unused leave.

PART III. CLASSIFICATION PLAN AND STAFFING PATTERNS

Rule 13. Classification Plan

(a) General. The state court administrator shall maintain a classification plan based on investigation and analysis of the duties of each position. The plan shall group all positions having comparable duties and responsibilities, and common requirements for filling positions assigned to the class. The plan shall be subject to approval of the supreme court.

(b) Class Specifications. The state court administrator shall prepare written specifications for every class of work in the personnel system. The specifications shall be based on a sound, systematic occupational analysis and position evaluation. They shall contain elements sufficient to distinguish the various classes. Duties as may be described in the specification shall not be construed to limit the assignment of other related duties by proper authority, subject to the notification provisions of rule 14(b).

(c) Class Title. The assigned class title shall be the official title for every position in the judicial system for personnel transactions and budget administration. Working or statutory titles may be used in the day-to-day business of the court.

(d) Changes to Class Specifications. When proposing, amending, or abolishing a class specification, the state court administrator shall provide administrative authorities and other interested parties with a notice of proposed changes and a copy of the changes or proposed specifications. The administrative authority shall make the content of the changes known to employees. The notice shall contain a specified time from the date of notice in which to file written objections with the state court administrator. The state court administrator shall consider the objections and may approve, modify, or disapprove the new or amended specifications or the abolishment of classifications.

(e) <u>Assignment of Duties</u>. The assignment of duties to a position, whether duties are primary or occasional, temporary or permanent, incidental or essential, shall be the responsibility of the administrative authority and the classification plan shall in no way limit or interfere with the administrative authority's responsibility for the assignment of duties.

(f) <u>Creation, Abolition and Reclassification of Positions</u>. (1) To create a new position, the administrative authority shall submit a request and a written job description to the state court administrator.

(2) The state court administrator shall investigate and analyze the duties proposed for any new position, allocate the position to its appropriate classification, and establish the effective date.

(3) The same procedure shall be followed whenever substantial changes in the duties and responsibilities assigned to a position are proposed.

(4) Any administrative authority may request a classification review of any position, if the position has not been reviewed within the previous twleve months. Such request shall be submitted to the state court administrator with a written job description setting forth the actual and essential duties of the position.

(5) Any employees may request, in writing, a classification review of his own position, if the position has not been reviewed within the previous twelve months. The administrative authority shall forward the request to the state court administrator within ten days.

(6) The state court administrator shall act on any request involving an individual position within sixty days after receipt and on any request involving several positions within one hundred and twenty days after receipt. If the reclassification review does not proceed in a timely manner, the employee may petition the reclassification review board for appropriate action.

(7) If a position is vacant, the state court administrator may review the classification of the position prior to appointment to determine the appropriateness of the classification.

(8) The administrative authority may re-

assign duties assigned to a vacant position and request a classification review, or reclassify the vacant position within limitations established by any prior written delegation of authority to reclassify vacant positions by the state court administrator.

(9) The effective date for reclassification actions shall be the first working day of the pay period following approval by the state court administrator or a ruling by the reclassification review board.

(g) Periodic Review. (1) Subject to the conditions of section (d) of this rule the state court administrator shall make periodic reviews of the classification plan and shall prepare new classes of positions, revise specifications of existing classes, changes in class titles, changes in grades of classes, and recommendations for abolishing classes for consideration by the supreme court.

(2) The state court administrator may also recommend to the supreme court other changes and revisions in the classification plan as changing conditions require.

(3) The state court administrator, with the approval of the chief justice, may contract to have such periodic reviews performed by persons outside the Colorado judicial system who are knowledgeable and experienced in public personnel policies and studies.

Rule 14. Reclassification of a Filled Position

(a) Basis for Reclassification. (1) A filled position may be reclassified when warranted by permanent substantial changes in the duties and responsibilities of a position subject to the provisions of Rule 13(f).

(2) Whenever permanent substantial changes are made in the duties and responsibilities of a position, the administrative authority shall notify the state court administrator in writing within thirty days. Such notification shall include a new written position or job description setting forth the actual primary duties and other essential duties recommended for assignment to the position.

(b) Procedure for Reclassification. (1) If the administrative authority requests reclassification of a filled position, such request shall be accompanied by the notification of changes in duties.

(2) Upon receipt of the request, the

state court administrator shall review the position and determine the class and grade to which the position should be assigned.

(3) The state court administrator shall submit his decisions to the requesting administrative authority.

Rule 15. Classification Appeals

(a) Right of Appeal - Time Limits. (1) When a certified employee objects to a reclassification action, he shall have the right of appeal.

(2) (i) When the classification results from a request for reclassification from either the employee or the administrative authority, an employee shall have thirty days to appeal to the reclassification review board from the time he is notified of such classification by the state court administrator.

(ii) When the classification results from a periodic review performed by the state court administrator, or by persons outside the judicial system, as provided in rule (13)(g)(3), an employee shall have ninety days to appeal to the reclassification review board from the time he is notified of such classification.

(b) Content of Appeal. (1) Appeals shall be made in writing setting forth:

(2) The reasons why the employee believes his classification to be in error;

(3) The classification which he feels is appropriate to his position and the reasons therefor; and

(4) Any further documentation in support of his case.

(c) Appeal Procedure. (1) The appeal should be transmitted by the employee to the administrative authority, who shall prepare and attach an evaluation of the appeal and his recommended action thereon.

(2) Within thirty days, the administrative authority shall transmit the appeal and accompanying documents to the state court administrator, who shall have any evaluation and recommendations prepared for the board. The evaluation shall be prepared on the basis of the application of classification standards and budgetary impact of the action.

(3) The reclassification review board may limit its consideration to the material presented by the employee making the appeal and recommendations

and supporting documents used as the basis for establishing the classification being appealed. It may request a desk audit or additional information from the employee, the administrative authority, or the state court administrator. The board may ask the employee to appear at a hearing.

(4) (i) The reclassification review board shall make its decision within thirty days after receipt of an appeal in writing, unless the employee making the appeal is requested to appear before the board.

(ii) If the employee is asked to appear, the board shall make its decision within thirty days after hearing.

(5) The decision of the reclassification review board shall be final.

(d) <u>Reclassification Review Board</u>. (1) (i) The reclassification review board shall be appointed by the chief justice and shall be constituted as follows:

(ii) For consideration of appeals from employees of trial courts, the board shall have three members - one shall be a trial court judge or an appellate court judge with trial court experience, one shall be a district administrator, and one shall be the state court administrator or his designee.

(iii) For consideration of appeals from employees of probation departments, the board shall have three members - one shall be an appellate or trial court judge with knowledge of probation department practices and operations, one shall be a chief probation officer, and one shall be the state court administrator or his designee.

(iv) For consideration of appeals from employees of appellate courts, the board shall have three members - one shall be a justice or appellate judge, one shall be the clerk of an appellate court other than the one from which the employee is making his appeal, and one shall be the state court administrator or his designee.

(v) For consideration of appeals from employees of the state court administrator's office, the board shall have three members - one shall be the chief justice or his designee, one shall be a chief judge serving on the advisory judicial council, and one shall be a district admininstrator with a demonstrated knowledge and understanding of the function of the state court administrator's office.

(2) When an appeal comes before the board involving an employee from the court or agency of one

of the board members, the member shall disqualify himself, and the chief justice or the state court administrator, if so delegated, shall appoint a replacement temporarily to hear the appeal.

Rule 16. Staffing Patterns and Position Allocations

(a) Content. (1) The staffing pattern for each location shall contain the number of authorized positions, the classification grade of each position, the position number, the official title, the pay range, and such other information as the state court administrator may determine. It shall also show the name of the incumbent, unless the position is vacant.

(2) The current salary of each incumbent shall be listed on the staffing pattern, as well as the salary he is to receive in the next fiscal year.

(b) Request for new Positions in the Current Fiscal Year. (1) Any request for a new position to be established before the succeeding fiscal year shall be submitted initially by the appointing authority to the administrative authority, if other than the appointing authority.

(2) The administrative authority shall submit the request to the state court administrator with a description of the duties to be assigned, an explanation of why the position is needed, and any other pertinent information or comments.

(3) Upon receipt of a request for a new position, the state court administrator shall examine the need for the position, including such on-the-scene study of the requesting court or agency as he deems appropriate.

(4) (i) Upon completion of this examination, the state court administrator shall recommend to the chief justice that the request for the new position be approved or denied.

(ii) The state court administrator's recommendation to the chief justice shall set forth the proposed salary classification, official title, the availability of funds, and the reasons for the recommendation.

(5) No new position shall be approved during a fiscal year, unless sufficient funds are available. Positions so created shall expire June 30, of the same year, unless fully funded in the subsequent fiscal year.

(c) Request for New Positions in Succeeding Fiscal Years. A request for a new position to be established in a succeeding fiscal year shall be included in the annual budget request.

(d) <u>Periodic Studies</u>. (1) The state court administrator shall conduct periodic studies of the work load, work systems, and personnel for each location.

(2) Upon request of the appropriate administrative authority, the state court administrator shall make such studies for the supreme court and court of appeals.

(3) Upon completion of a study, the state court administrator shall submit his recommendations on work system organization, position allocation, and staffing patterns to the chief justice and the administrative authority.

(4) The administrative authority shall have thirty days to respond to the state court administrator.

(5) Recommendations approved by the chief justice shall be put into effect as soon as practicable, and the staffing pattern amended.

(e) <u>Hiring Unauthorized Staff</u>. No personnel shall be hired in excess of the number authorized, in job classes other than those authorized, nor in grades other than those authorized.

PART IV. APPOINTMENT OF EMPLOYEES

Rule 17. Qualifications of New Employees

(a) <u>Determination of Qualifications</u>. (1) (i) The initial determination as to whether a person meets the specified qualifications for appointment shall be made by the administrative authority after review of the person's academic credentials, work experience, examination results if required, and any other pertinent information.

(ii) This determination shall be subject to review and approval by the state court administrator.

(iii) The effective date of any appointment shall not precede such review and approval by the state court administrator.

(2) Written or oral examinations may be required to determine whether the qualifications for a position have been met by an applicant or appointee pursuant to rule 19.

(b) <u>Exceptions</u>. Alternative or lesser qualifications may be approved by the state court administrator, if he determines that it is not possible to fill the position at the required qualification level in a reasonable length of time.

(c) <u>Unqualified Applicant</u>. A person shall not qualify for a position if the administrative authority or the state court administrator finds the presence of any of the conditions enumerated in rule 19(h), except that any person terminated from prior employment shall not be disqualified from employment in the Colorado judicial system solely on the grounds of prior termination.

(d) <u>Application to Confidential Employees</u>. The qualifications specified in the judicial system personnel plan shall apply to the confidential employee of a justice or judge.

Rule 18. Appointing Authority

(a) <u>Office of State Court Administrator</u>. The employees of the state court administrator's office shall be appointed by the state court administrator, subject to the approval of the supreme court.

(b) <u>Supreme Court</u>. (1) The clerk of the supreme court, the reporter of decisions, and the supreme court librarian shall be appointed by the supreme court.

(2) Other employees of the supreme court clerk's office shall be appointed by the clerk, subject to the approval of the supreme court.

(3) Other employees of the reporter of decisions' office shall be appointed by the reporter of decisions, subject to the approval of the supreme court.

(c) <u>Court of Appeals</u>. (1) The clerk of the court of appeals and the reporter of decisions shall be appointed by a majority of the judges of that court. If a majority of the judges cannot agree, the authority for making the appointment may be delegated to the chief judge by the chief justice.

(2) The other employees of the court of appeals clerk's office shall be appointed by the clerk, subject to the approval of the chief judge.

(d) <u>District Court</u>. (1) Judicial district administrators and clerks of the district courts shall be appointed by a majority of the judges of the district court, except that appointments in grade 47 and above shall be subject to the approval of the chief justice. If a majority of the district judges cannot agree on the appointment, the authority for making the appointment may be delegated to the chief judge by the chief justice or the appointment may be made by the chief justice.

(2) (i) In districts having a judicial district administrator:

(ii) Employees of the county court in grade 27 and above shall be appointed by a majority of the judges of the county court after consultation with the district administrator and the clerk of the county court and subject to the approval of the chief judge. If a majority of the county judges cannot agree, the appointments shall be made by the presiding judge with the approval of the chief judge.

(iii) Employees of the county court in grade 26 and below shall be appointed by the clerk of the county court after consultation with the district administrator and subject to the approval of the presiding judge of the county court and the chief judge.

(3) In districts without a judicial district administrator, employees of the county court shall be appointed by the presiding judge of the county court, subject to the approval of the chief judge.

(f) Confidential Employees. (1) The confidential employees of a justice or a judge shall be appointed by the justice or judge.

(2) Confidential employees of each justice of the supreme court and judge of the court of appeals shall include a secretary and a law clerk.

(3) Confidential employees of a district, probate, superior, or juvenile court judge may include a reporter, division clerk, and either a bailiff or a bailiff-law clerk and none other.

(4) Confidential employees of a county judge in a multi-judge county court may include a reporter, division clerk and a bailiff, or bailiff-law clerk, and none other, except that if mechanical recording equipment is used, the employee shall be a clerk stenographer rather than a reporter.

(5) Positions which are in the classified service may not be changed to confidential positions, unless the position is vacant, or the incumbent in the position agrees to such a change in writing, after being advised as to the change in employee rights. Any written agreement signed by an employee to change to confidential status must contain a statement that he has been advised as to the change in employee rights.

(g) Probation Departments. (1) Chief Probation officers of adult or combined adult and juvenile probation departments of a judicial district shall be appointed by a majority of the judges of the district court, except that such appointments in grade 47 and above shall be subject to the approval of the chief justice. If a majority of the district judges cannot agree, the authority for making the appointment may be delegated to the chief judge by the chief justice.

(2) The chief probation officer of a probation department which serves more than one district shall be appointed by a majority of the chief judges of those districts, subject to the approval of the chief justice. If a majority of the chief judges cannot agree, the appointment shall be made by the chief justice.

(3) Chief probation officers of juvenile probation departments shall be appointed by a majority of the chief judge and the judges handling juvenile jurisdiction, except such appointments in grade 47 and above shall be subject to approval of the chief justice. If a majority of these judges cannot agree, the authority for making the appointment may be delegated to the chief judge by the chief justice.

(4) In those districts with a chief probation officer or a chief adult probation officer, adult probation department employees shall be appointed by the chief probation officer or the chief adult probation officer, subject to the approval of the chief judge.

(5) In those districts without a chief probation officer or a chief adult probation officer, adult probation department employees shall be appointed by the chief judge, after consultation with the judges handling criminal jurisdiction.

(6) In those districts with a chief probation officer or a chief juvenile probation officer, juvenile probation department employees shall be appointed by the chief probation officer, subject to the approval of the chief judge.

(7) In those districts without a chief probation officer or a chief juvenile probation officer, probation department employees shall be appointed by the chief judge, after consultation with the judges handling juvenile jurisdiction.

(h) Denver Probate Court. The clerk, confidential employees, and other employees in grade 28 and above of the probate court of the city and county of Denver shall be appointed by the presiding judge, appointments in grade 47 and above shall be subject to the approval of the chief justice.

(i) Denver Juvenile Court. (1) The director of court services, who shall have overall responsibility for administration and probation services of the juvenile court of the city and county of Denver, shall be appointed by the judges of that court, subject to the approval of the chief justice.

(2) The director of court services shall appoint all other non-confidential employees subject to the approval of the presiding judge.

(j) <u>Denver Superior Court</u>. (1) The clerk of the superior court of the city and county of Denver shall be appointed by the judge of that court, subject to the approval of the chief justice.

(2) The clerk shall appoint all other non-confidential employees, subject to the approval of the judge.

Rule 19. Examinations and Qualification Reviews

(a) <u>Application of Examinations</u>. (1) Subject to the approval of the chief justice, the state court administrator shall determine which positions in the judicial system require written or oral examinations to establish eligibility for appointment or promotion.

(2) The state court administrator, upon request of an administrative authority, may establish a different examination to determine eligibility for appointment or promotion to a specific position.

(3) (i) In lieu of written or oral examinations, the determination of eligibility for appointment or promotion shall be based on an evaluation of education, experience, references, interviews, and job related elements.

(ii) Interviews shall be conducted by the administrative and appointing authorities. The state court administrator may also interview prospective appointees upon request of the administrative authority.

(b) <u>Non-Discrimination</u>. Applicants shall not be discriminated against on the basis of race, religion, sex, national origin or political affiliation. Applicants or employees capable of performing the duties of a position shall not be discriminated against because of a physical handicap.

(c) <u>Responsibility</u>. The administrative authority shall be responsible for recruitment, examining, and referral activities in connection with vacant positions and competitive or promotional examinations, except that the state court administrator shall assist in recruitment as provided in rule 21(a)(1). The administrative authority may request the assistance of the state court administrator in examining and referral activities.

(d) <u>Announcement of Examinations</u>. (1)

Announcements shall be distributed to inform interested persons of the opportunity to apply. Announcement shall include such information as the title of the class, grade, the work location of positions covered by the examination, qualifications and standards applicants must meet, primary duties, time limits, and any other pertinent information.

  (2) Examination announcements shall be advertised throughout the Colorado judicial system. They shall be posted in the offices of all state courts and in such other places where eligible persons might reasonably be expected to read them. Districts shall post examination announcements in places known by and available to employees.

  (3) Positive efforts shall be made by the administrative authority and the state court administrator in all examination and recruitment efforts to advertise employment opportunities in state courts to minority groups and to seek out and employ qualified minority candidates.

  (4) When any substantial change is made in an announcement, such changes shall be distributed and posted, and a new time limit shall be set for filing applications.

 (e) <u>Extension of Filing Date</u>. Whenever it is found that an insufficient number of applications have been received from qualified persons on any announced examination, the filing date may be extended.

 (f) <u>Filing of Applications</u>. (1) All applications for examination shall be made upon forms approved by the state court administrator.

  (2) The applicant's signature on the application shall constitute his certification that, to the best of his knowledge, all information he entered on the application is true.

  (3) Applications must be submitted within the time period specified in the announcement.

  (4) Late or incomplete applications may be considered, if the time schedule permits.

 (g) <u>Oral Examinations</u>. When competition in an oral examination is announced as limited to the best qualified applicants, as determined by preliminary screening or testing, admission to the oral examination may be restricted to the top ranking applicants.

 (h) <u>Reason for Rejection</u>. (1) An application may be rejected if the applicant:

  (2) Lacks the prescribed qualifications;

  (3) Is physically or mentally unfit to perform the duties of the class;

  (4) Has reached the mandatory retirement

age, unless he is currently employed by the judicial system;

    (5) Has a recent history of excessive use of alcohol, narcotics, or other drugs which may affect job performance;

    (6) Has a prior record of unsatisfactory employment;

    (7) Has made false statements of any material fact or has practiced or attempted to practice deception or fraud in his application or his test; or

    (8) Has violated these rules or has been found guilty of violation of any law which affects the applicant's ability to perform the job.

    (i) <u>Content of Examinations</u>. (1) The state court administrator shall determine the content of examinations and shall prepare examinations for use as required.

    (2) Examination content shall be based on the job elements of the position for which the examination is conducted.

    (3) The state court administrator may prescribe alternate clerical or typing tests or other job related tests and may authorize that these tests be administered by the administrative authority or his designee.

    (4) The state court administrator may prepare lists of questions to serve as guides for boards conducting oral examinations.

    (5) In preparing such lists of questions and determining examination content, the state court administrator shall consult with judges and appropriate court personnel and may establish advisory committees for this purpose.

    (6) Test materials shall be confidential and shall be so handled by the state court administrator, members of his staff, and any other persons having access to this material.

    (j) <u>Conduct of Examinations</u>. (1) The administrative authority shall administer written examinations as he deems appropriate to meet the personnel needs of his judicial district.

    (2) The administrative authority shall determine the general qualifications and composition of examining boards in oral examinations and shall compile a list of appropriate oral examiners after contacting each one to ascertain his willingness to serve. A copy of this list shall be filed with the state court administrator.

    (3) When an oral examination has been requested for a position, the administrative authority

shall select a panel of three examiners from the list of appropriate oral examiners.

(k) <u>Eligibility for Examinations.</u> (1) A person shall be eligible to take a written or oral examination if he meets the educational and experience standards for the position or if alternative standards are allowed pursuant to rule 17(b).

(2) The determination of whether the specified standards are met or whether alternative standards are to be accepted shall be made by the administrative authority, subject to the approval of the state court administrator.

(3) (i) Attainment of age sixty-five shall be the maximum age for admittance to an examination, unless waived by the state court administrator.

(ii) Except as may otherwise be required by law or supreme court rule, a person must have attained the age of eighteen years to be eligible for an examination.

(l) <u>Rating of Applicants.</u> (1) (i) The administrative authority shall be responsible for rating applicants of all written examinations, subject to the guidelines established by the state court administrator, and for notifying the state court administrator of the results within fifteen days after conclusion of the examination.

(ii) The state court administrator shall establish a minimum passing grade for each written examination.

(iii) When a written examination consists of more than one part, the state court administrator may establish weights for each part of the examination and establish a passing grade for each part of the examination.

(2) (i) Each oral examination board shall rank applicants according to qualifications and suitability for the position, indicating applicants considered not qualified.

(ii) The oral board's evaluation shall be transmitted to the administrative authority, the appointing authority, and the state court administrator.

(iii) The appointing authority shall make his selection, subject to the approval of the administrative authority, from the top three candidates submitted to him.

(iv) In the event of a tie score amongst the top three positions on an examination, only the top three applicants may be considered, unless the tie occurs in the third position. If there is a tie for third position, all the applicants tied for third may be considered along with the persons in the first and second positions.

(m) Examination Records. The state court administrator and the administrative authority shall maintain examination records, including examination results, applications and test papers for each examinee, names of oral examiners, summary data on number of applicants and examination results, and such other information as he deems pertinent.

(n) Discretion of Administrative Authority. Any one of the top three persons who is admitted to and receives a passing grade on an oral or written examination may be appointed to a vacant position pursuant to rules 18 and 21. The administrative authority shall be responsible for informing all applicants of the examination results.

(o) Veterans Preference. Veterans who, for other than training purposes, served on active duty in any branch of the armed forces of the United States during any period of any declared or undeclared war or other armed hostilities against an armed, foreign enemy or served on active duty in any such branch in any campaign or expedition for which a campaign badge is authorized and who were separated under honorable conditions, and the unremarried widows of such veterans, shall have 5 points added to a passing grade on open competitive examinations. Such a veteran, who because of disability incurred in line of duty is receiving monetary compensation or disability retirement benefits by reason of public laws administered by the department of defense or the veterans administration or any successor thereto, shall have 5 additional points added to a passing grade on open competitive examinations. Applicants claiming such points shall submit the necessary documentation upon request.

Rule 20. Employment Eligibility Lists

(a) Establishment of Eligibility Lists. (1) (i) The state court administrator and administrative authority shall establish and maintain the following employment eligibility lists:

(ii) Examination lists, consisting of persons who have applied for and are eligible to take an examination;

(iii) Qualified applicant lists, consisting of persons who have received a passing grade on an examination or whose educational and experience credentials have been evaluated and were found to

meet the qualifications of the position applied for;
    (iv) Promotion lists, consisting of judicial system employees who have received a passing rating on an oral or written examination;
    (v) Reinstatement lists, consisting of certified employees who were separated in a lay off and who are entitled to priority reinstatement for a period of one year; and
    (vi) Reemployment lists, consisting of employees who terminated in good standing and who are entitled to reemployment for a period of one year.
    (2) Eligibility lists shall show the name of the person, his last known address, the position for which eligible, and the date eligibility was established.
    (3) A person may be carried on an eligibility list for two years, unless the period is extended by the state court administrator. Failure to respond to an official communication from the administrative authority shall result in removal from an eligibility list.
    (4) The administrative authority shall furnish a copy of all eligibility lists to the state court administrator.
    (b) Use of Eligibility Lists. (1) Employment eligibility lists shall be made available on request to all administrative authorities by the state court administrator.
    (2) When a vacancy occurs, appointing authorities may appoint a person from the top three qualified applicants on the eligibility list without further examination or evaluation of his credentials.
    (3) Appointments from an eligibility list shall be reported to the administrative authority and the state court administrator.

Rule 21. Recruitment and Filling Positions

    (a) Recruitment. (1) When a vacancy exists or is anticipated the administrative authority shall notify the state court administrator and shall request assistance in recruiting applicants.
    (2) The appointing authority shall recruit locally for a position. The vacancy shall be publicized locally, including notification to local newspapers when necessary and posting of the vacancy notice in a public place in the courthouse and all offices of clerks of court in the judicial district.
    (3) (i) Positive efforts by the administrative authority and the state court administrator

shall be made in recruitment to advertise employment opportunities to minority groups, and agencies specializing in the placement of minority group members, and to seek out, contact, and employ qualified minority candidates.

(ii) Ethnic and racial information on all applicants for positions in the Colorado judicial system shall be collected and transmitted to the state court administrator on the prescribed application for employment form.

(iii) This information shall be treated with strict confidentiality.

(b) No recruitment may be made outside of the state of Colorado without the prior approval of the state court administrator.

Rule 22. Probationary Period

(a) Probationary Period. A newly appointed employee shall serve a six-month probationary period in the position to which he is appointed.

(b) Dismissal or Reduction. (1) Any employee on probationary status may be dismissed at any time for failure to perform his duties properly or any other good and sufficient cause.

(2) Dismissal of a probationary employee shall be final and not subject to review.

(c) Attainment of Certified Status. (1) At the conclusion of the six-month probationary period, if the employee's performance is satisfactory, he shall be certified in the position, and officially notified by the administrative authority in writing of his certification.

(2) In exceptional cases, probationary status may be extended by the state court administrator for an additional period of time not to exceed three months upon written request and justification from the administrative authority.

(3) On appointment to a class for which satisfactory completion of a training program approved by the state court administrator is required, the probationary period shall be for the length of the training program, but not to exceed one year.

Rule 23. Trial Service Period

(a) Trial Service Period. A promoted employee shall serve a four-month trial service period in the position to which he is promoted.

(b) Reversion. (1) (i) Any employee serving a trial service period, may revert to the position to which he was previously certified if his performance is unsatisfactory. Such reversion shall be in accordance with the provisions outlined in Rule 27 (h)(2).

(ii) Employees who are certified to their classifications, and who have been reduced in classification due to the reversion process, shall have a right to return to that classification to which they have been certified when the first vacancy occurs, providing, that the vacancy occurs in the department in which the reversion occurred.

(2) Any employee who has received a promotional transfer shall not revert to his former position.

(c) Salary Adjustment. Salaries for employees receiving promotions or promotional transfers shall be governed by rule 7.

PART V. EMPLOYEE EVALUATION AND DISCIPLINE

Rule 24. Performance Evaluation

(a) Annual Evaluation. Each certified employee shall be rated annually on his job performance. The evaluation shall be initiated at least sixty days prior to the employee's anniversary date.

(b) Evaluation Report Content. (1) The evaluation report shall indicate whether the employee's performance is superior, satisfactory, or unsatisfactory.

(2) The report shall include, but not be limited to, an evaluation of job performance strengths and weaknesses as measured against normal standards, as well as recommendations for improvement.

(c) Responsibility for Evaluations. (1) The evaluation of each employee shall be made by his immediate supervisor. Evaluation of a confidential employee shall be made by the justice or judge to whom he is directly responsible.

(2) The evaluation report of each employee shall be forwarded through the appointing authority to the administrative authority or his designee.

(3) The appointing authority shall review the report and discuss it with the immediate supervisor, after which a review conference with the employee shall be held. Copies of the evaluation form shall be placed in the employee's file,

given to the employee, and relevant information contained in the report shall be forwarded to the state court administrator with the personnel action form for the anniversary increase.

(d) Employee Appeal. (1) A certified non-confidential employee may appeal his evaluation in writing to the administrative authority.

(2) The administrative authority shall review the evaluation and the appeal, including interviews with the appellant and rating officials as deemed appropriate for a satisfactory resolution of conflicting judgments. Within thirty days, the administrative authority shall render a decision in writing, which shall be final.

(e) Effect of Evaluation. (1) An employee must receive a written rating of satisfactory or superior ro receive his anniversary increase.

(2) If an employee's rating is unsatisfactory, he shall be placed on probationary status for three months.

(3) If, at the end of the probationary period, the employee's overall job performance is rated as satisfactory, he shall be certified with his anniversary date and anniversary increase determined as provided in rule 8.

(4) If, at the end of the probationary period, the employee's overall job performance is still unsatisfactory, he shall be subject to corrective or disciplinary action pursuant to rule 25. Any corrective or disciplinary action for confidential employees shall be determined by the justice or judge to whom they are directly responsible.

Rule 25. Employee Discipline

(a) Corrective Actions. Corrective actions are written warnings, reprimands, and censures which are taken to correct and improve an employee's job performance and do not affect current pay, current status, or tenure.

(b) Disciplinary Actions. (1) Disciplinary actions are taken to penalize an employee for an offensive act or poor job performance and affect current pay, status, or tenure.

(2) Disciplinary actions may include suspension, demotion, pay adjustment to a lower step in the assigned pay grade, dismissal as provided in rule 26, or any other appropriate action affecting the current pay, status, or tenure of an employee.

(c) Responsibility for Administering Corrective or Disciplinary Actions. (1) Except for confidential employees, the responsibility for initiating and administering corrective or disciplinary actions is vested in the administrative authority after considering recommendations from the appointing authority and the immediate supervisor.

    (2) The responsibility for initiating and administering corrective or disciplinary actions applicable to a confidential employee is vested in the justice or judge to whom the employee is responsible.

  (d) <u>Causes for Corrective or Disciplinary Actions</u>. (1) Causes for initiating corrective or disciplinary action shall include, but are not limited to:

    (2) Violation of, or failure to comply with, the state constitution or statutes, supreme court rules and regulations, or local court rules and regulations;

    (3) Failure or refusal to comply with a lawful order or to accept a reasonable and proper assignment from an authorized supervisor;

    (4) Documented inefficienty, incompetency, negligence, or brutality in the performance of duties;

    (5) Under the influence of or unauthorized possession of alcohol, narcotics, or other drugs while on duty;

    (6) Medical evidence of physical or mental incapacity to perform duties;

    (7) Careless, negligent, or improper use of state property, equipment, or funds;

    (8) Use of undue influence to gain, or attempt to gain, promotion, leave, favorable assignment, or other individual benefit or advantage;

    (9) Failure to obtain and maintain a current license or certificate as a condition of employment, if required by law, supreme court standards, or these rules;

    (10) Conduct unbecoming to a state officer or employee;

    (11) Chronic absences or tardiness in reporting to work; or

    (12) Taking unauthorized leave.

  (e) <u>Procedure for Corrective or Disciplinary Actions</u>. (1) Prior to initiating corrective or disciplinary action, the administrative authority shall meet with the employee to discuss the matter and to give him the opportunity to respond to the charges or present mitigating evidence.

    (2) If a corrective action is imposed, the administrative authority shall advise the

employee at a conference and in writing of his errors or failures, the corrective actions he should take, and the consequences he will face if he fails to follow corrective instructions. A copy shall be placed in the employee's personnel file.

(3) If a disciplinary action is imposed, the administrative authority shall advise the employee at a conference and in writing of the specific disciplinary action being imposed; why it is being imposed, including specific details of the offense; and the corrective actions to be taken and the consequences he will face for future violations. Copies shall be placed in the employee's personnel file and forwarded to the state court administrator.

(f) <u>Corrective and Disciplinary Action Limitations</u>. (1) An employee may not be corrected or disciplined more than once for a single specific act or violation, but he may be corrected or disciplined for each additional act or violation of the same or similar nature.

(2) No more than two corrective actions shall be imposed on an employee in any consecutive twelve-month period. Disciplinary action shall be taken for any further violations or offenses during the same period.

(3) A second disciplinary action disciplining an employee in any consecutive twelve-month period shall be cause for dismissal.

(4) Suspension of an employee without pay shall be limited to thirty calendar days, except as provided by section (g) of this rule.

(g) <u>Suspension of Employees Under Indictment</u>. (1) An employee who is charged with any felony or with a misdemeanor involving moral turpitude shall be indefinitely suspended pending outcome of the action, including any appeal thereon.

(2) If the employee is found guilty, unless later reversed on appeal, he shall not be compensated for the period of suspension and shall be dismissed.

(3) If he is found not guilty, or if the conviction is reversed, he shall be restored to his position and granted full pay and service credit for the period of the suspension.

(h) <u>Charges Filed by Private Citizens</u>. (1) Any private citizen who believes he has been aggrieved or adversely affected by the actions of a non-judicial employee of the judicial system in the performance of his job may file a complaint against the employee with the state court administrator. The charges shall be in writing and include the name of the employee, the name of the court or judicial agency, and the specific details of the act or acts upon which the charges are based.

(2) The state court administrator shall refer the matter to the proper administrative authority for investigation and appropriate action.

(i) Right of Review. Any certified employee who is disciplined pursuant to this rule, except a confidential employee or an employee suspended pursuant to section (g) of this rule, may request review of the action taken, as provided in rules 45 and 46.

(j) Expungement. (1) Any certified employee who has received a corrective action may request in writing to the administrative authority that action be expunged from his personnel file after a period of two years of satisfactory performance.

(2) The administrative authority may then expunge a corrective action.

Rule 26. Involuntary Termination
(Dismissal)

(a) Grounds for Dismissal. (1) A certified employee may be dismissed for any of the reasons enumerated in rule 25(d), whether or not disciplinary action of a lesser nature was taken prior to the dismissal action.

(2) (i) A certified employee shall be dismissed:

(ii) If found guilty of any felony or any misdemeanor involving moral turpitude; or

(iii) If the subject of two disciplinary actions within any twelve month period.

(3) Any district administrator or other employee to whom fiscal authority has been delegated by the chief judge who knowingly overspends the budget for the district or his court or agency without the approval of the chief judge shall be subject to immediate dismissal by the chief justice.

(b) Responsibility for Dismissal. (1) Dismissal of certified employees shall be the responsibility of the administrative authority after consultation with and upon recommendation of the appointing authority.

(2) Dismissal of confidential employees shall be the right and responsibility of the justice or judge for whom they work.

(c) Right of Review. Except for those listed in rule 46 any certified employee who is dismissed pursuant to this rule may request review of the action taken as provided in rules 45 and 46.

Rule 27. Layoff Procedures

(a) Initiation of Layoff. When permanent positions cannot be continued because of lack of work, lack of funds, or reorganization, the state court administrator shall determine the number and classes of positions to be abolished or vacated by layoff.

(b) Status Groups. (1) (i) For layoff purposes, judicial system employees shall be classified into the following status groups:

    (ii) Certified employees;
    (iii) Confidential employees; and
    (iv) Probationary employees.

(2) (i) Temporary employees shall be terminated prior to initiating layoff procedures and shall not constitute a status group for layoff purposes.

(ii) Grant funded employees shall be terminated upon the expiration of their grant and shall not constitute a status group for layoff purposes, except employees in positions which became state funded shall have the full rights of the layoff procedures.

(c) Seniority. Employees shall be laid off in reverse order of length of service within each status group.

(d) Veteran's Preference and Rights. (1) An honorably discharged veteran, eligible for veteran's preference under Article 12, Section 15(d)(a) and (b) of the Colorado constitution, shall have preferred retention over nonveterans with equal service in the same status group and class series.

(2) If, prior to entering judicial service, employees in the Colorado judicial system served in any branch of the armed forces of the United States, for other than training purposes, during any period of any declared or undeclared war or other armed hostilities against an armed foreign enemy or served on active duty in any such branch in any campaign or expedition for which a campaign badge is authorized, and were separated under honorable conditions, they are entitled to use such military service as judicial service in determining seniority for layoff purposes.

(3) A husband's or wife's military service shall be counted in determining seniority for an unremarried widow or widower of a veteran entitled to veteran's preference. The same provisions and limitations outlined for veterans above apply.

(e) **Preferred Status of Certified Employees.** All probationary employees within the same class shall be terminated prior to laying off any certified employees in that class.

(f) **Continuous Services.** (1) Continuous service shall include all continuous time served in the judicial system in certified, probationary, or temporary status. A regular part-time employee shall have seniority computed on the equivalent amount of full-time service.

(g) **Order of Retention Rights.** (1) Within his status group, an employee shall have retention rights based on seniority in the following order:

(2) At his work site or place of employment over all other employees with less continuous service in the class from which he is being laid off.

(3) If there are no employees as delineated in subsection (2), then over all other employees with less continuous service in the class from which he is being laid off in the judicial district in which he is employed.

(4) If there are no employees in the categories delineated in subsections (2) and (3), then the employee may exercise his demotion rights to a lower class in the same series to which he is certified at his work site or place of employment, under section (h) of this rule.

(5) If there are no persons over whom he can exercise demotion rights, then he may exercise his retention rights based on seniority in the last previous class series to which he served within four years preceding the date of layoff.

(h) **Demotion in Lieu of Layoff.** (1) Certified employees scheduled to be laid off shall have the right to request a voluntary demotion in lieu of layoff.

(2) (i) In a lower class in the same series in the judicial district in which they are employed, they are entitled to be certified to:

(ii) Fill vacant positions,

(iii) Displace probationary employees, or

(iv) Displace certified employees with less continuous service.

(3) The continuous service of employees being demoted shall include all continuous time in the judicial system, including that time credited at a higher level.

(4) At the discretion of the administrative authority and with the approval of the state

court administrator, a certified employee due to be laid off may voluntarily be demoted to a position in a lower level "related" class in a different series of classes to fill a vacant position, but he shall not displace an employee.

(5) (i) Certified employees who are laid off may request a transfer or voluntary demotion to another district.

(ii) Such action must be initiated by the employee and approved by the receiving district and the state court administrator.

(iii) No employee in the receiving district shall be laid off or demoted to permit such action.

(i) Notification to Employee. When it is determined that an employee is to be laid off, the administrative authority shall notify the state court administrator not less than forty-five days prior to the effective date of the layoff. The state court administrator shall notify the employee at least thirty days in advance, advising him of his retention rights consistent with these rules. The notification may be presented and receipted for in person or sent by certified mail to his home address.

(j) Exercise of Rights by Employee. An employee shall notify the state court administrator of his intention to exercise his retention rights within five days after receipt of the registered or certified notification from the state court administrator.

(k) Declination by Employees. If an employee declines all rights specified herein, he shall be terminated.

(l) Positions with Special Qualifications. Employees filling positions with bona fide special qualifications shall not be displaced by employees exercising retention rights, unless the employee exercising retention rights has those same special qualifications.

Rule 28. Resignations

(a) Written Notification Required. (1) When an employee resigns, he shall notify his superior, and the appointing authority or the administrative authority, in writing fifteen working days prior to the effective date.

(2) Failure of an employee without good cause to submit a written resignation may result in the termination being administered as a dismissal.

(3) (i) An employee who resigns for

reasons other than disciplinary action may be reemployed without loss of certification within a period of one year after termination.

(ii) If the resignation is due to a change in residence within the state, the employee may apply and be accepted for a similar position in his new place of residence within one year without loss of certification.

(4) The administrative authority or appointing authority may request an exit interview with an employee who resigns.

(b) Withdrawal of Resignation. For good cause and upon approval of the appointing authority, an employee shall have the right to withdraw his resignation before the effective date.

(c) Effect of resignation While Under Suspension or Disciplinary Action. An employee who resigns while under suspension or while under or awaiting disciplinary action shall forfeit all rights to be granted a review, shall not be eligible for reemployment, and shall not be eligible for appointment or admittance to an examination.

Rule 29. Outside Employment

(a) Outside Employment. (1) Judicial system employment shall be the principal vocation of full-time employees.

(2) (i) An employee may engage in outside employment, subject to the following conditions:

(ii) It does not interfere with job performance;

(iii) It does not conflict with the interests of the judicial system or the state of Colorado; and

(iv) It is not the type of employment which could reasonably give rise to criticism or suspicion of conflicting interests or duties.

(b) Approval of Outside Employment. No full-time employee may engage in outside employment without approval of the administrative authority. Outside employment by a confidential employee shall be approved by the justice or judge to whom he is responsible.

Rule 30. Political Activity

(a) Political Activity. Judicial system employees may not hold public office nor office in a political party, nor may they take an active part in the campaign or management of any political party or candidate for public office, except that any employee holding a public office on January 1, 1970 may complete the term for which he was elected or appointed.

(b) Leave without pay to engage in partisan political activity or to serve in an elected office shall not be granted, except that an employee holding an elected office on January 1, 1970 may complete the term for which he was elected and may be granted leave without pay therefor.

Rule 31. Employee Organizations and Representation

(a) Employee Organizations. Judicial employees shall have the right to join employee organizations of their choosing and at their own expense.

(b) Employee Representation. Employees shall have the right to counsel of their choosing at their own expense during classification appeals, grievance procedures, and review procedures.

PART VI. LEAVE, HOLIDAYS, RETIREMENT, AND OVERTIME

Rule 32. Annual Leave

(a) Annual Leave Accrual. (1) Permanent full-time employees shall earn and accrue annual leave as follows:

Years of Service	Days Earned Per Month	Maximum Accrual
1st Yr.	1	12
2nd-10th Yrs.	1-1/4	30
11th-15th Yrs.	1-1/2	36
16th Yr. & Over	1-3/4	42

(2) Permanent part-time employees shall earn and accrue annual leave on a prorated basis.

(3) Each year of consecutive service in an appellate court, trial court, related court agency, or other Colorado state agency, shall be counted in determining years of service for the accrual of annual leave.

(4) A year shall be considered completed on the first day of the month following actual completion of twelve months of service, except that if twelve months of service is completed on the first working day of the month, that day shall be the completion date.

(5) Employees eligible for annual leave must work or be on paid leave for sixteen scheduled working days in a month to earn annual leave for the month.

(6) Employees on leave without pay in excess of six working days in a month shall not accrue annual leave for that month.

(7) Employees shall earn and accrue annual leave from their date of initial employment; however, they shall not be granted or compensated for accrued annual leave until they complete six full months of service.

(8) Former employees who are reemployed shall earn and accrue leave as though their date of reemployment is the date of initial employment.

(9) Employees shall not earn annual leave for a period in which they are credited with leave-without-pay for any duration for disciplinary reasons.

(b) <u>Granting of Annual Leave</u>. (1) An employee may take annual leave only when authorized by the appropriate administrative authority or his designee.

(2) An employee who takes unauthorized annual leave, without a reason acceptable to the administrative authority, shall be subject so suspension without pay for a period equal to twice the amount of leave used and will not be paid for such unauthorized leave. Repeated violations or unauthorized leave for five days or more shall subject the employee to dismissal.

(c) <u>Annual Leave Accrual</u>. (1) An employee may accrue annual leave above the maximum permitted under section (a)(1) of this rule, but such additional annual leave must be taken in the calendar year in which it is accrued. Any additional unused leave shall be lost. Responsible supervisory and administrative authorities shall make every effort to avoid the loss of accrued leave by their employees through no fault of their own.

(2) Each January 1, the accrued annual leave of each employee shall be adjusted, so that no employee begins a calendar year with more annual leave credited to his account than the maximum accrual permitted under section (a)(1) of this rule.

(d) <u>Other Limitations and Conditions</u>. (1) Employees shall earn annual leave during periods of authorized leave, except that leave shall be credited only when they return to work, and leave earned during such periods shall be forfeited if they fail to return to work.

(2) Forfeiture of accrued annual leave as a disciplinary action shall not be authorized.

(3) No employee shall lose accrued annual leave when promoted, demoted, or transferred, except

as provided in section (c)(2) of this rule.

(e) Compensation for Accrued Annual Leave. (1) Upon termination or retirement, an employee shall be compensated for unused accrued annual leave. The maximum amount of unused accrued annual leave for which an employee shall be compensated shall be based on length of consecutive service as specified in section (a)(1) of this rule.

(2) Upon the death of an employee, the compensation for unused accrued annual leave shall be paid to the surviving spouse. If there is no surviving spouse, the payment shall be to the estate of the deceased.

(3) The employee's position shall be left vacant during the period of such payment, unless funds for this purpose have been appropriated or are available.

(f) Transfer of Annual Leave. (1) The judicial system shall accept any transferred annual leave from an employee transferring from another state agency.

(2) No leave shall be accepted which exceeds the maximum amounts permitted under this rule.

Rule 33. Sick Leave

(a) Sick Leave Accrual. (1) Permanent full-time employees shall earn and accrue sick leave with pay at the rate of one and one-fourth days per month.

(2) Permanent part-time employees shall earn and accrue sick leave on a prorated basis.

(b) Other Limitations and Conditions. (1) An employee must work or be on paid leave for sixteen scheduled working days in a month to earn sick leave for that month.

(2) An employee shall not earn sick leave during unauthorized periods of leave without pay.

(3) An employee shall not lose accrued sick leave when promoted, demoted, or transferred.

(4) Forfeiture of sick leave as a disciplinary action shall not be authorized.

(5) An employee shall earn and accrue sick leave from the date of initial employment, but shall not be granted sick leave until completion of one full month of service.

(6) Sick leave shall be used only for a bona fide illness or injury, or for medical or psychiatric examination or treatment.

(7) Employees on leave without pay in excess of six working days in a month shall not accrue sick leave for that month.

(8) The maximum number of sick days which may be accrued is one hundred and eighty.

(c) Exhaustion of Sick Leave. When an employee has used all of his accrued sick leave and accrued annual leave and is unable to return to work because of illness or injury, he may be granted sick leave without pay for a period not to exceed one year at the discretion of the administrative authority, subject to the approval of the state court administrator, if so delegated by the chief justice.

(d) Certificate of Continuing Illness. An employee on sick leave in excess of five consecutive days may be required to provide a certificate from a physician verifying the illness or injury. If the requested certificate is not provided, sick leave shall be terminated and the employee placed on leave without pay and ordered to return to work by a specific date or be subject to dismissal.

(e) Compensation for Accrued Sick Leave. (1) Upon termination or retirement, an employee shall be compensated for one-fourth of his accrued unused sick leave. Such compensation shall not exceed forty-five days.

(2) Upon the death of an employee, compensation for unused accrued sick leave shall be paid to the surviving spouse. If there is no surviving spouse, the payment shall be to the estate of the deceased.

(3) The employee's position shall be left vacant during the period of such payment, unless funds for this purpose have been appropriated or are available.

(f) Transfer of Sick Leave. Up to fifteen days of sick leave may be accepted by the judicial system from an employee transferring from another state agency.

Rule 34. Maternity Leave

(a) Maternity Leave. When, due to pregnancy or childbirth, an employee's physical condition is such that her continued employment may be injurious to her, as supported by a physician's statement, or if she is unable to perform the duties of her position, she shall be granted maternity leave without pay. Sick leave must first be exhausted, and then annual leave must be used before maternity leave is granted. The total period of sick leave, annual leave, and maternity leave cannot exceed six months.

(b) Medical Certification. The appointing authority may require the employee to present medical certification of fitness to resume work.

Rule 35. Injury Leave

(a) Granting of Injury Leave. (1) An employee who is injured or who contracts a compensable illness in the line of duty shall be granted injury leave with pay, if the illness or injury is determinted to be compensable under workmen's compensation.

(2) Injury leave with pay shall be granted for a period not to exceed ninety days, if the employee assigns his temporary workmen's compensation payments for this period to the judicial system.

(b) Other Limitations and Conditions. (1) If an employee is unable to return to work after ninety days of injury leave, he shall be placed on sick leave with pay. Upon exhausting his sick leave, he shall be placed on annual leave.

(2) If temporary compensation payments are continued to the judicial system during the period the employee is on sick leave or annual leave with pay, the amount of sick leave or annual leave charged against the employee shall be prorated according to the proportion the compensation payments bear to the full salary of the employee while he is on sick leave or annual leave with pay.

(3) If an employee is unable to return to work after using all of his accrued sick and annual leave, the appointing authority may place the employee on sick leave without pay for a period not to exceed one year, if it appears that the employee will eventually be able to return to full-time employment.

(4) When sick leave without pay is granted to an employee because of an injury or compensable illness in the line of duty, the employee does not have to assign temporary payments to the judicial system.

Rule 36. Funeral Leave

(a) Granting of Funeral Leave. (1) At the discretion of the administrative authority, an employee may be granted a maximum of five days funeral leave with pay to attend the funeral of an immediate member of his family or his spouse's family. Immediate members of the family include: a wife, husband, child (including adopted), parent, son-in-law, daughter-in-law, grandchild, grandparent, brother, sister, brother-in-law, sister-in-law, niece, or nephew.

(2) The amount of funeral leave shall be determined according to the distance to be traveled.

(b) Limitations. Funeral leave shall not be granted for settlement of estates, nor for any other reason except the required time to travel, attend, and return from a funeral. Any leave taken in excess of that required to attend the funeral shall be charged to annual leave.

Rule 37. Continuing Education

(a) Policy. Employees are encouraged, and shall be afforded the opportunity, to continue their education outside normal working hours. Local administrative authorities may also authorize flexible work schedules on an individual basis to permit employees to attend job-related courses during normal work hours.

(b) Granting of Educational Leave. When recommended by the administrative authority and approved by the chief justice, an employee may be granted educational leave with full or partial pay for a period not to exceed twelve months. The educational course shall be directly related to court employment or court administration and be designed to improve the employee's performance.

(c) Limitations and Conditions. (1) Upon completion of educational leave, an employee shall return to employment in the judicial system for a period at least equal to the time granted for educational leave. The employee shall sign an agreement to this effect prior to being granted educational leave.

(2) An employee on educational leave with pay shall be credited with service toward anniversary increases.

(3) An employee on educational leave with pay shall earn annual leave and sick leave, which leave shall be credited to him when he returns to work.

Rule 38. Leave Without Pay

(a) Granting of Leave Without Pay. When recommended by the administrative authority and approved by the chief justice, an employee may be granted leave without pay for justifiable personal reasons for a period not to exceed twelve months.

(b) Other Conditions and Limitations. (1)

Leave without pay shall not be granted until all accrued annual leave has been exhausted.

(2) No type of leave shall be earned during periods of leave without pay, and periods of leave without pay shall not be credited as service for anniversary increases, increased earning of annual leave, or any other benefits.

Rule 39. Administrative Leave

(a) <u>Granting of Administrative Leave</u>. (1) For good and sufficient reason, and with the approval of the administrative authority, an employee may be granted administrative leave with pay to attend clinics, seminars, and classes which are job related.

(2) This authority may not be delegated.

(b) <u>Granting of Leave for Jury Duty</u>. (1) Upon presenting a summons for jury duty, an employee shall be granted administrative leave with pay for the duration of such compulsory service.

(2) Leave for jury duty shall be paid leave, but the employee taking such leave shall remit to the judicial department any and all payments for such service.

Rule 40. Military Leave

(a) <u>Granting of Military Leave</u>. (1) Upon presenting proper military orders, an employee who is a member of the national guard or military reserve shall be granted a maximum of six months to attend military training. Of this amount of time, a maximum of fifteen calendar days in any calendar year shall be military training leave with pay and shall not be charged as any part of annual or compensatory leave.

(2) Military training leave shall commence the first working day the employee is on military leave from his job and terminate on the last calendar day he is in a military training status, as evidenced by a copy of the military orders covering the leave period.

(b) <u>Military Leave Without Pay</u>. (1) Any employee who enters active military service of the United States in war or national emergency shall be granted military leave without pay for the duration and one year after the expiration of such active service.

(2) An employee who fails to return at the end of this period shall be deemed to have resigned.

(c) _Other Conditions and Limitations._ (1) Employees granted military leave shall be entitled to all rights and benefits granted such employees by state statutes.

(2) All accrued annual leave shall be paid an employee granted military leave before he is placed on leave without pay, regardless of his length of service.

Rule 41. Holidays

(a) _Holiday Designation._ (1) The following days are designated by statute as legal holidays in Colorado and shall apply to judicial system employees: New Year's Day; Lincoln's Birthday; Washington's Birthday; Memorial Day; Independence Day; Colorado Day; Labor Day; Columbus Day; Veterans' Day; Thanksgiving; Christmas; and general election day in even-numbered years.

(2) Additional legal holidays when designated by the President of the United States or the governor shall not be considered a legal holiday, unless the declaration so states that it is extended to the judicial system by order of the chief justice.

(3) A special day of observance declared by the President of the United States or by the governor shall not be considered a legal holiday, unless the declaration so states that it is extended to the judicial system by order of the chief justice.

(b) _Holiday Leave._ (1) Any permanent full-time or part-time employee who is required to work on a legal holiday shall be granted a day of holiday leave at a time determined by the administrative authority.

(2) Upon retirement or termination, an employee shall be compensated for unused accrued holiday leave in the same manner as for accrued annual leave.

(3) Any employee who is on paid leave on a legal holiday falling on a working day shall be granted an additional day of leave.

(c) _Other Conditions and Limitations._ (1) To be granted holiday leave, an employee must work or be on paid leave the last working day before and the first working day after the holiday, except:

(2) A new employee or an employee returning from leave without pay in a month with a legal holiday on the first regularly scheduled work day of the month shall be granted holiday leave for the day, if he works or is on paid leave on all other scheduled work days in the month.

(3) A terminating employee and an employee taking leave without pay in a month including a holiday on the last scheduled work day of the month shall be granted holiday leave for the day, if he works or is on paid leave on all other scheduled work days in the month.

Rule 42. Retirement

(a) <u>Retirement Age</u>. All employees, including confidential employees, are required to retire upon reaching age seventy.

Rule 43. Hours of Work and Overtime

(a) <u>Hours of Work</u>. The normal work week for full-time employees shall be forty hours.

(b) <u>Overtime</u>. (1) (i) Employees in the classes listed in paragraph (ii) of this subsection shall be paid overtime at one and one half times the normal hourly rate for each hour of work in excess of forty hours in any one work week.

(ii) The classes eligible for overtime payment are: law library assistant I, law library assistant II, computer operator I, computer operator II, key punch operator I, key punch operator II, PBX operator, microfilm operator I, microfilm operator II, court clerk I, court clerk II, court clerk III, division clerk, division clerk I, division clerk II, court accounting clerk I, court accounting clerk II, court accounting clerk III, unit clerk I, unit clerk II, administrative secretary I, administrative secretary II, administrative secretary III, clerk steno I, clerk steno II, clerk typist I, clerk typist II, bailiff, street worker trainee.

(2) All requests for overtime and payment for overtime work shall be approved in advance by the administrative authority.

(3) Overtime shall be limited to the greatest extent possible by administrative authorities and appointing authorities.

PART VII. GRIEVANCE AND REVIEW PROCEDURES

Rule 44. Grievances

(a) <u>Right to File</u>. (1) Except as otherwise provided in subsection (3) of this section, any employee who is aggrieved by an action relating to his working conditions, court policies, or rules and regulations, which action is not appealable under other provisions of these rules, and which cannot be resolved through informal discussions with his immediate supervisor, may file a grievance.

(2) This rule shall apply only to actions occurring subsequent to its effective date.

(3) (i) Employees in the judicial system who do not have the right of grievance procedures are:

(ii) District administrators;
(iii) Chief probation officers;
(iv) Confidential employees;
(v) Employees of the state court administrator's office in grade 43 and above;
(vi) Clerk of the supreme court;
(vii) Clerk of the court of appeals;
(viii) Clerk of the superior court;
(ix) Clerk of the probate court;
(x) Director of juvenile court services;
(xi) Clerk of district and county courts;
(xii) Supreme court reporter of decisions;
(xiii) Court of appeals reporter of decisions;
(xiv) Probationary employees;
(xv) Supreme court librarian;
(xvi) Marriage counselors;
(xvii) Court psychologists;
(xviii) Legal staff assistant III's;
(xix) Legal staff assistant IV's;
(xx) Grievance committee counsel and staff;
(xxi) Law examining board secretary; and
(xxii) Water referees.

(b) *Matters Subject to Grievance Procedure.* Grievances shall include, but are not limited to, such matters as employee-supervisor relationships, duty assignments not affecting job classification, shift and job location assignments, hours worked, working facilities and conditions, policies for granting leave, and similar matters. Only the grievance presented originally shall be considered on appeal and a copy shall be filed with the state court administrator.

(c) *Procedural Requirements.* Any employee may be represented in a grievance procedure by a party of his choosing and at his own expense. Failure of the employee to proceed as prescribed shall terminate the grievance procedure.

(1) If a grievance is filed, it shall be processed in the following manner:

(2) First an employee shall discuss his grievance with his immediate supervisor and shall also request redress of the grievance.

(3) If redress is not granted by the immediate supervisor, or if the grievance is a complaint against actions of the immediate supervisor, the employee may appeal in writing to the administrative authority of the district where he is employed.

(4) The administrative authority may either resolve the appeal informally or appoint a board of three district employees or a disinterested examiner and render a decision on the appeal within thirty days from the date of filing. Decisions shall in all cases be made in writing to the employee.

(5) The employee may appeal to the state court administrator, acting for the chief justice, from the decision of an administrative authority. The appeal to the state court administrator shall be filed within fifteen days of the date of the chief judge's decision.

(6) (i) The state court administrator shall appoint and convene a three member grievance review board to hear the appeal and shall render a decision on the recommendations within thirty days from the date of filing. Decisions of the board shall be final.

(ii) Members of the grievance review board shall include a district judge or county judge, a district administrator, and the state court administrator or his designee.

(7) An aggrieved employee shall have the right to appear in person or be represented by a party of his own choosing in all hearings convened by an appropriate hearing examiner or board regarding the appeal.

Rule 45. Board of Review

(a) <u>Board Established.</u> (1) There is hereby established the judicial system personnel board of review, which shall be composed of five members appointed by the chief justice. Terms of the board shall be three years, except that the initial terms of the district administrator shall be for two years and the employee representative, other than a district administrator, shall be for one year.

(2) (i) One member shall be a supreme court justice who shall serve as chairman.
(ii) One member shall be a district judge other than a chief judge.
(iii) One member shall be a county judge other than a presiding judge in a multi-judge county court.
(iv) One member shall be a district administrator.
(v) One member shall be a court employee other than a district administrator.
(3) At least three of the five board members shall meet for the hearing.
(b) Vacancies. Vacancies on the board of review shall be filled by the chief justice for the unexpired terms.
(c) Disqualification. When a matter comes before the board involving an employee from the court of one of the board members, he shall disqualify himself, and the chief justice shall appoint another person who occupies the same type of position as the person disqualified.
(d) Jurisdiction. (1) The board shall have jurisdiction over employee requests for review concerning discharge, demotion, suspension, or involuntary termination, as provided in rule 44.
(2) All decisions of the board shall be final and binding on all parties.
(e) Hearing Examiner. The board shall appoint one or more hearing examiners, who shall be attorneys who have practiced law in Colorado for at least five years, to conduct hearings in review cases. A hearing examiner may be appointed for a two year term to handle such cases as the board may refer to him during his term. He shall be compensated on the basis of the actual time spent on board matters at a rate to be established by the board, in addition to reimbursement for actual expenses incurred. A hearing examiner and any board member shall have the power to administer oaths and to issue subpoenas duces tecum for hearings conducted under these rules.

Rule 46. Review Procedure

(a) Limitation on Review. Requests for review shall be limited specifically to the circumstances described in section (b)(1) of this rule.
(b) Grounds for Review. (1) Any certified employee, as defined in rule 4(a)(7), may file a complaint requesting review by the board of any action demoting, suspending (except pursuant to rule

25(a)), discharging the employee, or requesting the employee's resignation, on the grounds that such action was without good and justifiable cause. Such complaint must be filed within fifteen working days from the effective date of the action.

    (2) (i) Employees in the judicial system who do not have the right of review procedures are:
    (ii) District administrators;
    (iii) Chief probation officers;
    (iv) Confidential employees;
    (v) Employees of the state court administrator's office in grade 43 and above;
    (vi) Clerk of the supreme court;
    (vii) Clerk of the court of appeals;
    (viii) Clerk of the superior court;
    (ix) Clerk of the probate court;
    (x) Director of juvenile court services;
    (xi) Clerk of district and county courts;
    (xii) Supreme court reporter of decisions;
    (xiii) Court of appeals reporter of decisions;
    (xiv) Probationary employees;
    (xv) Supreme court librarian;
    (xvi) Marriage counselors;
    (xvii) Court psychologists;
    (xviii) Legal staff assistant III's;
    (xix) Legal staff assistant IV's;
    (xx) Grievance committee counsel and staff;
    (xxi) Law examining board secretary; and
    (xxii) Water referees.

    (c) *Procedure.* (1) The employee seeking review shall file a written complaint with the board chairman requesting review and stating all facts the employee deems necessary to show why the action complained of was improper and should be modified or reversed. The employee shall transmit copies of his complaint to the administrative authority whose action is the subject of the complaint and to the state court administrator.

    (2) The administrative authority whose action is the subject of the complaint shall file an answer to the employee's complaint with the board chairman within ten days following receipt of the complaint, responding to the allegations of the complaint and stating the reasons for taking the action.

    (3) The employee shall be entitled to

counsel of his own choosing at his own expense. The administrative authority whose action is complained of shall be represented by the staff legal officer of the judicial system.

(4) (i) One member of the board, selected by rotation of the board members, shall consider the complaint and answer and shall recommend to the board either that the allegations of the complaint and answer justify a hearing or that the matter should be ruled upon by the board without a hearing. The board shall thereupon decide whether or not to hold a hearing.

(ii) If the board determines not to hold a hearing, it shall so notify the parties, stating the matters considered and reasons for denying the hearing. The board shall then decide the matter of the employee's complaint upon the documents submitted by the parties without a hearing and shall dismiss the complaint or order such remedial action as the board deems appropriate in the circumstances, including, but not limited to, reinstatement of the employee to his former status. The board shall notify the employee and the administrative authority whose action is the subject of the complaint of the board's decision. The decision of the board is final.

(iii) If the board determines to hold a hearing, it shall so notify the parties, the hearing examiner, and all other interested and concerned parties. The hearing examiner shall set a convenient date and place for the hearing, to be held within thirty days after notification by the board. Hearings shall be open to the public, unless a closed hearing is requested by the employee or ordered by the hearing examiner and shall be recorded verbatim either stenographically or electronically.

(iv) Hearings shall be conducted in accordance with the provisions and procedures prescribed by CRS 1963, 3-16-4, as amended, and the hearing examiner shall have the power therein granted, except that where such provisions are in conflict with the provisions of these rules, these rules shall control.

(v) The hearing examiner shall conduct the hearing and shall afford the parties opportunity to introduce evidence, including testimony and statements of the complaining employee, his representative, the person whose action is complained of, the administrative authority, their representatives, and other witnesses, and to cross-examine witnesses. The testimony shall be under oath or affirmation.

(vi) Rules of evidence shall not be applied strictly, but the hearing examiner shall exclude irrelevant or unduly repetitious evidence.

(vii) The burden of initially going forward to show jurisdiction and the factual basis for the review requested shall be upon the complaining employee. If the hearing examiner is satisfied that the employee has met this burden after hearing the employee's evidence, he shall so rule, and the burden of going forward shall then shift to the administrative authority whose action is complained of to show that such action was based upon good or justifiable cause.

(viii) Upon hearing the evidence and statements of the parties, and after such deliberation as necessary, the hearing examiner shall make findings and a recommended decision on the issues of whether or not the action of the administrative authority complained of was without good or justifiable cause, and what, if any, remedial action should be ordered, or whether the complaint should be dismissed. The decision of the hearing examiner shall be based upon the greater weight of the evidence.

(ix) The hearing examiner shall issue a written decision and send copies thereof to the board and to the parties and their representatives. The decision shall contain findings, recommendations for any corrective action required, and notification of the right of either party to appeal to the board. The decision shall include an analysis of the findings and a statement of the reasons for the conclusions reached. Unless an appeal is filed as provided in subsection (5) of this rule, the decision shall become the decision of the board and shall be carried into effect within twenty calendar days after issuance by the examiner. If an appeal is filed, the decision may not be given effect until the board has adjudicated the appeal.

(5) (i) Either party is entitled to appeal the decision of the hearing examiner to the full board. Such appeal shall be filed with the supreme court justice serving as board chairman. An appeal to the board shall be in writing, setting forth the reasons for the appeal, and shall be filed with the board within fifteen calendar days after the receipt of the decision of the hearing examiner. The board may extend this time limit when a party shows that circumstances beyond his control prevent the filing of the appeal within the time limit.

(ii) The board shall review the record of the proceedings, all relevant written representations, and the decision of the hearing examiner. The record of proceedings may include such portions of the transcript of the hearing as may be necessary to consider the exceptions. Such transcript shall be furnished by the party appealing. The board may, in its discretion, afford the parties opportunity to appear and present oral arguments and representations.

(iii) The board shall issue a written decision, which may consist of an affirmation without comment of the decision of the hearing examiner, and shall send copies thereof to the parties and their representatives. The decision of the board is final, and there is no further right to appeal. When remedial action is ordered, the administrative authority shall report promptly to the board that the remedial action has been effected.

Appendix E-2

MAINE COURT SYSTEM

PERSONNEL POLICY AND PROCEDURES MANUAL

Effective July 1, 1977

PROMULGATED BY THE MAINE SUPREME JUDICIAL COURT

1.0 PURPOSE AND SCOPE OF THE SYSTEM

1.1   System Purpose

This Manual prescribes the personnel policies and procedures of the Maine court system as promulgated by the Supreme Judicial Court of Maine.

1.2   System Scope

The policies and procedures described in this Manual apply to all State court system employees except justices and judges.

2.0 RESPONSIBILITIES OF SYSTEM PARTICIPANTS

2.1   Responsibilities of the Supreme Judicial Court

The Maine Supreme Judicial Court is responsible for the establishment of the Maine Court Personnel System through the promulgation of the rules and procedures contained in this Manual. The Court is also responsible for promulgating any subsequent modifications to the system.

Individual Justices of the Court are responsible for the hiring and periodic review of their secretaries and law clerks in accordance with established system procedures.

2.2   Responsibilities of the State Court Administrator

The State Court Administrator (SCA) is responsible for the implementation, maintenance and operation of the Court Personnel System including:

2.2.1 Determining that all potential court system employees meet minimum standards as defined in the Classification Plan. Such determination will be made prior to the individual being hired.

2.2.2 Ensuring that all court system employees are evaluated at least once each year. Actual evaluations, other than for employees of the Administrative Office of the Courts (AOC), are not the responsibility of the SCA.

2.2.3 Conducting periodic interviews and audits to ensure that the Classification and Compensation Plans are current and accurate.

2.2.4 Maintenance of personnel records, including payroll records, leave balances and personal histories.

Each of these responsibilities may be delegated by the SCA.

2.3   Responsibilities of the Regional Court Administrators
Responsibilities of the Regional Court Administrators (RCAs) have the following personnel system responsibilities within their region:

2.3.1 Determining that all potential court system employees within the region meet minimum standards as defined in the Classification Plan. Employee recruitment and selection, although the responsibility of each clerk's office, will be supervised by the RCAs.

2.3.2 Ensuring that each employee in the region is evaluated at least once each year in accordance with established procedures.

2.3.3 Evaluating the performance of each clerk and court reporter in the region at least once each year in accordance with established procedures.

2.3.4 Serving as liaison between region personnel and the AOC in all matters relating to personnel. This will include the collection and forwarding of leave data, employee evaluations and employee discipline proceedings as well as data concerning all other personnel transactions.

2.3.5 Conducting periodic interviews, audits and organizational analyses of the various offices within the region.

2.4   Responsibilities of the Justices and Judges
Superior Court Justices and District Court Judges are responsible for conducting annual evaluations of secretaries and law clerks working directly for them.
Justices and judges will provide written input to the RCAs in the annual evaluation of clerks and reporters.

2.5   Responsibilities of Clerks
Clerks of Superior or District Courts have the following personnel system responsibilities for employees of their office:

2.5.1 Recruiting and selecting employees to fill job vacancies in accordance with minimum standards defined in the Classification Plan, and under the supervision of the RCAs; submitting statements of their qualifications to the AOC for approval.

    2.5.2 Conducting an evaluation of each employee at least once per year, and reviewing such evaluation with the RCA.

    2.5.3 Providing orientation and training to employees as appropriate.

    2.5.4 Performing disciplinary actions as necessary and in accordance with established procedures.

    2.5.5 Collecting and forwarding to the RCA data regarding all personnel transactions, such as leave, resignations and disciplinary actions.

2.6   Responsibilities of all Court System Employees

All court system employees are responsible for adherence to all policies and procedures of the Court Personnel System.

3.0 COMPENSATION PLAN

3.1   Compensation Plan Objectives

The primary objective of this Compensation Plan is to contribute to the attainment of the goals of the Personnel Management System. (See Section 1.1) Supporting objectives include:

    3.1.1 To achieve pay levels which help attract and retain the best people available for each job.

    3.1.2 To pay employees for the contribution each one makes to the work of the Maine Court System.

    3.1.3 To support attainment of the highest possible productivity within the Court System.

    3.1.4 To have each employee understand how pay is determined and what he or she can do to affect his or her pay.

    3.1.5 To deliver what the plan promises.

The Compensation Plan consists of four parts, each of which helps translate these objectives eventually into individual pay. These parts are:

> General Pay Policies
> Salary Grades
> Procedures for Determining Individual Pay
> Implementation Steps (transition from one
>   compensation plan to another)

3.2   General Pay Policies
The following policies will form the basis for compensation:

    3.2.1 Salaries for employees in the Personnel Management System will be based on these factors:

        3.2.1.1 The value of the employee's job relative to the value of other jobs in the Court System.

        3.2.1.2 The value of the job indicated in the relevant job market.

        3.2.1.3 The degree to which the employee has learned the job.

        3.2.1.4 Individual performance within the assigned job.

        3.2.1.5 The value of extensive experience.

    3.2.2 Jobs will be fitted into a set of ordered pay grades. Assignment of each job to a grade will be based on consideration of internal equity and market value.

    3.2.3 Individual pay will be related to performance against established goals and measures.

        3.2.3.1 Employees who are learning their job will be paid to reflect the extent of their learning.

        3.2.3.2 A fully-trained employee whose performance is satisfactory will be paid "at the market" - i.e., a salary equivalent to an assessment of what similar jobs are paid in the relevant market place.

        3.2.3.4 A fully-trained employee whose performance is superior will be paid significantly above the market.

3.2.4 Within the scope of available funds, salary levels (salary grade ranges and individual salaries) will be adjusted regularly to reflect both changes in the marketplace and purchasing power.
Note that the State Legislature decides how much money will be available for compensation. Therefore, implementation of this policy depends on legislative appropriation. The Administrative Office of the Courts will always request an appropriation which meets this policy.

3.2.5 Insurance and retirement benefits will be the same as those provided to employees of the Executive Department.

3.2.6 All aspects of this Compensation Plan will be examined annually to determine the degree to which they support the Plan's objectives and these general policies. Changes in the Plan will be made as necessary to achieve the objectives of the Personnel Management System.

3.2.7 This Compensation Plan will conform to wage and salary guidelines or controls issued by the Federal Government.

3.3   Salary Grades
Construction of salary grades, assignment of dollar values to these grades, and assignment of jobs to the appropriate grade are three methods which carry the Compensation Plan's general policies into effect.

3.3.1 Salary grades have many purposes. Since a grade is a group of jobs which are alike in their contribution to the work of the organization, a set of grades brings order and consistency to what otherwise might be subjective pay decisions. Another purpose is to express differences in the relative value of jobs in a measurable way. A third is to make possible a comparison of jobs to the market. A fourth is to set minimum and maximum values on each job.

3.3.2 Each salary grade has a salary range associated with it. The salary ranges have been constructed in the following manner:

3.3.2.1 Each range has as its key

point a figure called the Target Salary. This figure is the salary which will be paid to a fully-trained, satisfactory performer whose job is assigned to that grade. Target Salaries for all grades are approximately 10% apart (e.g., the Grade 2 Target is 10% above the Grade 1 Target). A set of 13 grades is sufficient to include all jobs which are part of the Personnel Management System.

   3.3.2.2 Each grade range has a Minimum and a set of salary steps between Minimum and Target. The number of salary steps increases at higher grade levels, to reflect the longer time needed to learn these jobs.

   3.3.2.3 With the exception noted below (3.3.2.5), each grade range has two Experience Recognition Steps. These are salary levels which may be attained by an employee with several years of satisfactory performance and experience in his or her job. One is 4% above Target Salary, the other is 8% above Target.

   3.3.2.4 Each grade range has a Maximum which cannot be exceeded. The Maximum is generally 25% above Target.

   3.3.2.5 Ranges for high-level professional employees have neither Experience Recognition Steps nor Maximums. Movement of employees in these grades beyond Target is possible (see 3.4.4).

   3.3.2.6 Salary grades for 1979 are found in Appendix B.

   3.3.2.7 The entire salary grade structure will be examined each year prior to January 1. Grade ranges may be changed up or down to reflect such factors as changes in relevant job markets and movement in the Consumer Price Index. The State Court Administrator will recommend a change in ranges based on these factors and on the amount of funds available.

   3.3.3 Once grades and ranges have been established, the next step is to assign each job within the Personnel Management System to the appropriate grade.

   3.3.3.1 A detailed description of

each job will be written and maintained by the Administrative Office of the Courts. Each description will contain representative examples of work to be performed, identification of the supervisor of the position, and identification of minimum education or experience requirements. Appendix A, CLASS DESCRIPTIONS, contains such descriptions for all current positions. The description will be reviewed and updated as necessary by the Administrative Office of the Courts whenever the job changes substantially and at least once a year. Jobs may be modified or eliminated at any time, at the discretion of the Administrative Office of the Courts.

3.3.3.2 The Administrative Office of the Courts will make the initial assignment of each job to the appropriate grade. Each job will be assigned to the Grade the Target Salary of which most closely approximates the market for that job as it is projected for the coming year. If there is no market comparison available for a particular job, it will be assigned to the same grade as other jobs with similar responsibilities and skill requirements.

3.3.3.2.1 Each job has a specific "market" which may differ from the market of other jobs. In general, the market for clerical jobs is considered to be a comparison to similar jobs in the public and private sectors in Maine communities. The market for professional and management jobs may include both Maine and national comparisons.

3.3.3.2.2 Initial assignments will be based on the results of a market survey conducted in June 1978, with information projected to January 1979.

3.3.3.2.3 Market information will be updated regularly. The information will be used as the basis for judgments about both grade assignments and movement of the entire salary grade structure (see Section 3.3.2.7).

3.3.3.3 The Administrative Office of the Courts will consider a change in the grade assignment of a job upon recommendation of the selecting authority for the position or at the request of an employee. The basis for such a request or recommendation must be either a significant change in the marketplace, an inequity in the grade assignment of one job as compared to the responsibilities of other jobs, or a substantial change in the responsibilities of the job. (Individual performance has no bearing on grade assignment).

3.3.3.4 Although the intent of the Compensation Plan is to include every job in a salary grade on the basis of market value and internal equity, there may be a few exceptions - i.e., employees whose jobs do not fit the system. In these cases, assignment of a grade or pay determination will be made by the Administrative Office of the Courts on the merits of the case, with the approval of the Chief Justice.

3.4 Procedures for Determining Individual Pay
This section describes the methods used to determine pay when the Compensation Plan is fully implemented. During the initial implementation of this Plan there may be some variance from these procedures. (See Section 3.5 for a discussion of the transition from the previous system.)

3.4.1 The first step is to separate employees in each job into two categories: those who are fully trained ("proficient") on the job, and those who are still learning ("trainees"). Each category is treated separately. The determination of who is fully trained will be made on an individual basis by the selecting authority in consultation with the Administrative Office of the Courts. The following time guidepoints will be used to determine that a person is fully trained:

Grade	Time on the Job
1	1 year
2-5	2 years
6-13	3 years

Note this is time in the current job, not total employment. An employee may be judged proficient in less time, of course. An employee who reaches the time guidepoint and is not considered proficient will be placed on probation for a time period determined by the selecting authority with the approval of the Administrative Office of the Courts.

3.4.2 Determining Salary for Trainees
The procedures outlined below are automatic, unless the employee's selecting authority

intervenes. See Section 3.4.2.3 for a discussion of this intervention.

3.4.2.1 An individual will be hired and promoted to the Minimum in a grade or to the step in the grade range which reflects his or her relevant knowledge, experience and skills. The decision will be made by the person's selecting authority, with the approval of the Administrative Office of the Courts.

3.4.2.2 The salary of a trainee will increase regularly according to the schedule outlined below. Note that the timing for the person's first increase in a new job may vary somewhat from the time shown in this schedule (see Sec. 3.4.2.3). Note also that any change in timing of one increase (see Sec. 3.4.2.3) automatically changes the timing of all future increases.

If an Employee is at:	**Movement takes place**	Then he or she moves to:
Minimum	After 6 months on the job	Step 2
Step 2	6 months after reaching Step 2	Step 3
Step 2 for Grade 1	6 months after reaching Step 2	Target
Step 3 for Grades 2 through 5	12 months after reaching Step 3	Target
Step 3 for Grades 6 through 13	12 months after reaching Step 3	Step 4
Step 4 for Grades 6 through 13	12 months after reaching Step 4	Target

In summary, the typical employee who starts at minimum will reach Target in Grade 1 after one year; in Grades 2 through 5, after 2 years; in higher grades, after 3 years.

3.4.2.3 The progression described in 3.4.2.2 above is automatic, unless the employee's selecting authority intervenes. The selecting authority may intervene in any of the following ways, with the approval of the Administrative Office of the Courts:

        3.4.2.3.1 On the basis of superior learning performance, move the employee's salary more than one step or move the salary earlier than at the indicated interval.

        3.4.2.3.2 On the basis of unsatisfactory learning performance, delay a salary change for an employee. If this is done, the employee must be placed on probation for a time to be determined by the selecting authority with the approval of the Administrative Office of the Courts. The move to the next step may be made whenever the selecting authority decides that learning performance is back on track or, if not, the employee will be terminated.

    3.4.3 Determining Salary for Proficient Employees

An employee who reaches Target Salary, or whose salary is above Target for any reason, is part of the proficient employee group. Proficient employees are divided into two categories: those whose performance is satisfactory and those whose performance is superior. (Definitions of "satisfactory" and "superior", and the methods for determining the evaluation of each employee, will be found in Section 6.0). The salaries of all proficient employees will be reviewed every twelve months, in December of each year.

        3.4.3.1 Employees who are rated satisfactory will be paid at the Target Salary. They may not exceed Target Salary, except as noted below.

        3.4.3.2 An employee in Grades 1 through 11 who has performed satisfactorily for five years at Target Salary is eligible to move to the first Experience Recognition Step in the grade range. An employee who reaches the first step and who continues to perform satisfactorily for another five years is eligible to move to the second Experience Recognition Step. In both cases, neither the move itself nor the timing is automatic. The decision to increase the salary and when to change is made by the employee's selecting authority, with the approval of the Administrative Office of the Courts, on the basis of a judgment about the value of the individual's additional experience.

3.4.3.3 An employee in Grades 1 through 11 who is rated superior may be paid above Target Salary, but not more than Maximum. The employee's salary will be set by his or her selecting authority, with the approval of the Administrative Office of the Courts. It is recommended that the individual be paid at least 10% above Target.

3.4.3.3.1 It is the intent of the Compensation Plan that every proficient employee who is at Target and then achieves superior performance be paid above Target. The Plan also recognizes that there is potential for distorting the system through pressure to pay above Target for reasons other than performance. To avoid the distortion, the following guidelines will apply:

3.4.3.3.1.1 There is no requirement that anyone be paid above Target.

3.4.3.3.1.2 The operating presumption will be that not more than 25% of proficient employees in each grade will be eligible to exceed Target for superior performance. In many circumstances, fewer than 25% of employees in a grade will earn superior pay.

3.4.3.3.1.3 The Administrative Office of the Courts will increase the 25% limit whenever it can be shown that more than 25% of the employees in a grade having achieved superior performance.

3.4.3.4 An employee at Target may be rated unsatisfactory. In this case his or her salary is frozen and probation is imposed. If, at the end of the probation period, the employee's performance has become satisfactory, his or her salary should be brought to Target if the salary is then below Target. If performance is still unsatisfactory, the employee should be terminated.

3.4.4 The salaries of employees in grade 12 and above will move beyond Target only at the discretion of the Supreme Judicial Court. The Supreme Judicial Court will be guided in its decisions about salaries for these employees by the principles and practices which apply to other employees in the Personnel Management System. The Court is not bound or limited by these principles and practices, however.

3.4.5 Salaries Above Target

It may happen than an employee is paid above Target in one year because of superior performance, then not earn a superior rating the next year. In that case, at the discretion of the selecting authority, the individual's pay may be frozen until the annual review period in which the Target Salary increases to a point above the frozen salary, or until the performance once again is superior, or until the employee is eligible for an Experience Recognition Step, or the salary may be reduced.

3.4.6 Promotions

An employee who meets the qualifications for a job opening may be promoted at any time during the year. The promoting authority should decide where in the new grade range the employee's salary should fall. As general guidelines:

3.4.6.1 A higher salary should be paid, if it is consistent with the points stated below. Of course, there should not be any decreases in salary.

3.4.6.2 A person at Target in the old range should be placed one or more steps below Target in the new range, since it is assumed that there will be a learning period on the new job.

3.4.6.3 A person above Target in the old range should be placed at or below Target in the new range.

3.4.7 Summary of Salary Increases

The procedures described above should make clear that the emphasis in this Plan is on the actual salary the employee receives, not the size of the increase. The size of the increase is irrelevant. To help understand how the system works, consider the instances in which an employee receives a higher salary.

3.4.7.1 When a trainee moves from one step to another.

3.4.7.2 When a proficient employee earns a superior rating or moves to an Experience Recognition Step.

3.4.7.3 When the entire salary grade range structure increases on account of market changes, inflation, and so on. In this case, the employee stays in the same step in the new range as he or she occupied in the previous range.

3.5   Implementation Steps

Because there are structural differences between this Compensation Plan and its predecessor, moving employees from one Plan to the other may cause some individual problems. Special arrangements and adjustments have been made to overcome these problems.

3.5.1 Transition will take place effective the first full pay period in December 1978. The next possible annual salary change will occur in January 1980.

3.5.2 Individuals will be assigned to the step in their range which best fits their training and performance. (Note that an employee may be moved to Target or to an Experience Recognition Step.) No employee's salary will decrease. See also 3.5.4 and 3.5.5.

3.5.3 No one will exceed Target at this time on account of superior performance. Time is required to develop the measurement system before making such judgments. In June 1979 employees will be eligible for a special review regarding superior performance.

3.5.4 A salary which is above Target for the new grade range will be frozen until the Target moves above the salary, the employee is paid above Target for superior performance, or he or she becomes eligible for an Experience Recognition Step. An individual whose salary is frozen is eligible for a special adjustment, as described below.

3.5.5 A special adjustment will be given during the November 1978 salary change period in recognition of changes in the marketplace and purchasing power since 1976.

3.5.5.1 Everyone will receive at least a 7% increase in total compensation.

3.5.5.2 If the individual's change in salary as a result of 3.5.2 is more than 7%, there is no special adjustment under 3.5.5.3.

   3.5.5.3 If the individual's change in salary is less than 7%, the difference between the amount of salary change and 7% will be paid as an "integrating adjustment". This adjustment will not be considered part of the employee's salary. It is a one-time amount designed to ease the person's transition to the new system. It will be paid in bi-weekly installments, and continues until the person is fully integrated into the system.

   3.5.5.4 It is expected that every employee's salary will be fully integrated into the new Plan by December 1979, i.e., his or her salary is at the point in the range which accurately reflects his or her training, experience and performance. But if an employee's salary is not fully integrated by January 1, 1980, there will be a continuing adjustment from year to year as necessary, calculated as in 3.5.5.3, except that the guaranteed increase shall be only half of any general salary increases granted under 3.3.2.7. For example: if the change in ranges for January 1980 is 6%, than the adjustment above the employee's current salary is not more than 3%.

4.0 ADDITIONAL COMPENSATION PROVISIONS

4.1 Overtime Compensation

No employee will work overtime without the prior approval of the selecting authority. Compensatory time for authorized overtime worked beyond the 37 1/2 hour week will be granted at straight time.

No employee in Grade 22 or above will receive compensatory time for overtime worked above the 37 1/2 hour week.

Compensatory time for authorized overtime worked must be taken within the calendar year earned.

4.2 Termination Compensation

A terminating employee, regardless of the nature of the termination, will be paid for each day of annual leave and for 50% of the sick leave accrued to the date of termination. Payment will be made at the salary level at the time of termination.

Employees who resign or are terminated during their six-month probationary period will not be compensated for accumulated annual and sick leave.

4.3   Holiday Compensation
Employees will be paid for holidays only if they are formally on the payroll and working the day prior to the holiday in the case of entering employees or the day immediately following the holiday for terminating employees. Part-time employees will be paid for holidays only if their regularly scheduled work hours fall on the holiday.

4.4   Accumulated Compensatory Time
Compensatory time accumulated by any employee is not transferrable either when the employee is hired into the system or transferred or promoted within the system.

4.5   Part-time Employees
Permanent part-time employees are those employees employed for a period exceeding thirty days, but for thirty hours per week or less. Such employees must be hired in accordance with the same procedures applying to full-time employees.
Permanent part-time employees are entitled to leave and have access to grievance and appeal procedures, and, if they work twenty (20) hours or more per week, are eligible for insurance and retirement benefits.

4.6   Temporary Employees
Temporary employees may be hired for a period not to exceed thirty (30) days, subject to the approval of the SCA. Such employees are not entitled to any benefits, and will be paid an hourly wage pro-rated from the approved compensation scales.

5.0   HIRING POLICIES AND EMPLOYMENT CONDITIONS

5.1   Selecting Authority
It is the policy of the Maine court system to have employees selected by the personnel who will be responsible for their subsequent daily supervision and evaluation. Determination of whether applicants meet the qualifications of the job classification in which they are being hired is the responsibility of the AOC.
Responsibility for employee selection is as follows:

5.1.1 Each Supreme Judicial Court Justice is responsible for selecting a secretary and law clerk. The SCA will be selected by agreement of the court. The Supreme Judicial Court will be responsible for selecting the RCAs in consultation with the appropriate justices.

     5.1.2 Superior Court Justices and District Court Judges are responsible for selecting personnel for secretarial and legal research duties. Where these positions are not allocated full-time personnel, the justices and judges will work with the appropriate RCA to make necessary arrangements.

     5.1.3 The SCA is responsible for selecting all AOC personnel and court reporters.

     5.1.4 RCAs are responsible for recommending for appointment Superior and District Court clerks in consultation with the appropriate justice or judge.

     5.1.5 Each Superior or District Court clerk is responsible for selecting those employees working in the clerk's office.

     5.1.6 The Clerk of the Supreme Judicial Court is responsible for selecting employees of that office.

5.2   Hiring Authority
It is the responsibility of each selecting authority to submit a written, employment application clearly stating the applicants experience and qualifications to the AOC in order that a review can be conducted prior to hiring.
    Regardless of where the responsibility for selecting potential employees resides, none will be hired without the prior approval of the AOC.

5.3   Applicant Testing
The SCA may establish appropriate testing procedures to facilitate the determination of employee qualifications.

5.4   Probationary Period
Once hired, each new court system employee will serve a six-month probationary period. During this period the employee can be terminated at any time at the request of the selecting authority and with the approval of the SCA. Any such termination is final and will not be subject to review or appeal.

5.5   Certification
Prior to the end of a new employee's proba-

tionary period the selecting authority must assess the employee's work performance to determine whether the employee should be granted certified status in the court personnel system. Certified status means that the employee is eligible for all the system benefits outlined in the policy and procedures manual, as well as responsible for adherence to all policies and procedures enumerated therein.

If the selecting authority determines that the new employee should be given certified status, he will so inform the Administrative Office of the Courts in writing.

If the selecting authority determines that the new employee should not be given certified status, the employee will be terminated pursuant to Section 5.4.

5.6   Recruitment
Selecting authorities will notify the AOC of any existing or potential position vacancies. Such vacancies will be posted within the court system by the AOC. Advertisement of vacancies is the responsibility of the Administrative Office of the Courts.

5.7   Employee Resignation
All employees will provide written notification of their intent to resign ten (10) working days prior to the final date of their employment.

5.8   Employment of Relatives
No person will be hired, promoted or transferred to a position where the selecting authority will be a relative of the employee.

5.9   Outside Employment
A court system employee may engage in outside employment if it does not interfere with job performance and does not conflict or appear to conflict with the interests of the Maine court system.

No employee may engage in outside employment without the prior knowledge and approval of the selecting authority.

5.10   Political Activity
No employee may hold public office or an office in a political party. They may not take an active part in the campaign or management of any political party or candidate for political office. Any employee holding such office on July 1, 1976 may complete the term for which he or she was elected.

Employees are prohibited from wearing campaign buttons and distributing campaign literature within the courthouse. Employees in Grade 10 and above are prohibited from participation in public political functions or making contributions.

5.11   Practice of Law
No court system employee may engage in the practice of law.

5.12   Equal Employment Opportunity
It is the policy of the Maine court system to recruit, select, train, promote, retain and discipline employees without regard to race, sex, religious creed, national origin, age, or physical handicap, unless related to a bonafide occupational qualification.

5.13   Promotion
Promotions must be the result of a competitive application process and must be approved by the Administrative Office of the Courts.

Employees promoted to a new job classification will serve a three-month probationary period. During this period, the employee can be reclassified to the position from which he was promoted.

With the approval of the Administrative Office of the Courts, the compensation of newly promoted employees may be raised one step.

6.0   EMPLOYEE EVALUATION

6.1   Responsibility for Evaluation
Each selecting authority is responsible for evaluating his or her employees' performance by the employee's anniversary date each year.

6.2   Evaluation Procedures
Each selecting authority will review the performance of each employee and submit a written evaluation to the AOC. RCAs are responsible for supervising the evaluation process within their regions. The written evaluation recommendations must indicate whether:

    6.2.1   The employee should be advanced one or more steps in grade (number of steps to be specified).

    6.2.2   The employee should be promoted in classification and grade (new classification, grade and step to be specified).

6.2.3   The employee should remain at his current classification and salary level.

If an employee is to be advanced more than a single step, the written evaluation must clearly state the circumstances warranting the action.
All promotions and salary increases must be approved by the AOC.
No advancements or increases will be executed without receipt of a written evaluation from the selecting authority, regardless of the period since the last advancement.
All salary increases will be authorized on a merit basis. Yearly increases are not to be considered automatic.

6.3   Unsatisfactory Evaluation
Any permanent employee receiving an unsatisfactory evaluation will be placed on probation for a period of three (3) months. If a subsequent evaluation at the conclusion of the probationary period also indicates unsatisfactory performance, the employee will be terminated.

6.4   Date of Evaluation
Each employee's anniversary date, or date of evaluation, will be the first of the month following his or her hiring or the first of the month following his or her last evaluation.

7.0   EMPLOYEE DISCIPLINE

7.1   Responsibility for Employee Discipline
The initiation of disciplinary action is the responsibility of the selecting authority.

7.2   Discipline Procedures
Where disciplinary actions beyond oral reprimands are required, the selecting authority may elect to:

7.2.1   Place a formal, written reprimand stating the specific disciplinary action in the employees official personnel file at the AOC.

7.2.2   Place the employee on disciplinary status, not to exceed three months.

7.2.3   Demote the employee in grade, step or position.

7.2.4 Place the employee in a suspended, leave without pay status.

7.2.5 Dismiss the employee.

In all instances disciplinary action will be documented in writing, specifically stating the circumstances warranting the disciplinary action, with a copy provided to the employee and a copy sent to the AOC. Copies of all disciplinary proceedings will be included in the employee's official personnel file.

Disciplinary actions cannot be executed without approval of the AOC.

7.3 Right of Appeal

All permanent full-time and permanent part-time employees have the right to appeal disciplinary actions in accordance with established grievance and appeal procedures. Probationary employees do not have the right of appeal.

8.0 HOURS OF WORK, LEAVE AND HOLIDAYS

8.1 Hours of Work

The standard work-week for full-time employees of the Maine court system is 37 1/2 hours. Normal clerk's office hours are to be from 8:00 to 4:30, however, the clerk's office will always be open when court is in session.

Deviations from this schedule must be approved by the Supreme Judicial Court.

8.2 Annual Leave

Annual leave will be earned by all full-time and permanent part-time employees from the date of their initial employment. State employees with uninterrupted state service, who transfer into the Judicial Department from either the Executive or Legislative Departments, will earn annual leave based on their entire period of State employment. Leave will be accrued as follows:

Period of Employment	Annual Leave	Accrual Rate in Days	Accrual Rate in Hours
Less than 5 years	12 days	1 day/mo.	7.5
5 to 10 years	15 days	1.25 days/mo.	9.5
10 to 15 years	18 days	1.5 days/mo.	11.5
15 years or more	21 days	1.75 days/mo.	13.5

In the case of permanent part-time employees, leave will be accrued proportionate to hours worked.

Annual leave for the month will accrue on the last day of each calendar month worked. Entering and terminating employees will accrue annual leave proportionate to the total hours worked during the calendar month.

An employee cannot carry forward from one calendar year to the next more than thirty (30) days leave.

8.3   Sick Leave

Sick leave will be earned by all full-time and permanent part-time employees at the rate of 12 days per year from the date of their initial employment. In the case of permanent part-time employees, leave will be accrued proportional to hours worked.

A maximum of ninety (90) days of sick leave can be accrued and carried forward from one calendar year to the next.

Maternity leave and funeral leave will be granted as sick leave. Once an employee's sick leave is exhausted, annual leave or leave without pay may be granted by the selecting authority.

Sick leave for the month will accrue on the last day of each calendar month worked. Entering and terminating employees will accrue sick leave proportionatal to the total hours worked during the calendar month.

8.4   Leave Without Pay

Leave without pay for a period not to exceed twelve (12) months may be granted an employee subject to the approval of the Chief Justice.

At the conclusion of the leave without pay period, the employee may return to a position similar to that which he or she left. Annual leave and sick leave will not be accrued during the leave period.

8.5   Military Leave

Military leave of two types will be allowable. Active service in any branch of the United States Armed Forces, Federal Reserves or National Guard, for a period not to exceed fourteen (14) working days within any calendar year, will be treated as active work time. During such periods the employee will receive his normal salary, accrue annual and sick leave and be entitled to all benefits accruing under this system.

Military service in excess of fourteen (14) days entered into during time of war or other national emergency or as a result of conscription, will be treated as leave without pay. The employee will not be entitled to salary, leave or benefits. However, he is entitled to return to a similar position within thirty (30) days of his release from the service.

8.6   Personal Leave
Each employee will be granted three days of personal leave per year. The purpose of this leave will be to handle personal business that cannot be accomplished outside working hours or to accommodate non-Christian religious holidays.
Personal leave will not abut other leave time or any holidays.

8.7   Transfer of Leave from Other Departments
State employees who transfer into the Judicial Department from either the Executive or Legislative Departments will be allowed to transfer their accrued annual and sick leave balances.

8.8   Leave Responsibility and Scheduling
It will be the responsibility of the selecting authority to approve employees' requests for leave.
All military leave and leave without pay must be requested in writing and approved by the Chief Justice.

8.9   Leave Records
The AOC is responsible for maintaining all leave records. Leave actions will be reported to the AOC monthly by the RCAs.

8.10   Transfer of Leave on July 1, 1976
At the effective date of this Manual, leave accrued by employees under a prior system as a result of employment by a Maine Superior Court, District Court or the Supreme Judicial Court, will be carried over to the new system (up to a maximum of thirty (30) days annual and ninety (90) days sick leave). Such leave must be certified by the county or district court.

8.11   Holidays
The following holidays will be observed.

   8.11.1 New Year's Day (January 1)

8.11.2 George Washington's Birthday (third Monday in February)

8.11.3 Patriot's Day (third Monday in April)

8.11.4 Memorial Day (May 30)

8.11.5 Independence Day (July 4)

8.11.6 Labor Day (first Monday in September)

8.11.7 Columbus Day (second Monday in October)

8.11.8 Veterans Day (November 11)

8.11.9 Thanksgiving Day

8.11.10 Christmas Day

8.11.11 The day of any statewide election, including primaries and the choice of presidential electors.

8.11.12 Any other days declared by the President or Chief Justice.

If a holiday falls on Sunday, the observance will be moved to the following Monday.

9.0 INSURANCE AND RETIREMENT BENEFITS

9.1 Insurance Benefits
All permanent full-time and part-time employees will be entitled to participate in the State of Maine's health insurance programs.
All permanent full-time and part-time employees who work an average of twenty (20) hours or more per week will be entitled to participate in the State of Maine's life insurance programs.

9.2 Retirement Benefits
All permanent full-time and part-time employees will be entitled to participate in the State of Maine's retirement program.

9.3 Retirement Age
All court system employees are encouraged to retire at the age of 65.

10.0 GRIEVANCE AND APPEAL PROCEDURES

10.1   Employee Right of Appeal
Permanent full-time and part-time employees have the right to file a grievance or appeal a position classification, adverse evaluation or disciplinary action.

10.2   Appeal Board
A court system Appeal Board consisting of a member of the Supreme Judicial Court, a Superior Court Justice, a District Court Judge, an RCA and three Judicial Department employees covered by the personnel system will be selected by the Chief Justice and will meet at the direction of the SCA.
The SCA will notify Board personnel concerning appeals when a meeting is required.

10.3   Appeal Process
The appeal process is as follows:

10.3.1 The employee must first attempt to resolve his grievance with his selecting authority.

10.3.2 If a satisfactory solution is not reached, the employee must notify the SCA in writing of his/her intent to appeal. Such notification must be made within ten (10) calendar days of the action being appealed. Upon notification, the appealed action will be suspended until the appeal is resolved.

10.3.3 Subsequent to notification of intent to file an appeal, the employee has ten (10) calendar days in which to file a formal appeal with the SCA. This appeal must include a statement of the problem, efforts made to date to satisfy the grievance and desired results. A copy of the appeal must be sent to the person against whom the appeal is filed. That person must file an answer within ten (10) days.

10.3.4 The Appeals Board will review the appeal and determine whether a hearing is justified.

10.3.5 If determined justified, a hearing will be conducted (within thirty (30) days).

10.3.6 A decision will be reached and the employee notified.

10.3.7 If a hearing is determined not to be

justified, the employee will be notified in writing.

If a hearing is to be conducted, the employee will be entitled to counsel at his own expense. Strict rules of evidence need not be followed in conducting the hearing. All grievances and their results will be documented and placed in the employee's personnel record.

COMPENSATION SCALE STRUCTURE

B.1   SALARY GRADE RANGES

The ranges which appear on the following pages depict annual, bi-weekly, and hourly salaries for each grade, together with the jobs assigned to each grade. Because the number of work days may vary from year to year, actual pay received may vary slightly from the annual figure. Numbers are rounded where necessary.

The ranges are constructed in the following manner:

B.1.1 Target Salary (hourly figure) for each grade is 10 percent above the Target of the grade below.

B.1.2 Maximum for superior performance for Grade 1 is 15 percent above Target.

B.1.3 Maximum for superior performance for Grades 2 through 11 is 25 percent above Target.

B.1.4 For Grade 1, Step 2 is 5 percent below Target. Minimum is 5 percent below Step 2.

B.1.5 For Grades 2 through 5, Step 3 is 5 percent below Target. Step 2 is 3.5 percent below Step 3. Minimum is 3.5 percent below Step 2.

B.1.6 For Grades 6 through 13, Step 4 is 5 percent below Target. Step 3 is 5 percent below Step 4. Step 2 is 3.5 percent below Step 3. Minimum is 3.5 percent below Step 2.

B.1.7 Experience Recognition Step 1 is 4 percent above Target; Step 2 is 8 percent above Target.

B.1.8 Bi-weekly figures are 75 times the hourly rate; the annual figures are 1950 times the hourly rate.

B.2   EFFECTIVE DATE

These ranges are effective December 3, 1978.

B.2 COMPENSATION SCALES

Jobs Assigned	Grade	Minimum	Step 2	Step 3	Step 4	Target Salary Maximum for Satis. Perform.	Exper. Recog. Step 1	Exper. Recog. Step 2	Maximum for Superior Perform.
Maint. Worker Court Officer	1-Annual Bi-weekly Hourly	5889.00 226.50 3.02	6181.50 237.75 3.17			6493.50 249.75 3.33	6747.00 259.50 3.46	7020.00 270.00 3.60	7468.50 287.25 3.83
Asst. Clerk	2-Annual Bi-weekly Hourly	6376.50 245.25 3.27	6591.00 253.50 3.38	6825.00 262.50 3.50		7156.50 275.25 3.67	7449.00 286.50 3.82	7722.00 297.00 3.96	8950.50 344.25 4.59
Asst. Clerk I	3-Annual Bi-weekly Hourly	7000.00 269.25 3.59	7254.00 279.00 3.72	7507.50 288.75 3.85		7878.00 303.00 4.04	8190.00 315.00 4.20	8502.00 327.00 4.36	9847.50 378.75 5.05
Acctg. Clerk Transcript. Typist	4-Annual Bi-weekly Hourly	7702.50 296.25 3.95	7819.50 300.75 4.01	8248.50 317.25 4.23		8658.00 333.00 4.44	9009.00 346.50 4.62	9360.00 360.00 4.80	10822.50 416.25 5.55
Asst. Clerk III Clerk I	5-Annual Bi-weekly Hourly	8463.00 325.50 4.34	8755.50 336.75 4.49	9067.50 348.75 4.65		9516.00 366.00 4.88	9906.00 381.00 5.08	10276.50 395.25 5.27	11895.00 457.50 6.10

Jobs Assigned	Grade	Minimum	Step 2	Step 3	Step 4	Target Salary Maximum for Satis. Perform.	Exper. Recog. Step 1	Exper. Recog. Step 2	Maximum for Superior Perform.
Sec. I Asst. Clerk of Law Ct. & Exec. Sec.	5-Annual Bi-weekly Hourly	8463.00 325.50 4.34	8755.50 336.75 4.49	9067.50 348.75 4.65		9516.00 366.00 4.88	9906.00 381.00 5.08	10276.50 395.25 5.27	11895.00 457.50 6.10
Acct. Asst. Clerk IV Clerk III Sec. II	6-Annual Bi-weekly Hourly	8872.50 341.25 4.55	9184.50 353.25 4.71	9496.50 365.25 4.87	9964.50 383.25 5.11	10471.50 402.75 5.37	10880.00 418.50 5.58	11310.00 435.00 5.80	13084.50 503.25 6.71
Clerk III Sec. III	7-Annual Bi-weekly Hourly	9750.00 375.00 5.00	10101.00 388.50 5.18	10452.00 402.00 5.36	10978.50 422.25 5.63	11524.50 443.25 5.91	11992.50 461.25 6.15	12441.00 478.50 6.38	14410.50 554.25 7.39
Clerk IV	8-Annual Bi-weekly Hourly	10744.50 413.25 5.51	11115.00 427.50 5.70	11505.00 442.50 5.90	12070.50 464.25 6.19	12675.00 487.50 6.50	13182.00 507.00 6.76	13689.00 526.50 7.02	15834.00 609.00 8.12
Clerk V	9-Annual Bi-weekly Hourly	11817.00 454.50 6.06	12226.50 470.25 6.27	12655.50 486.75 6.49	13279.50 510.75 6.81	13942.50 536.25 7.15	14508.00 558.00 7.44	15054.00 579.00 7.72	17433.00 670.50 8.94

B.2 COMPENSATION SCALES (cont'd)

Jobs Assigned	Grade	Minimum	Step 2	Step 3	Step 4	Target Salary Maximum for Satis. Perform.	Exper. Recog. Step 1	Exper. Recog. Step 2	Maximum for Superior Perform.
	10-Annual	12987.00	13435.50	13903.50	14605.50	15327.00	15931.50	16555.50	19149.00
	Bi-weekly	499.50	516.75	534.75	561.75	589.50	612.75	636.75	736.50
	Hourly	6.66	6.87	7.13	7.49	7.86	8.17	8.49	9.82
Court Reporter	11-Annual	14293.50	14781.00	15307.50	16068.00	16867.50	17550.00	18213.00	21079.50
	Bi-weekly	549.75	568.50	588.75	618.00	648.75	675.00	700.50	810.75
	Hourly	7.33	7.58	7.85	8.24	8.65	9.00	9.34	10.81
Clerk of the Law Court	12-Annual	15717.00	16263.00	16828.50	17686.50	18564.00			
	Bi-weekly	605.50	625.50	647.25	680.25	714.00			
	Hourly	8.06	8.34	8.63	9.07	9.52			
Reg. Court Admin. Fiscal Dir.	13-Annual	17296.50	17901.00	18525.00	19441.50	20416.50			
	Bi-weekly	665.25	688.50	712.50	747.75	785.25			
	Hourly	8.87	9.18	9.50	9.97	10.47			

Appendix E-3: Circuit Court of Oregon, Multnomah County, Personnel Plan

SECTION I: PERSONNEL PLAN

1. Purpose: The purpose of this rule is to establish the objectives of the court's personnel management system.

2. Intent: The intent of the court's personnel management system is as follows:

   (a) To provide a comprehensive, fair and effective personnel management system for court employees;

   (b) To insure that personnel are compensated fairly in accordance with the quality of performance of the work assigned;

   (c) To insure that personnel performing the same work are classified equally;

   (d) To insure that employee standards of performance are developed and maintained;

   (e) To insure that the court remains an equal opportunity employer, and complies with affirmative action goals set by the court as adopted within the plan maintained by Multnomah County.

ALLOCATING POSITIONS/DUTIES

1. Purpose: The purpose of this rule is to establish the procedure for allocating new positions or duties to positions already existing within the administrative operation of the court.

2. Allocating Positions/Duties:

   (a) When a new position is to be established, or the duties of an existing position are to be altered, modified or changed, the administrator will:

   (1) be responsible for properly classifying the position in consort with the duties assigned;

   (2) if necessary, seek the approval of the Board of County Commissioners to add new positions;

   (3) insure that compensation is commensurate with the classification of the position.

   (b) Duties of a position are only descriptive of the position, and not restrictive to the duties to be performed.

   (c) Newly allocated positions will be assigned to the various units of the court's administrative operation by the administrator only.

   (d) Permanent employees shall have the right to request, in writing, to the administrator that their positions be evaluated for classification. The decision to proceed/deny rests solely with the administrator, and must be communicated in writing to the employee.

   (e) The employee's written request must include the rationale and supportive evidence which, in the employee's opinion, warrants the evaluation.

   (f) A denial to proceed, presented to the employee in writing, is appealable to the Presiding Judge, in writing, only when:

   (1) the administrator's action is in violation of the existing personnel rules, or

(2) the administrator's action was unwarranted by evidence presented, procured by fraud, coercion or the improper conduct of any party in interest.

(g) The Presiding Judge may act upon any and/or all evidence presented for the purpose of the appeal, or may deny it outright.

(h) The administrator, based upon the employment needs of the court, may underfill a vacant budgeted position provided the underfill salary level is properly classified in consort with the duties to be performed. By definition, underfill shall mean to employ a person in a permanently budgeted position to perform work for the court at a salary level below the minimum salary level established for that budgeted position. There shall be no time limit on the underfilled position.

PERSONNEL SELECTION

1. Purpose: The purpose of this rule is to establish the policy for selection of administrative personnel. This rule is established on the basis of the court being and maintaining its status as an equal opportunity employer. As stated in the rule concerning Promotion, the intent of the court shall be to develop its employee's proficiency and skills from within the organization.

2. Personnel Selection:

   (a) Announcement of vacant positions shall be made in such manner as to insure the widest circulation amongst potential applicants.

   (b) An applicant, to be considered for employment, must meet the qualifications established for the position for which they apply. Failure to do so will cause the application to be rejected.

   (c) All applicants shall be required to complete whatever application forms are required by the court.

(d) All applicants shall be initially screened by the court's personnel analysts. Secondary interviews will be conducted by the unit supervisor/coordinator, who will make the final selection.

(e) A selected applicant will be required to serve a six-month probation period prior to granting of permanent status. Such applicant may be dismissed from employment at any time during the probation period by the appointing authority. Such a dismissal shall not be appealable.

(f) All applicants must be 18 years of age and a citizen of the United States.

(g) It shall be the policy of the court to discourage the employment of more than one member of the immediate family.

(h) Personnel employed by the court shall be considered in the following categories:

   (1) <u>Judicial appointees</u>: secretary-bailiffs, courtroom clerks, and court reporters.

   (2) <u>Permanent employees</u>: those employees who have successfully completed probation and are occupying a permanently budgeted position.

   (3) <u>Part-time employees</u>: any employee who is not so defined in (1) and (2) above. May include WIN, CETA, College Work Study students, temporary personnel, PSE grant employees, emergency personnel, etc.

(i) Part-time employees shall be appointed as needed by the appointing authority in order to complete work assignments commensurate with their abilities.

(j) Judicial appointments shall serve at the pleasure of the judge who appoints them.

(k) Continued employment with the court shall be based upon the employee's satisfactory performance of assigned work.

COMPLIANCE WITH PERSONNEL RULES

1. Purpose: The purpose of this rule is to establish employee compliance with personnel rules of the Circuit Court.

2. Compliance with Personnel Rules:

    (a) Employees of the Circuit Court are required, as an accepted condition of employment with the court to comply with the personnel rules in effect.

    (b) Failure to comply with the personnel rules shall subject the employee to disciplinary action.

RULES OF CONDUCT

1. Purpose: The purpose of this rule is to establish the policy regarding conduct of employees during their performance of assigned duties.

2. Rules of Conduct:

    (a) Except as otherwise provided for by the personnel rules, by court rule, or by statute, no employee of the court shall engage in any activity which by the nature of its duties, requirements or qualifications shall cause that employee to incur any obligation or perform any act which is in conflict with the discharge of the employment obligation to the court.

    (b) No employee shall utilize, by direct or indirect activity, their position to secure special privileges or exemptions for themselves or others.

    (c) No employee shall directly or indirectly receive, or agree to receive, any compensation, gift or reward or gratuity for any matter connected with or related to the duties of their position unless expected by this rule or by receiving prior written approval from the court administrator.

(d) Honoraria, expenses paid, consulting fees provided for papers, lectures, demonstrations, seminars, or appearances made by employees on their own time, and not in violation of Oregon Law, shall not be deemed a violation of this rule.

(e) All employees giving lectures, a series of lectures, or speeches before groups during normal working hours, and for which a fee is paid may retain the fee. All such appearances require written approval in advance of the event, by the court administrator. The court administrator may require the employee to make up the lost time; grant the employee leave without pay; or both.

(f) No employee shall engage in or accept other employment which may reasonably impair or preclude the discharge of official duties.

(g) No employee shall conduct themselves in a manner which shall reflect negatively upon the court or the employee's official duties. Some examples of such manners are:

   (1) drinking or utilizing dangerous drugs while on duty;

   (2) misappropriation or abuse of court property, funds or equipment;

   (3) engaging in any form of criminal activity;

   (4) providing special services to litigants or the public outside those services established by or governed by law, rules of the court or by approved policy.

ROLE OF THE COURT ADMINISTRATOR

1. Purpose: The purpose of this rule is to define the role of the court administrator in the court's personnel management system.

2. Role of the Court Administrator:

    (a) The administrator is responsible for development, implementation and maintenance of the personnel management system.

    (b) The administrator may delegate functions of the personnel management system to management staff.

    (c) The administrator will prepare and recommend rules and policies governing personnel management to the General Committee.

    (d) The administrator will insure that complete personnel records are maintained on all employees of the court.

    (e) The administrator will insure that personnel actions taken prior to the effective date of new, abolished or amended rules will not be altered or cancelled by the newly adopted policy.

    (f) The administrator will perform those specific duties assigned by the personnel rules.

    (g) Classification of positions is the duty of the administrator, who has the authority to amend, modify, or initiate the job duties so long as the classification assigned to the affected position is commensurate with classification requirements in force.

ROLE OF THE GENERAL COMMITTEE

1. Purpose: The purpose of this rule is to define the role of the General Committee of judges in the court's personnel management system.

2. Role of the General Committee:

   (a) The Committee is an advisory committee to the Presiding Judge for personnel rules/policy matters.

   (b) The Committee will entertain those personnel rules/policy matters prepared and recommended by the court administrator. Such matters will be heard by the Committee at its regular monthly meeting.

   (c) The Committee may initiate or approve, modify, reject or approve as modified, the rules/policies prepared and recommended by the administrator.

   (d) Judges of the Court acting as appointing authorities, may establish a set of rules for the purpose of handling personnel matters of their individual departments.

WORK HOURS, BREAK PERIODS
LUNCHEON PERIOD

1. Purpose: The purpose of this rule is to establish the policy for work hours, break periods and luncheon periods.

2. Work Hours:

   (a) The regularly scheduled work week for all administrative employees except for those assigned to judicial departments shall be thirty-seven (37) hours and thirty (30) minutes.

   (b) The normal work day for such employees, except those assigned to judicial departments and the Recognizance office shall be either:

      (1) 8:00 a.m. to 4:30 p.m. or,

      (2) 8:30 a.m. to 5:00 p.m.

   (c) Responsibility for determination of the individual employee's work day shall be the duty of the employee's supervisor, and shall be the result of evaluating the working requirements of the court, the work unit and the individual's reasons for requesting an alteration in the work day.

3. <u>Break Periods</u>:

    (a) Employees are entitled to two (2) fifteen (15) minute break periods during the work day, one (1) in the morning hours, and one (1) in the afternoon hours.

    (b) Since it is not practical for everyone to be away from their work station at the same time, the unit supervisor shall establish and publish a schedule of assigned break period times.

    (c) Break periods shall not be accumulated to either extend the lunch hour or reduce the work day.

4. <u>Luncheon Period</u>:

    (a) Each employee is entitled to a one (1) hour luncheon period each work day, to be scheduled between the hours of 11:30 a.m. and 2:00 p.m.

    (b) Since it is not practical for everyone to be away from their work station at the same time, the unit supervisor shall establish and publish a schedule of assigned luncheon periods.

5. <u>General</u>:

    (a) Tardiness in returning to work from breaks and luncheon periods will cause an adjustment in the employee's time sheet. Repeated abuse shall result in appropriate disciplinary action, which may include discharge from employment.

    (b) The administrator, in conjunction with the unit supervisor, shall have the right to:

        (1) Alter, modify or establish break or luncheon schedules.

(2) Establish an appropriate work schedule for the unit.

(3) Establish new working shifts for units.

(c) An employee, grieved by working hours, must incorporate in the grievance petition that the working hours assigned do not interfere with the working requirements of the court or the work unit.

DEFINITIONS

1. Purpose: The purpose of this rule is to establish definitions for key words utilized in the personnel rules. Definitions may be added at any time without requiring voted approval. However, no definition, once added, may be altered or deleted without voted approval.

2. Definitions: The following terms, whenever used in the personnel rules, shall mean the following

   (a) Administrator: Circuit Court Administrator.

   (b) Administrative Personnel (or employee): Nonjudicial employees of the Circuit Court exclusive of those working directly for judges as judicial appointees or judicial staff.

   (c) Allocation: The original assignment of an individual position to the appropriate class on the basis of the work performed.

   (d) Appeal: A petition by an employee to the Appeal Board (PEP); to the Grievance Board (personnel); or to the Presiding Judge (denial of request for reclassification) for a hearing on an issue directly affecting that employee.

   (e) Appointing Authority: The judges of the court, or the court administrator, or other person delegated to make appointments to positions in court service.

(f) Appointment: A regular appointment to a position established within the court.

(g) Board: Board of County Commissioners of Multnomah County.

(h) Class: One or more positions grouped in accordance with duties or work performed; responsibilities assigned; qualifications or experience required; and for which the same salary schedule applies.

(i) Classification: The act of grouping positions into classes.

(j) Compensation: The salary paid for work performed.

(k) Compensator: The agent, authority, political unit, or activity which pays for services rendered.

(l) Coordinator: The supervisory titles assigned to the Criminal, Civil, Domestic Relations and Administrative Services units of the court's administrative operations. Coordinators are supervisory and managerial.

(m) County: Multnomah County.

(n) Court Administrator: The Circuit Court Administrator.

(o) Day(s): Unless otherwise specified, means working days.

(p) Demotion: A change by an employee from a position in one class to a position in a lower class.

(q) Disciplinary Action: Action taken to reprimand an employee.

(r) Employee: Unless otherwise specified, means a permanent employee.

(s) General Committee: The General Committee of Circuit Court judges in Multnomah County.

(t) Grievance Board: The board which hears appeals concerning personnel rules of the court.

(u) Judicial Appointment: The direct employment of courtroom staff, consisting of courtroom clerk, secretary-bailiff and court reporter.

(v) Lay Off: Employees who have been separated from service due to a lack of work or lack of funds and without delinquency or misconduct on their part.

(w) Permanent Employee: An employee in court service who has successfully completed the probation period. All other employees are temporary employees.

(x) Probation Period: A working test/training period during which a newly-hired employee must demonstrate fitness for the position.

(y) Promotion: A change by an employee from a position in one class to a position in a higher class.

(z) Reallocation: A reassignment; change in duties of a position; or movement of a position within the court's administrative structure.

Additional Definitions:

(a) Reduction in Force: A mandatory reduction in the number of employees due to an imposed budgetary cutback or reduction.

(b) Reinstatement: Appointment of a former employee who was laid off, reduced in force, or was previously terminated in good standing to a permanent position.

(c) Supervisor: Any court employee who occupies a position which involves supervision of employees.

(d) Suspension: A temporary lay off of an employee for disciplinary reasons.

(e) Transfer: A change by an employee from one position to another in the same class or to another class in the same salary, usually involving similar duties or qualifications.

SECTION II COMPENSATION

1. Purpose: The purpose of this rule is to define the requirements of the court's compensation plan.

2. Compensation:

   (a) The rate of compensation (or salary) paid to any court employee shall be in accordance with the compensation schedule in effect and adopted by the court, and if necessary, approved by the Board of County Commissioners.

   (b) Beginning salary paid upon appointment to a position with the court shall be determined by the administrator. However, for new employees, the beginning salary shall not exceed Step 3 of the compensation schedule for the class of the position.

   (c) Salary increases within an established range shall be awarded in accordance with the court's Merit Plan.

   (d) Review of compensation schedules is a duty of the administrator, and shall be accomplished at least annually.

   (e) Compensation shall be paid for actual time worked.

RATES OF PAY

1. Purpose: The purpose of this rule is to establish the rates of pay, or salary, to be paid to employees.

2. Rates of Pay:

   (a) Employees shall be paid at the rate of pay appropriate to the step and classification of the position for which they are regularly employed.

(b) The rate of pay shall be determined by the compensation schedule in effect at the time of employment, promotion, demotion or reinstatement, whichever is appropriate.

(c) In the event of reclassification, an employee's rate of pay shall change only if the rate of pay scheduled is below that of the reclassification rate of pay or if any other arrangement is negotiated between the appointing authority and the compensator.

(d) Employees who are affected by new compensation schedules shall be brought "on-to-step" on their anniversary date.

(e) Under no circumstances, unless negotiations between the compensator and the appointing authority dictate to the contrary, will an employee receive a reduction in salary due to a new compensation schedule or reclassification being in effect. Such employees shall be frozen until such time as the compensation schedule base passes their rate of pay.

(f) At time of employment, the employee's rate of pay shall be set within the range or steps appropriate to the classification of the position by the appointing authority.

(g) Any employee who is demoted, shall receive the rate of pay assigned by the appointing authority, according to the range or steps appropriate to the classification of the position to which the employee is demoted.

(h) At time of reclassification to a higher class, the employee's rate of pay shall be set within the range or steps appropriate to the classification. Such rate will be based upon the employee's performance, anniversary date and discretion of the appointing authority. Under no circumstances can the rate exceed the third step of the range.

COMPENSATION FOR WORK OUT-OF-CLASSIFICATION

1. Purpose: The purpose of this rule is to establish payment for work performed by employees who temporarily work out-of-classification. Out-of-classification is defined as any temporary work performed by an employee either in a higher or a lower classification.

2. Compensation for Work Out-of-Classification:

    (a) An employee, required to temporarily perform duties of a higher classification to which the employee is temporarily assigned.

    (b) An employee, required to temporarily perform duties of a supervisor for a period of more than five (5) consecutive work days, shall be compensated at the highest step of the highest classification of employees who are not in classified service (Office Assistant IV).

    (c) An employee, required to temporarily perform duties of a lower classification shall not lose compensation because of the temporary assignment.

    (d) An employee who performs new or additional work within the same class shall not receive additional compensation.

OVERTIME COMPENSATION

1. Purpose: The purpose of this rule is to establish policy under which overtime compensation is authorized.

2. Compensation for Overtime:

    (a) Overtime shall be paid to an authorized employee only if approved in advance by the supervisor.

    (b) The administrator has the right to except certain employees from overtime, and has the right to authorize compensatory time in lieu of overtime. Such compensatory time shall be granted in the following manner: straight time compensation compensatory time for each hour of overtime worked, unless approved otherwise.

(c) The following shall constitute overtime work:

(1) Work in excess of eight (8) hours in any work day.

(2) Work in excess of ten (10) hours in any work day for a four-day-a-week employee.

(3) Work in excess of forty (40) hours in any work week.

(d) Overtime shall not be paid for weekend work if those days fall within the regular working schedule of the employee.

(e) All courtroom personnel, recognizance staff, and those persons compensated within the County's management (or unclassified service) plan are excepted from overtime compensation.

MERIT PLAN

1. <u>Purpose</u>: The purpose of this rule is to establish the policies for applying the court's merit increase program.

2. <u>Merit Plan</u>:

(a) The court's merit plan is designed to effectively match employee renumeration [sic] (salary increases) to their individual work performance (as determined by PEP). Consequently, the merit plan is directly related to the results measured by PEP. PEP provides the chronological performance evaluation data upon which the annual merit decision will be made. The decision to grant a salary increase will be made in accordance with pre-determined formulae developed in this plan. It is important to understand three key points:

360

(1) Merit increase/denial decisions are annual only; not automatically progressive.

(2) PEP evaluates performance, not merit; merit recommendations are only made (once annually, unless excepted to by the administrator) based upon the total PEP process (3 ratings/year; based upon anniversary dates).

(3) There is only one merit increase opportunity per rating year. Unlike the step increase system utilized in previous years, the merit plan ties such step increases to work quality; not job longevity. Only cost-of-living benefits are automatic (even though a PEP element will cause cost-of-living to be denied as well).

(b) The basic elements of the merit system are as follows:

(1) <u>All</u> administrative employees covered by PEP are included, even those hired after April 30, 1976 (who would go on the step system effective July 1, 1978).

(2) Step increases are awarded solely upon one year's performance as established and evaluated by the PEP system. Step increases are no longer granted for longevity reasons.

(3) Step increases are awarded based upon criteria in this merit plan.

(4) Cost-of-living increases remain automatic awards to every employee except those who are o Below Average PEP probation.

(5) Budgeted funds for step increases not awarded, general wage increase funds not awarded, and not more than 50% of unexpended personal services funds will be pooled for merit awards to those top-of-the-step employees who

cannot receive step increases. The amount of the merit award will be determined by the amount of funds available and the number of employees eligible. Responsibility for such merit awards rests solely with the court administrator.

(c) Merit awards are determined at the end of the individual employee's rating year (based upon anniversary date) as follows:

   (1) Steps 1-4: The employee must receive an Average rating (PEP) for a minimum of two of the three PEP ratings during the rating year. No Below Average ratings can be received during the rating year.

   (2) Steps 5 and above: The employee must receive an Above Average rating (PEP) for a minimum of two of the three PEP ratings during the rating year. No Below Average ratings can be received during the rating year.

   (3) Employees at Top Step: The employee already at the top step is eligible for a merit bonus (one time only per rating year) from the pool discussed in item (5). Eligibility is the same as for Steps 5 and above since employees who have achieved this step must theoretically be evaluated continuously as Above Average employees.

   (4) Cost-of-living: Awarded automatically to all employees, based upon achievement of Average or Above Average ratings. An employee who receives a Below Average rating will not receive any cost-of-living increase for the duration of the probationary rating period immediately following the rating. This is due to the employee being placed in a 120-day probation status pending either termination or improved performance sufficient to remove the rating and achieve reinstatement.

(d) Each employee's merit rating at the end of an anniversary rating year determines the step increase entitlement. Since the rating is determined from PEP ratings, it is easy for the employee to determine the level of performance needed to achieve a step increase. In fact, by utilizing their individual copies of PEP ratings, each employee can plan their program in conjunction with their supervisor.

Since the step rating formulae are known in advance, employees at the critical step 4 level can undertake to plan a program to achieve step 5. The same is true for those already at the top step, who desire to achieve a bonus award from the merit pool. Thus, the key for making the merit plan work for you is to plan ahead, and to discuss your performance with your supervisor openly and honestly.

(e) Under PEP, new employees serve a six-month probationary period. Two PEP ratings are developed during this period. The first, after three months, measures progress only and provides the base from which the second three month's training requirements are developed. The second, completed at the end of the six months' probationary period, not only measures progress, but is also utilized to determine if the new employee will be granted permanent status or be terminated.

(f) To the new employee, these two initial ratings are critical. To the supervisor, they represent the critical determinator of the new employee's ability to contribute and perform assigned duties effectively. As such, the ratings are as effective as those of permanent employees, and are definitely usable in making the merit decision.

(g) At this stage, six months remain before the new employee, now a permanent member, reaches their first anniversary date. That time period represents 1.5 rating periods for a permanent employee; but is only one rating period for the new employee. Thus, the merit plan <u>does not</u> create a disadvantage for the new employee: the granting of permanent status represents, at a minimum, an Average PEP rating (otherwise, the person would be terminated). Achievement of a second Average rating would qualify the employee, at the minimum, for the increase to the next step in the salary range.

PERFORMANCE EVALUATION

1. <u>Purpose</u>: The purpose of this rule is to establish the court's performance evaluation system.

2. <u>Performance Evaluation</u>:

    (a) It is the policy of the court to financially reward its employees based upon their demonstrated work performance.

    (b) The court administrator shall maintain, amend, and enforce a personnel evaluation system which will conform to the intent of the policy in (a) above. Such evaluation system shall be with the court's approval.

    (c) The performance evaluation plan, shall be printed and distributed to each employee affected by the plan, and copies shall be available from the administrator's office.

PROMOTION

1. <u>Purpose</u>: The purpose of this rule shall be to establish promotion policy and procedure.

2. <u>Promotion</u>:

    (a) The promotion policy of the court shall be to promote from within whenever possible. Promotion from within shall mean that the employee who seeks promotion or transfer to the open position must be selected on the basis of qualification, experience and demonstrated performance.

(b) Every employee of the court shall be eligible to compete for promotion regardless of their employment status except for those employees who are serving probation for below average work performance.

(c) Every employee who applys, and meets the criteria in (a) and (b) above, will be interviewed by the unit supervisor and/or the section coordinator, who shall make the final selection.

(d) If none of the employees who apply are selected, the position shall be deemed vacant and the external hiring process may begin.

(e) A vacant position to which an employee may be promoted or transferred shall be announced internally in writing to every employee for a period of not more than five (5) working days. Such announcement period shall be indicated on the notice.

TRANSFER

1. Purpose: The purpose of this rule is to establish the procedures and policy for position transfer. A transfer is defined as a job change within the court administrative structure from one unit to another, and involving no increase in salary or classification.

2. Transfer:

   (a) An employee may be transferred under the following circumstances:

   (1) at the discretion of the appointing authority;

   (2) at the request of the employee, providing the position to which transfer is requested is vacant and the transfer meets with the approval of the unit supervisor, unless superceded by (1) above; or

   (3) due to a reduction in force or lay off.

(b) An employee is not eligible to request transfer if they are on probation, serving in a temporary or part-time capacity, or working under an employment grant. However, such a transfer may be made by the appointing authority.

(c) A transfer is not appealable unless the transfer was made as described in 2 (a) (1) above. Under these circumstances, an appeal may be made to the Grievance Board.

EMPLOYEE BENEFITS

1. Purpose: The purpose of this rule is to set forth those employee benefits and qualifications for same available to employees of the court, exclusive of Retirement Benefits.

2. Employee Benefits:

    (a) Health and Welfare benefits available to court employees shall be the same as those available to Multnomah County employees, with eligibility requirements being the same. Employee benefit information is available from the administrator's office.

    (b) Worker's Compensation benefits shall be the same for court employees as they are for employees of Multnomah County, and the same rules shall apply.

    (c) Every effort shall be made by court employees to utilize County vehicles for travel purposes on official court purpose. Arrangements must be made with the administrator's office in sufficient time to insure a vehicle reservation. Under no circumstances, unless written approval is received from the administrator, will employees be compensated for use of their personal transportation while conducting official court business. Approval by the administrator will authorize the employee to collect, upon submission of proper records, a rate of fifteen (15¢) per mile for the first three hundred (300) miles, and ten cents (10¢) per mile for all miles thereafter.

RETIREMENT BENEFITS

1. **Purpose:** The purpose of this rule is to establish the employee's entitlement to retirement benefits.

2. **Retirement Benefits:**

   (a) So long as the employees of the court are compensated by Multnomah County, they shall be entitled to receive whatever rights, benefits, and privileges are extended to employees of Multnomah County by the Employee's Retirement Fund.

   (b) Employees shall be required to contribute from their salaries whatever contribution rate is in effect and agreed to by Multnomah County.

   (c) If non-participation by employees is allowed, employees may so do through whatever process is required by the Employee's Retirement Fund.

AUTHORIZED LEAVES OF ABSENCE WITH PAY

1. **Purpose:** To establish the Policy for authorized leaves of absence with pay exclusive of sick leave, maternity leave and vacation leave.

2. **Authorized Leaves of Absence With Pay:**

   (a) **Court Leave:** Any employee subpoenaed to appear as a witness or called and selected to serve as a juror shall be granted leave to appear with full pay. If the employee is excused or dismissed prior to the time that would normally equal completion of one half (½) of the employee's work day, the employee must report for work. Fees are to be turned over to the Court.

   (b) **Military Leave:** Any employee who is a member of any Reserve or National Guard component of the military forces of the United States shall be granted thirty (30) calendar days per fiscal year when ordered to active duty for such training periods as are necessary to maintain their participation in the Reserve training program. Such military leave shall not be deducted for vacation benefits.

(c) Voting: Employees are allowed two (2) hours to vote on any regularly scheduled election day if their normal work hours would prevent them from exercising this right.

(d) Bereavement Leave: An employee shall be granted not more than three (3) day's leave of absence with pay in the event of a death in their immediate family. Immediate family shall include spouse, parents, children, brothers or sisters, grandparents, aunts or uncles, nieces or nephews, and in-laws. Leave taken beyond the allowable three (3) days shall be charged as designated by the administrator.

(e) Conference or Training Leave: Employees are authorized leave with pay to attend conferences, seminars, training sessions, institutes or meetings when it is determined such attendance is in the best interest of the Court. Such attendance shall not be deducted from any other leave time. Such attendance shall be approved in advance by the Section Coordinator.

(f) Leave of absence with pay other than the foregoing will not be authorized unless written approval is obtained from the appointing authority.

AUTHORIZED LEAVES OF ABSENCE WITHOUT PAY

1. Purpose: The purpose of this rule is to establish the policy for authorized leaves of absence without pay except for maternity leave.

2. Policy:

   (a) Leaves of absence without pay for a limited period, not to exceed thirty (30) days, shall be granted for any reasonable purpose, and may be renewed upon written request of the administrator.

(b) Request for leaves of absence shall be in writing, and submitted through the supervisor to the administrator, who shall have the final authority to approve/disapprove. Requests shall include the reason(s) for the leave, the dates of absence, whether a replacement is required, and any supportive documentation directly applicable to a rationale of approval. Granting of the leave shall not involve usage of sick leave or vacation time.

(c) Requests for such leave must be submitted thirty (30) days prior to the initial absence date. Requests may be granted provided suitable replacement(s) are available; that the leave is in the best interests of the court or the individual; or that such leave will enhance the future career development of the employee.

(d) Employees granted such leave of absence must recognize that the loss of their services to the court may impair their return to the job position vacated. However, the court assumes the responsibility to accept the employee back to work at whatever salary rate or position classification (whichever is appropriate at the time of return) was held by the employee when the leave officially began.

(e) In the event of a reduction in force, the court assumes the responsibility to protect the employee's reemployment right commensurate with positions and duties available at the time of reemployment, provided the employee reports for work when so notified.

(f) Military leave of absence without pay shall occur whenever the employee is required to involuntarily report for active military service, or is so ordered to such active service as required by the United States Government. Reemployment rights guaranteed by federal law shall prevail. This provision does not apply to required Reserve Annual Training.

(g) Full-time, temporary or probationary employees may apply for sick leave without pay for the entire period of disability because of sickness or injury. A certificate from the attending or designated physician is required. In the event of a failure or refusal to provide the certificate, or if the certificate does not substantiate the request, the administrator may cancel such leave and order the employee back to work. An employee's failure to appear for work on the date specified shall be considered as a discharge from employment.

(h) The administrator shall have the final authority to approve/disapprove any other special leaves without pay not specified by this or any other policy in effect at the time the special leave is requested.

CANCELLATION/REINSTATEMENT OF LEAVE

1. Purpose: The purpose of this rule is to establish the policy for cancellation of leaves and for reinstatement from leave.

2. Cancellation of Leaves:

(a) The administrator has the authority to cancel any and all forms of leave granted to any employee. Such a cancellation may be done orally or in writing, and must specify a reasonable reporting date.

(b) Justification for cancellation is not required. However, such cancellation may be imposed if the employee is found to be abusing the leave for purposes other than those specified at time of approval.

3. Reinstatement of Leaves:

(a) Reinstatement from leave requires, unless otherwise specified elsewhere in these rules, the employee to be returned to employment with the same class in which service was being rendered at the time the leave was granted. This condition will be observed, **unless the position was abolished, and no person with less seniority is employed in the same class in the same** department, unit or section on the date the leave expired. Subject to the earlier exception noted, such employee may be returned to employment at any tiem prior to the expriation date by authority of the administrator.

HOLIDAYS

1. Purpose: The purpose of this rule is to establish the policy for holiday observance.

2. Holidays:

   (a) Eligibility--employees, other than part-time or temporary, must be on the payroll on the work day immediately preceding and immediately following a holiday to be eligible for holiday benefits.

   (b) Whenever any full time employee is required by the nature of assigned duties to perform work on a scheduled holiday, he/she shall be compensated according to the overtime compensation policy.

   (c) Holidays which occur within an employee's vacation or sick leave shall not be charged against that leave.

   (d) Holidays to be observed are those declared by the President of the United States, the Governor of the State of Oregon, the Chief Justice of Oregon's Supreme Court or the Presiding Judge; and those declared by statutes. Each calendar year, the administrator shall publish a list of holidays to be observed.

INCLEMENT WEATHER

1. Purpose: The purpose of this rule is to establish the policy concerning reporting for work during periods of inclement weather.

2. Inclement Weather Policy:

   (a) An employee who, in the interest of their own personal safety during a period of inclement weather, decides not to report for work, and so notifies their supervisor or the administrator's office, will be assessed an approved absence charged either to vacation or personal holiday.

(b) If the employee fails to notify their supervisor or the administrator's office of their decision to remain away from work due to inclement weather, the absence shall be charged as "leave without pay".

(c) Notification of the supervisor or administrator's office must occur within two (2) hours of the employee's scheduled starting time for work.

(d) During an inclement weather period, the tardiness policy will not be applied during the first two (2) hours of the employee's scheduled work starting time.

(e) Should the Court, on the basis of a decision by the Presiding Judge, declare a judicial holiday due to inclement weather conditions, the administrator shall insure that employees are compensated as if they appeared for, and completed, a normal work day.

(f) Employees who have no accrued vacation time or personal holidays available, and opt not to report for work, will be assessed a day as "leave without pay".

(g) Sick leave will not be used for absence due to inclement weather.

MATERNITY LEAVE

1. Purpose: The purpose of this rule is to establish the policy regarding maternity leave taken by employees of the court. This rule shall be the sole guide for maternity leave.

2. Maternity Leave:

(a) Maternity leave, not to exceed 6 consecutive months, shall be granted to any court employee upon written request to the court administrator. Such written request shall be submitted in sufficient time to allow for a temporary replacement to be acquired. In any event, sufficient time shall not be less than 21 days.

(b) Maternity leave is leave without pay. However, if the employee so requests, accrued vacation and accrued sick leave time may be utilized as an inclusive part of the 6 months of maternity leave, but shall not be used to extend the maternity leave period of 6 consecutive months. Such request inquires approval of the court administrator.

(c) Utilization of accrued sick leave and vacation shall only be in the amount accrued at the time maternity leave begins, and shall be utilized only from the day maternity leave begins.

(d) An employee who requests maternity leave shall reasonably specify the amount of maternity leave to be taken. Should the time requested and approved be insufficient, the employee must request additional time at least 30 days prior to the expiration of the original leave. Under no circumstances shall the amount of additional time requested, when combined with the time originally granted, exceed 6 consecutive months from the date maternity leave began.

(e) Should the employee require an extension of maternity leave beyond the 6 months grant, medical evidence is required from the attending physician to support the request. The administrator is under no obligation to grant such a request beyond the initial 6 consecutive months. However, if approval of the additional time is in the best interest of the court, it may be approved.

(f) Any extension beyond the initial 6 consecutive months shall be as leave without pay, and shall not exceed 3 months from the date of expiration of the original 6 consecutive months grant.

(g) An extension beyond the original 6 consecutive months shall cause the employee to relinquish any right to automatic reemployment unless such automatic reemployment is granted as a condition of the extension. A return to work under such conditions is mandatory. If the employee fails to report for work, and without proper medical release, on the specified date, the employee will be terminated.

(h) Any employee who returns to work from maternity leave must have a written medical release from the attending physician.

PERSONAL HOLIDAYS

1. Purpose: The purpose of this rule is to establish the policy concerning personal holidays.

2. Personal Holidays:

   (a) Each Administrative employee is entitled to two (2) personal holidays per fiscal year.

   (b) Before taking a personal holiday, the employee must request to do so, in writing, on a Request for Absence Form provided by the administrator's office. Such requests must be approved both by the supervisor and the administrator, and must be submitted by the employee at least one (1) week prior to the date requested.

   (c) Personal holidays shall be granted only at the convenience of the court's workload, and not solely at the convenience of the requestor.

SICK LEAVE

1. Purpose: The purpose of this rule is to establish the policy for sick leave.

2. Policy:

   (a) Sick leave coverage may be utilized by the employee for illness to himself/herself or any member of the immediate family household.

   (b) Absence due to illness in excess of three (3) consecutive days must be verified by a licensed physician's certificate at the request of the court.

(c) Sick leave shall not apply during any period for which the employee has already received authorized leave.

(d) Sick leave is not authorized as maternity leave.

(e) Part-time or temporary employees shall not accrue sick leave benefits. Those part-time or temporary employees who are subsidized by funds or contracts which specifically authorize compensated sick leave shall be allowed such benefits according to provisions of their funding agent or contract.

(f) Sick leave is authorized for medical/dental/psychological appointments. However, employees must make every reasonable effort to schedule such appointments so as to not interfere with their work responsibilities. Utilization of sick leave for this purpose requires written approval, and must be submitted at least three (3) days prior to the appointment.

(g) For illness as described in 2(a), such shall be honored if the employee notifies their supervisor within two (2) hours of their regular work starting time. Failure to report to the supervisor shall cause the employee to be assessed a day without pay.

(h) Abuse of sick leave may result in appropriate disciplinary action.

(i) At time of retirement or termination, the employee shall be compensated for accrued, but unused, sick leave on the basis of whatever formula is utilized by the compensating public employer at the time of retirement or termination.

(j) Sick leave shall always be charged to the nearest half hour.

(k) Sick leave charges in excess of earned sick leave credits may be charged to earned vacation or leave without pay upon written approval of the appointing authority.

VACATION

1. <u>Purpose</u>: The purpose of this rule is to establish the policy for vacations.

2. <u>Vacation</u>:

    (a) Each full-time non-management employee is entitled to accrue vacation benefits at whatever accrual rate is in effect for that class of employee, and may be utilized by that employee upon receipt of an approved written request.

    (b) Accrued vacation time may be taken by any full-time employee once they have completed six (6) calendar months of employment with the court.

    (c) Vacation benefits shall not accrue during a leave of absence without pay.

    (d) Eligible employees shall be permitted to choose their vacation times consistent with the needs of the court. Selection shall be based upon seniority unless an employee has already requested and received permission to utilized vacation at the same time.

    (e) Eligible employees may be requested to forecast vacations in advance. Under such circumstances, such forecasts are to be considered as guides only. However, in the case of disputes over vacation times, the forecast will be utilized to determine who shall receive the benefit of the time requested.

    (f) Eligible employees are required to request written approval to utilize vacation benefits. Such requests are to be submitted at least two (2) weeks in advance through the supervisor to the administrator, who is the final authority for approval/disapproval.

    (g) Eligible employees may utilize vacation benefits for any type of leave authorized as leave without pay except for maternity leave.

(h) No employee shall be allowed vacation leave for more than thirty (30) consecutive calendar days or to take such vacation leave at the rate of one (1) or two (2) days per week over several succeeding weeks without prior written approval.

DISCIPLINARY ACTION

1. Purpose: The purpose of this rule is to establish authority for disciplinary actions to be taken by personnel so authorized.

2. Disciplinary Action:

   (a) Disciplinary action shall be taken in any form prescribed by this rule, for any violation of the personnel rules. Disciplinary action shall be taken only with the approval of the court administrator.

   (b) Personnel authorized to administer disciplinary action are:

   (1) Court Administrator

   (2) Coordinator

   (3) Supervisor

   (c) In degrees of severity, the following actions are prescribed:

   (1) Oral reprimand;

   (2) Written reprimand;

   (3) Suspension;

   (4) Second suspension for the same infraction; or

   (5) Dismissal

   (d) In any case where disciplinary action is taken, the administering person shall insure that a written record is placed in the personnel file of the employee disciplined. The written record shall contain the name of the employee, the cause for the action, the date the action was taken, the action taken, and the name of the person who administered the action.

(e) Such written records shall be maintained as follows:

(1) Oral reprimand - one year

(2) Written reprimand - two years

(3) Suspension - three years (for any type).

(4) Dismissal - permanent

(f) Employees shall not be held accountable for disciplinary actions taken against them for which there is no written record.

(g) Under no circumstances shall the grievance procedure be utilized to cause disciplinary actions to be taken.

DEMOTION

1. Purpose: The purpose of this rule is to establish the conditions which an employee may be demoted. Demotion shall be defined as a reduction in classification or a reduction in salary within the same classification.

2. Demotion:

    (a) A demotion can occur only upon such action by the appointing authority.

    (b) A permanent employee may be demoted under the following conditions:

    (1) reduction in force;

    (2) loss of position due to budgetary action (position deleted from the budget);

    (3) upon request of the employee and the positions to which the employee requests demotion is vacant; and for

(4) failure to perform effectively in a position to which the employee has been promoted and the probationary period is still in effect.

(c) A demotion is appealable to the Grievance Board only in case (4) above. In such an appeal, the employee shall justify that the demotion is unwarranted. See Grievance Procedure.

(d) A demotion shall be done by written notice to the affected employee, and shall cite the position and salary of the position to which that employee is demoted.

(e) A demotion shall remain in effect during the grievance process.

DISMISSAL
(Administrative Personnel)

1. Purpose: The purpose of this rule is to establish the policy regarding dismissal from employment. By way of definition, dismissal is a form of disciplinary action.

2. Dismissal:

   (a) No employee who has permanent status shall be dismissed from employment except for just cause. Such just cause may arise from disciplinary actions, non-compliance with personnel rules, insubordination, criminal activity, conflict of interest, or failure to adequately perform assigned work.

   (b) Any employee who is dismissed shall receive a written notice of termination.

   (c) Any dismissed employee shall have five working days from the date of dismissal to appeal to the Grievance Board except when such dismissal is for failure to adequately perform assigned work (see Grievance Procedure and Grievance Board) which is not appealable.

   (d) Employees not in permanent status may be dismissed at any time by the appointing authority.

(e) An employee who has permanent status, but is in a probationary status as the result of a transfer or promotion to a new position is excepted from this rule.

(f) Reasons for dismissal shall include, but are not limited to:

    (1) Physical or mental difficulty which prevents assigned work from being accomplished;

    (2) incompetence;

    (3) insubordination;

    (4) misconduct;

    (5) abuse of leave;

    (6) excessive tardiness; or

    (7) any cause, which if so deemed by the court, reflects negatively upon the constitutional duty of the court or its ability to effectively carry out its judicial functions under the laws of the State of Oregon.

GRIEVANCE PROCEDURE

1. Purpose: The purpose of this rule is to establish the grievance procedure to be utilized by administrative personnel. This process applies in all grievance matters except for the Performance Evaluation Plan (PEP). The PEP appeal process is final, and this grievance procedure shall not be utilized to appeal PEP decisions.

2. Grievance Procedure:

    (a) The following shall constitute grounds for filing a grievance:

        (1) A request for interpretation of the personnel rules.

        (2) A suspension without pay for more than five (5) working days.

(3) A discharge from employment (that is in violation of personnel rules).

(4) A personnel action taken which is contrary to, or is in violation of the personnel rules.

(b) Grievances which only seek interpretation of personnel rules shall be referred by the employee's supervisor directly to the administrator for resolution.

(c) All grievances shall be submitted in writing to the immediate supervisor, and shall describe the grievance and facts surrounding the employee's opinion that he/she has been grieved.

(d) The employee and their immediate supervisor shall have five (5) working days to resolve the matter or bring it to the administrator's attention.

(e) If not so resolved, the administrator shall have ten (10) working days to resolve the matter, or forward it to the Grievance Board for resolution. See Personnel Rule _____ for the Grievance Board.

(f) Any resolution of a grievance shall be in writing and directed to the parties to the matter. A copy of the resolution shall be kept on file in the administrator's office and in the personnel file of the grievant. Grievance Board decisions are to be kept in a separate file.

GRIEVANCE BOARD

1. Purpose: The purpose of this rule is to establish the activity, membership and authority of the Grievance Board.

2. Grievance Board:

    (a) The Grievance Board shall hear all grievances referred to it by the administrator, and its decisions shall be final.

(b) Membership on the Grievance Board is limited to five (5) members as follows:

    (1) Supervisors: two (2) from units other than the grievant's.

    (2) Employees: two (2) from units other than the grievant's.

    (3) Coordinator of Administrative Services shall be a permanent member (unless the grievant is from a unit supervised by the coordinator).

(c) When the grievant is from a unit supervised by the Coordinator of Administrative Services, the Board shall be composed of two (2) employees as described in 2(b), (2) and the Coordinators of the Civil, Criminal and Domestic Relations units.

(d) The Board's voting shall be by secret ballot. A majority vote of the Board is required to overrule the administrator's decision.

(e) The Board's decisions shall be in writing, and directed to all parties in the matter. Seven (7) working days from the date of referral shall be allowed to resolve the grievance. Decisions shall be kept on file in the administrator's office.

(f) The Grievance Board shall not have the authority to waive, suspend, alter or delete an existing personnel rule. However, the Board may recommend in its decision that the rule(s) be reviewed in order to insure equity.

LAY OFF

1. *Purpose*: The purpose of this rule is to define the lay off procedure utilized by the court. Lay off may also mean a required reduction in force.

2. Lay Off:

   (a)   Any employee may be laid off from work by reason of abolition of position, shortage of work, budgetary reduction, shortage of funds or other reasons outside the employee's control.

   (b)   A lay off shall not be construed as a discredit on the service of the employee.

   (c)   The duties of a laid off employee may be redistributed to other employees by the appointing authority, or may be discontinued.

   (d)   The order of lay off shall be as follows:

        (1)   First consideration shall be given to conserving to the court the services of employees deemed most valuable.

        (2)   Performance, experience and potential for minimal training shall be considered.

        (3)   Seniority shall be considered in so far as the value of service the employee may contribute toward conserving essential services for the court's judicial functions.

   (e)   Lay off shall be by written notice to the employee at least five working days prior to the lay off date.

   (f)   Laid off employees shall be maintained on an eligibility list and called back to work as there are openings in their job classification or work available based upon their experience.

RESIGNATION

1. Purpose: The purpose of this rule is to establish the policy concerning resignations from employment with the Court.

2. Resignation:

   (a) Any employee shall have the right at any time to resign from employment with the court.

   (b) Any resignation shall be in writing, given to the immediate supervisor, and be submitted at least 14 working days prior to the scheduled termination date. However, an employee may request, in writing, an earlier resignation date. The appointing authority shall be under no obligation to honor same.

   (c) Any employee in a supervisory position or position which the appointing authority has declared as being critical to the operations of the court must provide at least 30 days notice prior to termination.

   (d) A resignation submitted by the employee may only be rescinded by the appointing authority.

   (e) Failure to submit a proper resignation shall shall cause a termination notice to be placed in the employee's file.

SUSPENSION

1. Purpose: The purpose of this rule is to establish the policy for suspension of administrative employees.

2. Suspension:

   (a) The appointing authority may suspend any employee, as a form of disciplinary action, for any reasonable period not to exceed 30 working days. Such a suspension may be with or without pay at the discretion of the appointing authority.

   (b) A suspension shall be in writing, and shall specify the number of days of suspension and the pay status.

   (c) No employee may be suspended more than twice in one year without the approval of the court administrator. The total amount of suspended working days shall not exceed 40 days in one year.

(d) A suspension in excess of five working days is appealable to the Grievance Board.

TARDINESS

1. Purpose: The purpose of this rule is to establish policy concerning tardiness by employees.

2. Tardiness: An individual who is tardy up to fifteen (15) minutes reporting to work either at the start of the work day or upon return from breaks or luncheon periods will be given an option of:

   (a) Making up the time that work day only.

   (b) Having the time reduced from their paycheck.

   Tardiness beyond the original fifteen (15) minutes may not be made up. For each fifteen (15) minute increment of tardiness beyond the initial fifteen (15) minutes, an employee will recieve a reduction in wages of one (1) hour.

3. Exceptions: The only exception to the tardiness provisions shall be inclement weather.

4. General: Abuse of this policy shall result in appropriate disciplinary action which may include dismissal from employment.

COURT PROPERTY

1. Purpose: The purpose of this rule is to establish the policy regarding usage and responsibility of court or county property.

2. Court Property:

   (a) Court or county property is public property, not to be abused or misappropriated for personal use.

   (b) Every employee is responsible for that equipment utilized in the performance of their assigned work. Such responsibility shall include maintenance, security, and assurance of proper usage.

(c) Upon termination of employment, every employee shall insure that all property is turned in or accounted for by the immediate supervisor.

(d) Misuse, abuse, or misappropriation of court or county property shall be subject to disciplinary action.

(e) Failure to comply with paragraph (c) above, shall cause the employee's final check to be held until an accountability is made.

EMPLOYEE PERSONNEL RECORDS-CONFIDENTIALITY

1. <u>Purpose</u>: The purpose of this rule is to establish the confidentiality of employee personnel records.

2. <u>Employee Personnel Records-Confidentiality</u>:

    (a) It shall be the policy that employee personnel records are confidential as follows:

    (1) Not open to public.

    (2) Not open to other employees except to supervisory staff during the process of consideration for promotion, transfer, or disciplinary action.

    (3) Open at any time during working hours to the employee.

    (4) Open to the Grievance Board during its action or deliberation.

    (5) Open to the Appeal Board of the Performance Evaluation System during its action or deliberation.

    (b) Nothing in this policy is to prevent access to such records by the court administrator's office for purposes of posting data to the file or to make an authorized removal of data.

(c) No employee may remove information from their file without the approval of the appointing authority.

(d) Every employee is encouraged to review their file at least once during the fiscal year. An annotation of the date and initials of the employee should be made upon each review.

PROFESSIONAL ATTIRE AND DEMEANOR

1. Purpose: The purpose of this rule is to establish the policy concerning the attire worn by employees during working hours, and the demeanor which shall be observed.

2. Professional Attire and Demeanor:

   (a) All employees are expected to dress in a manner which is appropriate both to the dignity of the court and to the nature of the work being performed.

   (b) The wearing of shorts, cut-offs, halters, T-shirts, tennis style shoes, thongs, etc. is prohibited.

   (c) There is no work within the court which requires the wearing of revealing or suggestive clothing, and such is not within the dignity of the court.

   (d) Hats shall not be worn in work environments.

   (e) All employees, regardless of their employment status, are required, as a condition of employment, to be well groomed and neatly dressed during work hours. The court administrator, coordinator or supervisor shall have the authority to send any employee home to change into proper working clothes. The time required to do so shall be without pay, and the employee must return to work that same day.

   (f) In the case of special work details or projects, the appointing authority may dictate a special uniform to be worn.

RELEASE OF INFORMATION

1. Purpose: The purpose of this rule is to establish the policy governing the release of information not subject to ORS, Chapter 192 and Chapter 7.

2. Release of Information:

    (a) The release of information concerning the business and activities of the court which is not subject to ORS, Chapter 192 (Oregon's public records law) or Chapter 7 shall only be done with the prior approval of the court administrator.

    (b) According to ORS, Chapter 7, all case files of the court are public record except secret indictments, adoption cases, filiation cases (paternity suits) or cases ordered sealed by the court. In accordance with Chapter 192, the internal operating records of the court are not public records. To simplify matters, any request for data other than case files, indexes, or fee records (including judgment dockets) should be referred immediately to the court administrator's office.

    (c) Employees should refrain from giving legal advice; expressing opinions about the court or its judges; or concerning lawyers or other officials, public or private.

    (d) As statutory clerk-of-the-court, the court administrator is the official who may release information; requestors shall be referred as outlined in (b) above.

    (e) Personnel records are confidential records, and not subject to public inspection or use.

    (f) Failure to comply with this policy is cause for disciplinary action.

Appendix F:
The Judicial Cost Model

(Colorado Judicial System
October 16, 1978)

The Colorado court system is highly diverse with its combination of rural and urban courts; its single and multi-county districts and its wide variance in workload represented in the various courts. Judges and administrators, while recognizing this diversity, have increasingly expressed their desire that the Judicial Department develop a management and budget system which would establish statewide workload and performance standards.

Through the work of the Judicial Planning Committee it was determined that what was necessary was an improved method for the determination of the needs of an efficient judicial system. The Committee recommended that this be accomplished by developing standards for:
1) workload and performance;
2) staffing;
3) case processing;
4) case reporting;
5) facilities; and
6) forecasting.

At first this seemed to be an overwhelming task. Again, with the help of the Committee, it was felt that a revised management and budget system should be the first step in accomplishing the objective. The system envisioned by the Committee was to be one which would compare the disparate court operations and determine attainable levels of performance.

A system with this capability, The Cost Model, is currently being developed by the State Court Administrator. The common measurement is cost, or dollars per case.

The underlying assumption of this approach is that at any established level and quality of the delivery of justice, the most efficient administration will provide those services at the lowest cost per case.

Cost per case as a measurement of performance assumes that all costs regardless of the source of the funds, are assigned to cases. This is illustrated in the Justice System Cost Model (see Attachment A).

Separate models can be developed for each of the components of the complete cost model. Attachment B illustrates the Judicial Cost Model currently under development for the Judicial Department. A further breakdown of the Judicial Cost Model (The Trial Court Personnel Cost Model) is shown in Attachment C. This portion of the Judicial Cost Model has been completed and is included in the Department's FY 1979-80 budget request. Analysis for judges and referees as well as for indirect court personnel has been completed.

In order to begin to evaluate alternatives for improving administration of the courts, it was first necessary to determine how the courts were actually performing with existing workload, staff, equipment, facilities and procedures. It was assumed that, on a statewide basis, the level and quality of services provided was satisfactory. It was also assumed that future performance should not be reduced if all factors remained constant.

The Trial Court Personnel Cost Model data was therefore analyzed to determine the status quo. The following assumptions were made:
1) The sole product of the judicial system is the resolution of cases. Therefore, all costs of the system are assigned to cases.
2) All personnel in the court, with the exception of judges, reporters and bailiffs, are concerned with indirect support for each court filing.
3) That the use of actual staffing and terminations for FY 1976-77 and FY 1977-78 realistically represent actual work accomplished with then existing procedures, equipment and facilities.

The analysis was conducted as follows:
1) The cost per termination was determined by the personnel categories shown on the model for each county in county court and for each judicial district in district court. Costs were based on average salaries for each personnel category.

2) Indirect support categories were totaled.
3) Costs were analyzed to determine if grouping of courts was supported by actual performance. This analysis showed that there were similarities in indirect personnel cost per termination that were comparable to known differences in size and operations. The results of the analysis attributed the differences to:

District Court   County Court

Urban   1 or more full-time judge
Rural   less than one full-time judge

4) Standards were established for the cost of indirect personnel per case by taking a reasonable average of all costs within the above groupings. The reasonable average was established by:
   a) evaluating all costs in the grouping;
   b) eliminating those costs that were significantly higher than the absolute average;
   c) averaging the balance;
   d) comparing the actual performance over the two years;
   e) selecting the average cost representing the highest performance level.
5) The determination of workload standards for judges and referees required a different methodology than that used for clerical staffing. It can be shown that productivity of a judge/referee will increase as workload (filings) increases, until, at a certain point, productivity will level off and will not increase with increased filings.

   This is confirmed by inspection of the graphs shown as Attachments I - L. The graphs illustrate the cost versus filings for the different categories of courts for the two fiscal years. The leveling off points represent actual performance by the judge/referees with sufficient workload. These points were, therefore, selected as the standard workload measures for judges and referees.

Attachment M represents the same analysis for urban district courts in chart form.
6) Cost per standards were converted to filings/terminations per FTE.

The first standards or performance goals based on workload actually performed are:

	Filings Per FTE Per Year			
Personnel	District Courts		County Courts	
Category	Urban	Rural	A & B	C & D
Judge and Referee	930	775	4,065	2,860
Indirect (Clerical)	255	210	1,181	897

These standards mean that the statewide trial court system, as of July 1, 1978, was adequately staffed and if there are no increases in filings from FY 1977-1978, no additional personnel will be needed. Thus, the standards are properly applied to projected filings to determine future staffing needs. The standards may be modified in the future as measurement of workload by case type is developed and as improvements in procedures, equipment and facilities are made.

Attachment D - G illustrate the cost per case calculations for the county and district courts.

Attachment D

DISTRICT COURT ANALYSIS
URBAN COURTS - INDIRECT STAFFING STANDARDS
10/15/78

District	Cost Per Case - Indirect Staff	
	FY 1976-77	FY 1977-78
1	$ 45.23	$ 53.35
2	70.71*	78.82*
4	41.89	42.85
8	66.07	68.62
10	57.74	56.27
17	44.52	49.41
18	59.51	57.35
19	73.74*	94.30*
20	46.30	49.52
21	31.63	33.34
TOTAL*	$ 392.89	$ 410.71
Standard (Avg.)*	49.11	51.33
Average Cost	12,525.00	13,000.00
Standard Filing/ FTE/Year	255	253

* Costs not included.

Office of the State Court Administrator
Colorado Judicial Department

11/1/78

Attachment E

DISTRICT COURT ANALYSIS
RURAL COURTS - INDIRECT STAFFING STANDARDS
10/15/78

District	Cost Per Case - Indirect Staff	
	FY 1976-77	FY 1977-78
3	$ 78.92	$ 69.71
5	77.69	63.94
6	45.01	46.56
7	60.81	58.92
9	82.70*	102.87*
11	46.28	50.98
12	78.81	70.33
13	78.60	79.42
14	99.44*	52.44
15	103.38*	112.04*
16	66.12	58.37
22	67.02	67.80
TOTAL*	$ 599.25	$ 618.47
Standard (Avg.)*	66.58	61.85
Average Cost	12,525.00	13,000.00
Standard Filing/ FTE/Year	188	210

* Costs not included.

Office of the State Court Administrator
Colorado Judicial Department

11/1/78

Attachment F

COUNTY COURT ANALYSIS
A & B COUNTIES - INDIRECT STAFFING STANDARDS
10/15/78

County		Cost Per Case - Indirect Staff	
No.	Name	FY 1976-77	FY 1977-78
1	Adams	$ 9.16	$ 9.38
3	Arapahoe	9.18	9.59
7	Boulder	10.85	10.79
10	Clear Creek	9.47	11.48
18	Douglas	9.00	10.50
21	El Paso	10.06	10.04
30	Jefferson	9.62	6.75
35	Larimer	14.82	15.62
39	Mesa	10.62	12.94
51	Pueblo	11.62	12.86
62	Weld	12.52	11.09
TOTAL		$ 117.02	$ 121.04
Standard (Avg.)		10.64	11.00
Average Cost		12,525.00	13,000.00
Standard Filing/ FTE/Year		1,177	1,181

Office of the State Court Administrator
Colorado Judicial Department

11/1/78

Attachment G

COUNTY COURT ANALYSIS
C & D COUNTIES - INDIRECT STAFFING STANDARDS
10/15/78

No.	County Name	Cost Per Case - Indirect Staff FY 1976-77	FY 1977-78
2	Alamosa	$ 12.95	$ 14.59
4	Archuleta	19.90	20.03
5	Baca	15.56	18.30
6	Bent	28.38*	24.30
8	Chaffee	9.22	12.19
9	Cheyenne	27.15*	30.10*
11	Conejos	8.74	6.53
12	Costilla	9.78	12.97
13	Crowley	20.17	15.90
14	Custer	24.61	22.61
15	Delta	13.78	9.47
17	Dolores	52.70*	89.43*
19	Eagle	16.07	13.90
20	Elbert	19.36	20.00
22	Fremont	17.84	18.94
23	Garfield	9.52	11.89
24	Gilpin	17.31	15.06
25	Grand	10.40	9.23
26	Gunnison	10.20	8.95
27	Hinsdale	69.38*	24.85*
28	Huerfano	14.72	15.84
29	Jackson	28.57*	31.14*
31	Kiowa	30.07*	31.10*
32	Kit Carson	14.40	13.68
33	Lake	10.14	9.83
34	La Plata	15.79	22.48
36	Las Animas	9.68	10.33
37	Lincoln	16.69	14.60
38	Logan	12.02	11.67
40	Mineral	12.55	10.80
41	Moffat	14.83	9.24
42	Montezuma	16.59	16.20
43	Montrose	10.37	9.40
44	Morgan	8.62	9.39
45	Otero	7.71	7.70

Attachment G (Cont'd)

County		Cost Per Case - Indirect Staff	
No.	Name	FY 1976-77	FY 1977-78
46	Ouray	$ 18.12	$ 14.28
47	Park	16.17	12.33
48	Phillips	20.75	25.77
49	Pitkin	17.59	14.04
50	Prowers	13.59	14.70
52	Rio Blanco	27.41*	19.43
53	Rio Grande	10.81	13.08
54	Routt	14.48	16.22
55	Saguache	8.76	8.82
56	San Juan	8.20	10.54
57	San Miguel	10.66	14.36
58	Sedgwick	18.91	20.50
69	Summit	14.07	12.65
60	Teller	10.74	9.50
61	Washington	15.74	16.34
63	Yuma	18.01	20.50
TOTAL*		$ 614.12	$ 683.83
Standard (Avg.)*		13.96	14.55
Average Cost		12,525.00	13,000.00
Standard Filing/ FTE/Year		897	893

* Costs not included.

Office of the State Court Administrator
Colorado Judicial Department

11/1/78

TEXAS A&M UNIVERSITY-TEXARKANA